BRAHMS AND HIS FOUR SY

BRAHMS
AND HIS
FOUR SYMPHONIES

Da Capo Press Music Reprint Series
GENERAL EDITOR
FREDERICK FREEDMAN
VASSAR COLLEGE

BRAHMS
AND HIS
FOUR SYMPHONIES

By Julius Harrison

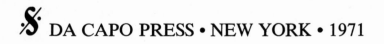 DA CAPO PRESS • NEW YORK • 1971

A Da Capo Press Reprint Edition

This Da Capo Press edition of
Brahms and His Four Symphonies
is an unabridged republication of the
first edition published in London in 1939.

Library of Congress Catalog Card Number 76-127285

SBN 306-70033-6

Published by Da Capo Press
A Division of Plenum Publishing Corporation
227 West 17th Street, New York, N. Y. 10011

BRAHMS
AND HIS FOUR SYMPHONIES

JOHANNES BRAHMS

After a pencil drawing by H. Varges.

(Reproduced by permission of Werckmeisters Kunsthandlung, Berlin)

BRAHMS
AND HIS FOUR SYMPHONIES

BY

JULIUS HARRISON

LONDON

CHAPMAN & HALL LTD.

11 HENRIETTA STREET W.C.2

First published
1939

CHAPMAN & HALL LTD
11 HENRIETTA STREET
LONDON, W.C.2

PRINTED IN GREAT BRITAIN BY THE WHITEFRIARS PRESS LTD.
LONDON AND TONBRIDGE
BOUND BY G. & J. KITCAT LTD., LONDON
Flexiback Binding Patent No. 441294

To my friend and colleague

ADRIAN BOULT

in appreciation of his
many fine performances
of the Master's Symphonies

" Therefore in order to find a criterium
of Good musick wee must (as I sayd) look
into nature it Self, and ye truth of things."

The Musicall Gramarian.
ROGER NORTH,
1650–1734.

CONTENTS

PREFACE

IT has proved by no means an easy task to plan this book on Brahms's Symphonies. To have analysed them from bar to bar with musical references alternating between the thematic structure and the orchestration would have been a comparatively simple matter. Yet the seeming simplicity of such a plan would, I fear, have been apparent only to the author of the book. For the reader it would have been confusion worse confounded because the amount of detail quoted would have wearied the brain out of all concentrated attention on the subject.

It has therefore been thought more practical to analyse the orchestration apart from the thematic structure and in the order given, since, in such a synthesized art as Brahms's, the music matters far more than its orchestral presentation. Needless to say, the difficulty has been to disentangle the one feature from the other, and so it must follow that cross-references are frequent. Yet, despite my inability to escape some redundancies here and there, occasioned by the adoption of this planning of the book, I feel that what I have done is infinitely preferable to cluttering up the reader's mind with a plethora of detail.

The aim of the book is to endeavour to give those interested a detailed account of the countless hidden beauties that lie in these four symphonies, like pearls in the bed of the ocean. I cannot pretend to a complete analysis because none of us can hope to capture the full essence of beauty. Could we do so, there would be nothing new under the sun and life would not be the joyous adventure it is.

There is much in this book that is not intended for the highly skilled musician, things that are understood by him long before I put my pen to paper. On the other hand there is a vast musical public that has not only a large heart to respond to the beauty of all good music, but, in addition, an intelligent head to appreciate the subtleties of effect and the great technical skill evinced by a composer of genius.

It is particularly in the hands of such music-lovers that I hope my book may find a resting-place.

My grateful thanks are here expressed to those Publishers who have permitted me to quote from books which will be found acknowledged in various footnotes; to Messrs. Novello and Co. Ltd., for the use of a copyright musical quotation; to my friend Eric Fenby for reading the proofs and for some valuable suggestions; and, lastly, to Mr. John L. Bale, of Messrs. Chapman and Hall, for his tireless patience in waiting five years for the final chapter of a book, which, but for recurrent ill-health, would have been completed in the Brahms centennial year.

J. H.

HASTINGS,
  October, 1938.

CHAPTER I

PARTLY BIOGRAPHICAL

"WHAT would become of biographies if they were always to be written with discretion?"

In such words Johannes Brahms once addressed himself in a letter to his cherished friend Clara Schumann.

She and her husband, Robert Schumann, had befriended the young Brahms in 1853, inviting him to their home in Düsseldorf and treating him almost as another son in a household that already had seven young children to its name. Brahms himself was little more than a boy at the time (he was born on May 7th, 1833, at Hamburg), a young romantic, spellbound by the compositions of the elder man whose mind ran so feverishly on fairy tales and the fanciful whimsies that found their outlet in music of a thousand moods.

He was soon to fall deeply in love with the composer's wife, although she was thirty-four and he but twenty at the time. And that love, which in due course of time was reciprocated, was to prove an all-important factor in the ordering of his life and work. It was much more than a boyish infatuation, for its roots lay deep down in an intellectual companionship which, come what might, would survive the many emotional crises through which both he and Clara were destined to pass before the end of their days. Other friendships with women a good deal younger than himself came his way, friendships sentimental and otherwise—one at least that hung precariously on the brink of matrimony—but never an one to equal that with his beloved Clara Schumann. When she died in 1896, an old woman of seventy-seven, he followed her in less than a year, a kindly providence seeming to decree that they should not be parted for long.

Grim tragedy was soon to cloud the happy triple companionship of those early years in the 'fifties, for less than a year after Johannes' first meeting with the Schumanns, Robert, in a fit of insanity, threw himself into the Rhine, and but for the timely intervention of the crew of a passing steamer would have been drowned. He was taken to an asylum at Endenich, where after two years of suffering during which demons of sound hammered incessantly at his crazed brain, he died on July 29th, 1856.

All this time Johannes and Clara were torn between the love which now had them in thrall and their unfailing devotion to the stricken composer. Whatever Clara's feelings for the younger man, there was no doubting her affection for her husband. Johannes' conduct, too, seemingly above reproach, was dictated as much by a genuine solicitude for the distressed wife and mother as by his natural desire to be as much as possible with the woman he loved. Yet when circumstances kept them apart neither attempted to disguise the real state of their feelings. We find him addressing her as " my beloved Clara," " most adored being " and " darling," telling her in many an ardent phrase that his soul is " tormented by longing and desire " and that he thinks of her " with the same love that grows stronger and heartier every day."

Of the numerous love-letters that passed between them the majority are lost, for in 1887 Brahms and Clara agreed to destroy all that were felt to be too intimate for publication. He, true to the compact, consigned hers to noble burial in the deep waters of the Rhine, with, we can surmise, many a poignant memory of her and poor Robert surging through his mind, and, almost needless to add, without a single thought for those biographies which could have been written with less discretion had the letters survived. She, lingering over a last perusal, found the task beyond her, and so, womanwise, saved from destruction some thirty or forty on which it has been possible to reconstruct in part the story of their love and its renunciation.

All this is of the greatest interest because of the remarkable change that crept into Brahms's music at the time of these tragic events. But for what happened this deeply sensitive, impressionable young composer might so easily have become just another of those weaker romanticists who had by now caught the ear of all Europe. He might have followed slavishly and without question in the footsteps of his early benefactor, composing long successions of *Noveletten, Romances, Nachtstücke* and all those other rich and warm examples of romantic music which, in an age of novelty and enormous change, sprang to life so readily in the perfervid imagination of Robert Schumann.

That Brahms was greatly attracted to Schumann's music goes without saying. Already, in his Opus 9, he had taken a theme by Schumann as the basis of a set of Piano Variations. " Clara speaks in one of them " the composer wrote to his friend Joachim, while, in a further similar set (Op. 23), written after Schumann's death in a spirit of reverence for the departed genius, there is actually woven a theme by Clara herself. This latter set was written in piano duet form on a theme which Schumann fantastically declared to have been presented to him by Schubert in a dream.

In circumstances such as these Brahms could scarcely have hoped to escape the effect of this close contact with the Schumann household. But recently he had met Liszt, and, as will be seen presently, for the younger composer it was an unhappy encounter. Whereas Robert Schumann regarded Brahms as a composer of his own school, Liszt had hailed the young Johannes as another apostle of that new realism which spurned the classic formalism of bygone days.

Brahms must have felt as if between two fires—the stark realism calling the way of Liszt, Wagner and Berlioz, and that gentler romanticism learnt from the Schumanns. Less apparent now was that strength of purpose which showed to such advantage in his three Piano Sonatas, Opp. 1, 2 and 5. It was evident that he had reached that fallow stage of life when mind and instinct are at variance, when seeds of distrust sown in the field of inspiration bring forth more tares than harvest.

Yet it would be rash to assume too readily that the tragic events of those early years affected to any large extent Brahms's ultimate career or the formation of his style as a composer.   He seems to have withdrawn from the outside world for long periods during the years 1854 to 1858 as much on purely musical grounds as on account of the circumstances of his private life.   In 1856 he accepted a post at the court of Prince Lippe-Detmold, where, little disturbed by the events of the day and unhindered by many musical duties of the perfunctory kind, he must have found that quiet atmosphere conducive to work of the creative order.   Here he wrote the two Serenades (Opp. 11 and 16) to which reference will be made.

That his acceptance of this post was determined or at least hastened by the tragic happenings in the Schumann household and the consequent upheaval in his and Clara's lives there can be little doubt.   Things had been driven to a climax by the death of Schumann.   Before this occurred Brahms had been wandering about from place to place, restless in body and mind, visiting the Rhine and Switzerland in company with Clara, seeking diversion here and there, unable to decide where to face his destiny.

Detmold was his salvation.   From this time onwards there was no turning back.   Severe self-criticism now began to cast disparaging eyes on the compositions of his youth, with the exception of the Variations on a theme by Schumann, and, strangely enough, the Four Ballades (Op. 10).   And this self-criticism proved to be the deciding factor that severed the remaining link between Brahms the weak romanticist and Brahms the new oncoming champion of the traditional classical school of composition.   None of his compositions was published between 1856 and 1859, a fact that suggests a partial cessation or suspension of his creative faculty or the desire to withhold what had been written until he was entirely sure of its value. Possibly this unproductive period was the result of the mental suffering he had experienced in those painful years of self-abnegation, while his musician's mind was at the same time tormented by doubt and despair and the knowledge that success could only come to him if he resisted all temptation to follow in the wake of the new German school of realism. The loneliness of Detmold gave him time to think ; convinced him that music, to be enduring, must be above self, must sing of the joys and sorrows of the world more than of the individual, and must find its highest expression through those sounds hallowed by time and usage by the great masters.

And so he chose the path he was to tread to the end of his days, eschewing the weak romanticism that had affected his earlier work and reforming his style in the classical manner of Bach, Handel and Beethoven. Thereafter his life was largely spent in quiet seclusion the while he laboured to create music that might rank worthily with the works of these giants.

In this respect he is unique. No other composer of his standing ever held such a soul-searching inquiry and then decided to start afresh on another safer road. In the case of Bach, Handel, Haydn, Mozart and Beethoven that road was departed from but rarely, if at all. And as for the others, did it really matter what road they chose to reach the goal of their extremely personal and divergent styles ? There were many roads to select from ; highways to the mountain-peaks of realism, paths to the valleys of romance, yet not a single one that led to the expression of something as noble as the music of the great selfless immortals.

The classical symphony had indeed fallen into neglect ; there had been nothing outstanding since Schubert's great Symphony in C major. Mendelssohn and Schumann had succeeded up to a point, but theirs was the music of a gentler age, scarcely worthy to be placed beside that of the greatest masters. But Brahms was another matter. He lived through a brief phase of youthful indiscretions that might have determined his style for good and all, and then, his music emerging from the twilight of morbid introspection into the full radiance of the classical style, became a man of action, secure in the knowledge that he could write symphonies which would endure to the end of time.

Everything seems to have led up to this point. Brahms's careful upbringing ; his lessons founded on the works of the great masters ; his admiration for those warmer romantic works by Schumann and others ; his searching examination of all the qualities that made and marred this later school of musical thought ; his eventual rejection of all extravagant emotions borrowed from the romantics that stood in the way of breadth of conception. Everything went to prepare the way for those Four Symphonies which, in many ways, are the most interesting examples of their kind ever composed.

Of the triumph of Brahms over his weaker romantic self nothing speaks with more eloquence than the history of the Piano Concerto in D minor. Originally intended as a Sonata for two Pianos, with, it must be presumed, Clara in mind as keyboard partner to the composer, it is soon metamorphosed into sketches for a symphony, only to be discarded and rewritten in the final form by which it is known. And, apart from the Concerto itself, this event seems to be of the utmost importance. We see in it Brahms's fixed intention to change to that musical style which was to be directly responsible for the birth of the symphonies.

Brahms's music rings true because his nature rang true, because he hated all sham, all false estimation of self, all the pettiness of mundane things, all the spites and professional jealousies that seem to be inseparable from music in high places. He would have none of them. He truckled to no one and so was called gruff and surly by musicians and people of his time whenever their ignorant advice or empty flattery provoked him to words which were resented because of the unforgivable truth contained therein. For he disliked intensely such things as the tawdry glitter of

Liszt's music, finding it pretentious and false at heart. He never forgot that first encounter with the great virtuoso who lived *en prince* at Weimar and about whom society flocked in all its insincerity and foolish hero-worship. When Brahms had ventured to refuse to play his own Scherzo in E flat minor to the great man, Liszt himself had read it at sight from the rather dreadful manuscript and was duly impressed by the originality and strength of the music. Whereupon he (Liszt) made the tactical blunder of entering into unpremeditated competition with the other composer by playing his own Sonata in B minor, during which performance the weary Brahms is said to have fallen sound asleep.[1] Liszt of course forgave him, for he was magnanimous by nature. But to Brahms the recollection of that competition must always have caused a sense of irritation. He, the other-worldly, saw through the shallow pretence of the older man's earth-bound music and had fallen asleep through sheer ennui. It must have hurt his pride or his sense of the fitness of things to hear his own earnest, God-fearing music played more or less as a prelude to such sophistry. And when Brahms could not forget, it was difficult for him to forgive. Liszt and what he stood for (more the latter) became increasingly antipathetic to him as the years rolled by. In 1860 we find Brahms's name as one of the four misguided signatories to an ill-timed manifesto which appeared in the Berlin *Echo*—a manifesto wilfully intended to be a direct attack on the music of Liszt and Wagner. This was indeed a sad departure from the usual reserve that characterized the thoughts and actions of Johannes Brahms. Yet it revealed the utter honesty of purpose of a man who could be so inflamed against the decadent tendencies which were beginning to disturb his art that he could break through his natural reserve and come out into the open as the champion of truth and

---

[1] " Brahms could sleep soundly at any hour of the day, if he wished to do so." *Recollections of Johannes Brahms*, by Albert Dietrich. (Seeley, London, 1899.)

righteousness in music, even if the outburst did bring him
(in company with Joachim and others associating in the
manifesto) into temporary ridicule with press and public
alike.

Germany was Wagner mad at the time. *The Flying
Dutchman, Tannhäuser* and *Lohengrin* were gaining adherents
by the thousand. *Tristan und Isolde* was published that year,
music that once provoked Brahms to say " Whenever I hear
that music I get bad-tempered." For him it was too
unhealthy, too chromatic, too self-centred—what a contrast
to his own music ! And at that time *Rheingold* and *Walküre*
were wholly, and *Siegfried* partly written. The air was full of
the palpitating "Sehnsucht" of *Tristan*. And Wagner's own
mind was steeped in the atmosphere of those primitives from
the *Nibelungenlied*, the *Nibelung Saga* and the *Edda*—primitives
who were but prototypes for the new militant Germania
that was arising. Small wonder that Wagner, who invested
these ancient legends with something of the warm blood of
modern Germany and who made the Siebengebirge on the
Rhine the haunt of the god Wotan, the Valkyries, the Rhine-
maidens and Siegfried, should achieve a national popularity
at the expense of an untheatrical composer who saw more
enduring beauty in music of the pure abstract order. By
nature Brahms was far from jealous : popular success meant
little to him. But he did feel the divine spark in what he
wrote and his whole spirit rebelled against the antichrist.
And for that dislike of the specious and unreal he gained the
enmity of the many and the friendship of the few. His
acerbity of manner was but the proud reserve of one who
knew where he was going, who was destined for a better
Valhalla than one peopled by warring gods and goddesses
and by those slain heroes whose actions when on earth had
merely coincided with the selfish interests of these deities.

Yet, for all his brusqueness, Brahms had a nature that
brimmed over with the common humanities. He never tired
of the company of children. At twenty-eight we find his
simple soul still delighting in the manœuvres of his own

battalion of tin soldiers ; many years later he is on his hands and knees disposing the army commanded by his landlady's boys. A hungry urchin looking into a cake-shop window was more than he could resist. His passion for a good cigar was the outward and visible sign of the camaraderie that made him seek the company of men at the " Red Hedgehog " in Vienna, and elsewhere, to indulge in lengthy argument on this and that aspect of art or philosophy. He would talk but little of his own music—how different from Richard Wagner ! He disliked the inquisitiveness of others who wanted to know what was going on in that inaccessible mind of his. He must have felt that any discussion of a half-finished work would blunt the inspiration, would make him self-conscious and critical at a time when mind and instinct must respond in sympathy to each other, like the bursting seed to the warm sunshine. He shared his musical secrets with few. In all he did there was an absence of vanity.

In such things lay the greatness of the man. Through his deep humanity and simple selfless nature the world was given music without which it would be incalculably poorer. Had I, personally, to take the choice between the utter destruction of Wagner's *Ring of the Nibelungs* and of the Four Symphonies by Brahms I should unhesitatingly consign the *Ring* to its fate, great as the pang might be. The Symphonies represent something which cannot be replaced, something that seems to have brought the wheel of absolute music full circle, something that is the quintessence of the beauty of sound springing from a nature devoid of all insincerity and desire for worldly gain. On the other hand, the *Ring*—marvellously wrought, the work of a Homer in sound—demonstrates through its babel-tongued mythologies the futility of terrestrial things. At the end it leaves the listener, despite the *Redemption by Love* motif, with but a material picture of Valhalla in flames and the bitter knowledge of inescapable oblivion for gods and mortals alike. Not through such pagan pictures can music survive the centuries.

But the contrast just drawn does not necessarily mean that

the greatest music must have a moral tag attached thereto or that we must only appreciate what " does us good." Far from it. We choose our music purely by personal reactions. But the time comes when most people need something which unconsciously elevates the soul above the body. That is only to be found in music which abjures all selfish expression, free from the tribulations of the world in which we live. Such music must of necessity be what is called *absolute* music. It goes beyond the limits of circumstance, time and space. It becomes other-worldly, is intangible, floating on the air like dapples in the sunlight. It is ethereal and seemingly of the spheres ; Pythagorean, in that we cannot hear its message in entirety. And of that kind of music Brahms was one of the greatest exponents.

CHAPTER II

THE ROAD TO THE SYMPHONY

HOW fortunate it was that these four masterly symphonies were written at a time before music was affected by the experiments of our modern age, before the whole-tone scale was exploited as a conscious, mannered thing, before luscious harmonies were falling on the ear in thick profusion, before the art, generally, had become the slave of atonalism, the slave of the rhythm fiends, the plaything of a non-classical post-war age, abused by all and sundry and revered by few. Fortunately, Brahms lived long before this mechanical age, before the days of speed, motors, aeroplanes, wireless, foxtrots, swing music and saxophones, before the years when everything went crazily into the melting-pot to come out tarnished and alloyed. He had time for the recollection of his emotions in tranquillity ; he was not captured by one gramophone company striving for supremacy over another, nor was he offered a fabulous sum to turn his more popular dance movements into another *Waltzes from Vienna*. And Hollywood was then unborn or it might have offered to film him opposite Robert and Clara.

Not that one can believe that Brahms would ever have succumbed to these decadent soul-destroying influences. But the unrestful conditions of our twentieth-century life might have interfered with his output to such an extent that less would have been written than was actually the case.[1]

The danger to Brahms in those days came from within, not from without. Did he not himself, at the time of the tragic years with the Schumanns, begin to sense the dangers,

---

[1] His compositions with Opus numbers amounted to 122. In addition, he transcribed, arranged and edited many works by the great masters.

the damning influence of a too fully-flavoured romanticism, tearing himself away from the world at the age of twenty-one (after several years of the greatest success in the public eye) in order that he could master the methods of Bach and Beethoven ?

He had already given to the world those remarkable early works. They were arresting in the development of their form, amazingly fresh and inventive in thematic material, intriguing in their harmonization and generally of such promise and achievement as to receive the warmest eulogies from Robert Schumann, who, no doubt, must on occasions have wanted to repeat his well-worn phrase about Chopin : " Hats off, gentlemen, a genius."

Yet neither the plaudits of the crowd nor the praise of that incurable romanticist Schumann could turn him from his slowly formed decision to temper his style and learn the way of moderation in all things.

He sensed the big faults in his early music ; he knew where certain tricks of harmony had got the upper hand and spoilt the whole effect intended. He must have argued that he could not have it both ways, that if harmony interfered with design his house of music would be divided against itself and not stand enduringly. In fact, he took stock not only of himself but of the world's output of music, making Bach and Beethoven his gods and placing most of the others on a plane less exalted. No doubt he pictured his own early works in company with the romantics, next Chopin, Mendelssohn and Schumann. However different their actual content might be, however much they might be admired for the touches of individuality scattered over their pages, yet he knew that these early essays were but another variety of the same flower—the same hot-house plants which had blossomed in such profusion since the days of Schubert and Weber. In Schubert's days the flowers of romantic music were unforced, an out-of-doors growth, lovely to the ear, natural offshoots of the classical tree, straining for no effects and artificialized by no unnecessary displays of the newer harmonies then coming into general use. A few years later when those new and exciting harmonies and nervously wrought rhythms were being exploited by Chopin, Schumann and others of that time, music was beginning to lose its open-air freshness ; much of it was under glass and becoming precious. Chopin was being petted by George Sand and her Parisian entourage, sentimentally busy translating the perfume of the salon and the boudoir into his Nocturnes *si ravissants ;* Mendelssohn was the fashion, fêted by royalty, writing tiny musical souvenirs called *Songs Without Words* for adoring admirers ; Schumann was still in the thirties, a vital force for good or evil, his *Papillons, Carneval, Blumenstuck, Nachtstücke, Kreisleriana, Waldscenen,* all the rage the while he was putting together those rather unsymphonic symphonies which attracted only the few.

In his youth Mendelssohn had entranced the world with those two beautiful but slightly sentimental symphonies, the *Scotch* and the *Italian.* Nevertheless, apart from a few such examples, instrumental music of the absolute order was fast becoming a shrinking quantity and new works of symphonic breadth and scope were less frequently written. A great proportion of the pieces then being composed could be printed on a page or two ; the spinal column of music was beginning to suffer badly from curvature ; it was more the age of miniatures than of masterpieces.

About this time the boy Brahms was engrossed in study with his teachers Cossel and the more famous Marxsen at Hamburg, and a good deal of the newer music must have come his way and influenced his most impressionable years to a certain degree, even if it did not (as was afterwards proved) weaken his love and reverence for the great classical masterpieces. Since this newer music was largely homophonic and less polyphonic, and had fascinating new harmonies as its most striking features, it follows that Brahms must have been affected in a way that would not altogether have accorded with lessons given by a teacher[1] who was

[1] Eduard Marxsen (1806–1887), one of the most famous teachers of the day.

a contemporary of Beethoven and, no doubt, brought up in the traditions of Haydn and Mozart. Counterpoint must have played the most important part in that early training, harmony coming second. And the latter, by falling within the scope of the other study, would take care of itself because of the true movement of the separate parts in the contrapuntal exercises.

As Brahms grew up and became less dependent on his teachers for advice, mixing more and more with the musicians of his day, he must have indulged in excited talk about the new romantic composers springing into popular favour with their highly coloured music. How he and his comrades must have dissected those harmonies and the highly-strung rhythms, analysing their value, admiring some, rejecting others—just as happened in my young days when we had the choice of Debussy, Sibelius, Elgar, Hugo Wolf and many others to whet our appetites. Was it humanly possible to escape these influences? It must be remembered that the advent of the out-and-out romanticists would have caused more than a mild sensation in the eighteen-forties. The new wave in its onward rush must have swept many off their feet and the *terra firma* of the classics would be often in danger from the flood of these sounds.

In the 'fifties, as we know already, Brahms went to stay with the Schumanns and felt the full effect of this romantic flood. But, happily for his art, he realized a fundamental truth and saw the way things would go unless a curb were put on a too adventuring style. Above all else he must have realized that harmony, improperly used, would be the greatest handicap to the true development of his music. Instead of being the servant it would become the master ; it would turn the house inside out, weaken the structure and eventually destroy it. His thoughts must have flown many times to Cossel and Marxsen.

There is no doubt that all the finest music that has survived the passage of time lives in all its strength and vitality by virtue of its economy in harmony. The composer uses just as much as his themes suggest and require ; nothing is redundant and yet nothing can be said to be lacking. Since Brahms's day things have gone astray in this respect. Harmony has been raised on too high a pedestal—an idol of clay, toppling over with each generation, raised by the next, smashed to smithereens by a few composers who have misguidedly gone too far in the other direction, yet always returning in a cheaply glorified way to deck out gaudily the compositions of those who lacked contrapuntal skill.

An untempered, indiscreet use of coloured harmonies is one of the first signs of weakness in a composer, for by such means he hopes (unconsciously perhaps) to deaden the critical ear to the paucity of his ideas or the absence of design. He can be quite sincere about it, too, probably knowing no better or, maybe, realizing his limitations and working within them. Yet he does a great deal of harm. Many talented composers of this type have come and gone in the last fifty years, all products of a later school of romanticism than that of Chopin or Schumann, but derived therefrom. Their number has increased enormously in the past few decades, and some of them, Debussy and Puccini in particular, have left a deep and dangerous mark on contemporary music. Imitators they have had by the hundreds, even thousands, and it can be said quite positively that a good proportion of the successful second-rate composers of today derive their wealth and their ideas from a close following of the styles and tricks of these gifted minor composers. Today the world is harmony and rhythm mad ; it must have the twopenny-coloured. Penny-plain does not go with post-war luxury and inertia ; it is too austere, forbidding, too brainy, too " horribly intellectual." It accords neither with night clubs, " hot music " bands, nor with musical comedies that depend on celestes, harps, vibraphones, mustel organs and other soft treacly sounds for their effect. The world has learnt to sip the cocktails of Puccini and his successors ; to imbibe the over-sweetened fruit-cups, the liqueurs of Debussy *et sui generis*. Nations languish in this post-war lassitude and only require to be ear-tickled by theme-songs or lulled to sleep by the pulsing of a languorous *Valse Lente* or something similar. Harmony of the sickly sentimental kind has ruined the world and will continue to do so until some dictator-reformer comes along and forces Parliament to pass a measure making the setting down on paper of redundant major ninths and thirteenths a capital offence.

Brahms now stood midway between the weaker romanticists and the oncoming Wagner, whose rich, dark-hued masses of sounds were beginning mightily to disturb the world. He was of neither party; was aloof, solitary, linked up with the hallowed past of Bach and Beethoven, owing all to them and as oblivious of contemporary influences as if he had been in another world. Fortunate it was for us that such early works as the three Piano Sonatas, the much-played Scherzo in E flat minor, the Trio in B for Piano, Violin and Violoncello[1] and the curious Ballades for Piano (in which we see a grim seriousness of purpose conflicting oddly with speculative harmonies and hesitant outlines) did not encourage him to go on and prosper in the path already mapped out for him by an admiring public. However, these early compositions served their purpose. Only in our appreciation of the later Brahms do we feel their irreality (fine as some of the works undoubtedly are) and the fulfilment of that genius which was bound to assert itself through those experiences of youth.

But for Brahms it was not sufficient just to go away and hide himself for a while with his beloved Bach and Beethoven and then emerge " fully armed like Minerva from the head of Jove "[2] with his Opus 15, the Pianoforte Concerto in D minor. Things had evidently been calculated by him far beyond his musical needs of the moment. This Concerto and the two Serenades would be but steps to a higher plane;

---

[1] Revised by Brahms in his later years.
[2] Schumann in the *Neue Zeitschrift für Musik*, October 28, 1853.

exercises in the severest classical outlines, noble preludes to undisputed mastery.

And so, with many chamber works of large calibre pointing the way, he goes from strength to strength, treading his own narrow path towards the goal of the First Symphony. Between the Piano Concerto (Op. 15) and the First Symphony (Op. 68) there are, taking them chronologically, but nine works that are written for orchestra or in which we find it. Of these, an *Ave Maria* for voices with orchestral accompaniment and the two Serenades are respectively labelled Opus 12, 11 and 16. Then comes a long break, and it is not until Opus 45 that Brahms employs the orchestra again in the magnificent *German Requiem*—a work for all time and all peoples. But the pace is now increasing and between this work and the First Symphony the orchestra is employed much more frequently—Op. 50, 53 (Alto Rhapsody), 54 (Song of Destiny), 55 and 56a (St. Anthony Variations).

Did this more frequent turning to the orchestra for self-expression mean that Brahms was now beginning to feel a compelling urge towards the highest manifestation of his signal powers? Was the momentum such that it had to gather speed through the motive power supplied by these various orchestral works until it could find its true outlet in his Symphony? Brahms's case is different from Beethoven's, for the Bonn master's First Symphony was only his Opus 21 (written at the age of twenty-nine, in 1799, when he was still under the Mozartian influence, or barely liberated therefrom) while Brahms deliberately avoided the symphonic form until his style was fully matured in every sense of the word in his Opus 68. There is therefore no such thing as an immature Brahms symphony (a case practically without parallel in the annals of music until Elgar wrote his Op. 55 in A flat) and so we can assess each one by the same standard without disadvantage anywhere.

Brahms enthusiasts often declare that the finest symphony in the world is *any one* of the four by their favourite, their predilection varying toward the one last heard. Adherents of Beethoven as the supreme master would scarcely agree and would vigorously defend against all comers the unapproachable grandeur of the *Eroica*, the Fifth, the Seventh, or the *Choral*, and I feel sure that none of us could swear that they were wrong. Yet than Brahms, with the possible exception mentioned above, there is no other composer whose symphonies have been so consistently mature from the very first note written, or so universally admired for their craftsmanship.

It is not only that we stand amazed at the mastery over form and ideas there displayed, but also at the peculiar appositeness of the orchestration.[1] There is hardly a thought anywhere that is not satisfactorily presented through the instruments employed. Ideas and their expression go hand in hand, each relying on the mastery of the composer to weld them into an unified whole.

Brahms had very definite ideas on the method of composing and once expressed his convictions to his great friend Sir George (then Mr.) Henschel. It was then he very modestly defined his belief in himself as being some kind of composer-medium able to give the world only what was originally prompted from without.

" There is no real creating without hard work. That which you would call invention, that is to say a thought, is simply an inspiration from above, for which I am not responsible, which is no merit of mine. Yes, it is a present, a gift, which I ought even to despise until I have made it my own by right of hard work. And there need be no hurry about that either. It is as with the seed corn : it germinates unconsciously and in spite of ourselves. When I, for instance, have found the first phrase of a song, I might shut the book there and then, go for a walk, do some other work, and perhaps not think of it again for months. Nothing, however, is lost. If afterward I approach the subject again, it is sure to have taken shape ; I can now really begin to work at it." [2]

[1] The orchestration is analysed in detail elsewhere.
[2] *Musings and Memories* by Sir George Henschel. (Macmillan, London.)

Herein lies the Brahms creed in its entirety. This extract tells us almost as much as a Beethoven sketch-book ; we are let into the secret of his working methods and only fall short of an understanding of the inspiration itself which, he reminds us, is no merit of his.

By "right of hard work" he completed his First Symphony in his forty-third year, after many years' deliberation on the subject. What monumental patience was needed to clarify the mighty ideas that must have surged so emotionally and so enthusiastically through his being from the moment he first felt "from above" the moving throb of that reiterated C on the tympani ! But his disciplined mind eventually harnessed the thoughts to their proper expression, and so gave to the world the first of those masterpieces that combine so unerringly symmetry of design, beauty of intellectual thought and romantic feeling of the right kind.

Evidence from early sketches shown to friends, including Clara Schumann, proves that it took him not less than twenty years to complete the task—a feat of mental endurance comparable to Wagner's twenty-eight years for the *Ring of the Nibelungs*. And Brahms's task appears all the more remarkable when we recollect that the symphonist was dealing with the co-ordination of abstract sounds unprompted by any programme ; that, unlike Wagner, he had no words nor yet dramatic situations on which partly to build his house of music. The mosaic *leit-motif* principles adopted by Wagner had no part in Brahms's scheme ; nor indeed could he have succeeded had his subjects and themes been no longer than most of the patchwork phrases used in the *Ring*.[1]

And so Brahms is regarded as one of the greatest absolutists among composers, a worthy compeer of Beethoven and Bach—incomparable immortals, standing on the heights of

[1] Perhaps the most *un*symphonic of all the well-known Symphonies is, for the reason just stated, the B minor (No. 2) by Borodin, where the continual repetition of tiny phrases that were never anything else but tiny phrases (particularly in the slow movement), is a travesty of the term Symphony.

Olympus with the old gods for company. No wonder he sought that seclusion wherein he could more closely study the methods of the other two Bs. He seems to have had a pretty shrewd idea of his predestination, to have felt that he was chosen by the Muses to join the company of inspired contrapuntists. His daily study of counterpoint would fit him for such an honour ; indeed there was hardly a day throughout his life of sixty-four years but that he prac- tised in the ways of Bach and the others, learning the freedom of their moving parts—parts that had, as their great characteristic, independent melodic writing when viewed *horizontally*, and yet which met *vertically* [1] in perfect harmonic agreement to cause that concord of sweet sounds which is the ultimate end of all true music.

Consequently, sheer polyphonic strength is the most convincing and ear-satisfying of all the features in his music. Examination of the symphonies later in this book points to an all but complete absence of anything that stagnates. It will be seen how each instrument lends its indispensable horizontal melodic line as a quota of sound contributing to the general sonority of the mass as heard vertically. More particularly is this independent movement noticeable in the bass line of the counterpoint, where, in writing so many virile leaping phrases and figurations Brahms must surely have had in mind that epigrammatic saying of old Karl Reinecke (nine years his senior) : " By their basses ye shall know them." In his later years he must have cast a very critical eye over the shortcomings in those early immature works, the Ballades for Piano— pale, expiring efforts of a self-confessed weak romanticist, promising works of youthful genius, somewhat cankered in the bud. Here was palpable stagnation of movement, of which the following example can be quoted with advantage to the argument.

[1] The use of the terms *horizontal* and *vertical* can refer, of course, only to the " look " of music on a printed page, since music falls on the ear independently of such distinctions.

Ex. 1

The mellifluous harmonies and the hesitant melodic outline in the right hand part need not detain us ; these are
referred to elsewhere. The melody begins with the Brahms
" hall-mark " notes F, A, F (8va.), which stand for the
phrase *Frei aber froh* (" free but glad ")—a device found
in many of his works. But the motto as used here is
too romantically obvious to be effective, not having the
freedom nor yet the *gladness* that we find in it elsewhere, most
particularly in the Third Symphony. Nor does the odd
length of nine bars save this melody from itself, it merely
prolongs the agony of dying what seems an unnatural death.
The double pedal-point of D and A throughout has hardly
the merit of a pedal proper. A pedal must have justification
and this seems to have none ; it merely stagnates. One can
hazard the guess that Brahms improvised this piece at the
Piano, sprawling over the keys with large extended right
palm, thumb busily giving a middle-pitch sonority to the
general plan of the sound, his romantic soul delighting particularly in the colour of those G chords against the A in the
left hand pedal.[1] I would recommend those interested to

[1] Since writing the above I have come upon the following passage in Vol. I.
of Ethel Smyth's *Impressions that Remained* (Longmans, Green & Co.) " . . .

study the other fourteen bars following this quotation, noting the discontinuity of the melodic phrases (mostly two-bar snippets), the hesitant left hand and the sickly perfume of further G major chords used as in the quotation above.

What a change there was to be from the moonshine of this Opus 10 to the breadth of style found in the Piano Concerto in D minor produced by Brahms at a Leipzig Gewandhaus concert on January 27th, 1859—some five years later than the Ballades ! So different was this work from those acclaimed so enthusiastically by Schumann that it left the audience utterly nonplussed and disappointed, chilling them to the marrow by its uncompromising severity of style and the absence of any concession to the prevailing bravura school of instrumental music. In place of the sensuous harmonies that characterized the Ballades there reigned a far greater economy of colour, allied at the same time to a more widely developed rhythmical scheme. Design, it will be seen, was now beginning to mean more to the composer than colour. The architecture of this Concerto was so big, and the mood so serious that it took no less than forty-seven minutes for it to have its say. But its length told against its success and it was badly cold-shouldered by the Leipzig public. Even today it is caviare to numbers of enthusiastic Brahms lovers, who read into it arid patches of cold formalism out of accord with its general character. It may be unequal in many ways (particularly in the orchestration) and too stretched in the length, but great music it undoubtedly is, especially the deeply spiritual slow movement.

The Serenades, published a year later, were more angular and square-cut, easier to grasp, lighter in the mood at times, but again notable for the absence of harmonic experiments.

Brahms had now gone to the other extreme, and it must be confessed that these works betray signs of having been written under the effect of a heavy brooding mental discipline that all but avoided sentiment and took account

when lifting a submerged theme out of a tangle of music he (Brahms) used jokingly to ask us to admire the gentle sonority of his ' tenor thumb.' "

only of directness of utterance.[1] At times they mortified the flesh ; they were indeed not far removed from a Trappist's " memento mori " ; full of good deeds but devoid of freedom in their speech. The scherzos, the *Adagio non troppo*, the minuets of the First Serenade are formal in the extreme, retrogressions into the simple language of Haydn, but dry and often inspirationless.

In the Second Serenade (Op. 16) Brahms discarded the use of the Violins, as if to imply that their higher-pitched sounds, their honeyed vibrations were too sweet for the purpose he had in mind. Was he, in making full use of the Violas here, unconsciously imitating the style of Bach's sixth Brandenburg Concerto or merely exploiting in exercise form those darker hues of this most expressive instrument as a prelude to the masterly effects which were to be achieved at a later date in the First Symphony ? Idle speculation will not help us. We cannot look into the unconscious workings of a composer's mind when in the act of creation. Nor, again, can we accurately piece together the whole circumstances of his life at any given time and say that this or that piece of music must have been written in a certain way because of some particular mental state brought about by a combination of events. Tchaikovsky, we know only too well, wore his feelings on his coat sleeve, for he was the most subjective of all composers. His griefs and despairs and black suicidal moods were for the world ; he could not keep them to himself when there was the chance to tell everyone through the power of his symphonies that he, Tchaikovsky, was the most miserable of all men.[2] Brahms was the reverse.

[1] In the autumn of 1859 Brahms made a copy of the score of the Serenade in A for Agathe von Siebold (see footnote, p. 70). Specht adds that the composer told Graedener, the Hamburg musician—" It might well please a maiden. Doesn't do it, however."

[2] Tchaikovsky felt little sympathy with Brahms's music although he held the composer in the highest esteem. He found it unreal. To him Brahms was " trying to be profound but had only attained to an appearance of profundity." That the composer of *Francesca da Rimini*, the *Pathetic* Symphony and the many other *cris du cœur* could not fathom the intellectual depths of the other man is self-explanatory. Their music, their methods, the outlook of Brahms *versus* the inlook of Tchaikovsky were as the poles asunder.

His aim, as was pointed out in the last chapter, was to rid himself of every particle of weak romanticism. The world, he must have argued, did not want to know anything about the intimate thoughts of one Johannes Brahms, son of a contrabassist at a Hamburg theatre. Nor, despite hidden allusions found here and there in his music, would he desire anyone to know the state of his feelings towards Clara Schumann or his more transient loves. His pride, his sense of a proper privacy in respect to matters of the heart would prevent his being autobiographical like his illustrious and somewhat shameless contemporary Wagner. His mission was higher—to perpetuate the glories of an art so great that it must transcend the individual giving it utterance and take him completely out of himself. That may be the reason why the Concerto and the Serenades swung a little too far in the other direction. There was that taint of the subjective and introspective to be kept rigidly under control. This could only be accomplished by severe penance and self-imposed flagellation of the spirit. Probably Brahms foresaw his own future ; was given an inkling of it by unconscious prevision. More than likely his general stocktaking after the Ballades convinced him that he of all men had it in him to continue from where Beethoven left off at the close of the Ninth Symphony. It has already been surmised that the change in his style was mainly due to his love of the classical masterpieces and to his dislike of everything meretricious and artificial. Bright glittering colours in music made little appeal to him. He preferred the simple dark shades that helped the listener to concentrate on the substance of the music itself without unnecessary distraction. For that reason the Violas in the second Serenade seem to foretell more than anything else the general kind of sounds that were beginning to interest him, to find, later, their joyful liberation in the First Symphony. Brahms is never happier than when he is writing those dark-shadowed sounds obtainable through the combinations of Violas, Bassoons, low-pitched 'Cellos and Contrabasses. These sounds per-

meate a great part of his work, they are his especial orchestral
trade mark, recognizable in a moment—much like his
F.A.F. motto.

Of course, the Violins, following their temporary discharge,
returned to the fold in the *German Requiem*, after Brahms had
used them solo-wise in some of his finest chamber-music,
written between the Serenades and the Requiem. By the
time the First Symphony was due he had extracted from
them all he wanted of the quality that appealed to his ear.
They were now ready to take their place in a work that
would need all their tenderness yet without any of their
cloying sweetness. Before the birth of the Symphony he
had made inspired use of them in the *St. Anthony Variations*,
wherein can be found nowhere any passage that does not
elevate them into the realms of the most poignant
expression.

I have touched prematurely on points in Brahms's orchestration since it has been necessary to show briefly by what
combination of *musical* circumstances the composer seems to
have gradually made his way to the goal of that immortal
First Symphony—hailed by the ardent Brahmsians of 1876
as " No. 10."

To sum up at some length. Brahms got rid of the weaker
elements in his harmonization, simplifying his methods by
rigid elimination of all extraneous matter and thereby toning
down the more vivid hues of his music to an extent that must
have proved sadly disconcerting to the advanced romanticists
of his day. This done, he proceeded to enlarge the design
and structure of his compositions to a degree that made
them somewhat wearisome to many and not a little hard
of understanding to some. He exchanged the painter's palette
for the draughtsman's pencil—a reversal of the usual order
of things which must have come as a real shock to the short-
sighted majority who were unable to measure the full length
of the Brahmsian idiom. Brahms's courage must have been
exceptional. He alone of the famous composers of the
day faced the classical direction, convinced he could best

serve his art that way. There were enough realists and romanticists in the Europe of 1855 to make any composer upholding this old order of things almost an object for ridicule. In addition to the romantic composers mentioned already there was Wagner, building up his pagan Valhalla with the aid of his Fafners, Fasolts and various serio-comic paraphernalia, adding gloriously to the drama and melo-drama of sound by making pseudo-play with the old *Nibelun-genlied* and other sagas of ancient memory, collecting whole families of tubas and other instruments and adding them to his orchestra to bear the weight of those stupid wranglings between divided deities and primitive tribes of wild back-woodsmen. To the realistic Teutonic mind this demanded large masses of inwoven harmonies (but less counterpoint) so that the stark primitiveness of the whole thing, so remini-scent of Attila and his hordes, could be heard in all its significance. Nor did Berlioz lag behind in the devising of such monster effects. His *Grande Messe des Morts*, written some eighteen years previously, required no less than four brass bands and several hundred orchestral musicians to give it its ideal performance.

Amid this maelstrom of romance, realism and revolution, Brahms, *mirabile dictu*, kept his head when the world might well have expected him to lose it. He then proceeded to work for twenty years at a First Symphony fashioned on classical lines. And for music such as this (although at an earlier date, 1855, we find him, in company with Cornelius, Tausig and others, assisting with the copying of *Die Meister-singer* [1]) he was soon to taste the venom of Wagner.

Actually that venom was in the nature of a tit-for-tat, for Brahms himself knew the art of invective ; knew, as that strange *manifesto* of 1860 went to show, how to taunt the

---

[1] Thus Wagner in *My life*. " Tausig also mentioned Brahms to me, recom-mending him as a ' very good fellow ' who, although he was so famous himself, would willingly take over a part of their work, and a selection from the *Meister-singer* was accordingly allotted to him. And, indeed, Brahms's behaviour proved unassuming and good-natured, but he showed little vivacity and was often hardly noticed at our gatherings."

leaders of the New German School : how, under cover of a solemn declaration of artistic faith, to pour anonymous yet pointed scorn on all modern realists not of his way of thinking.

His last desire was to write music of a programmatic or theatrical kind ; that was abhorrent to his nature. He felt he could save the art more permanently by a further development of the classical forms ; of the symphony, the sonata, variations, songs, chamber-music and choral and instrumental pieces. And to this end he applied himself with the same intensity and concentration that Wagner gave to his music-dramas and Liszt to his symphonic poems.

Wagner was twenty years older than Brahms : a man of great genius and experience, one whose achievements were lauded by the whole of Europe long before the younger man had left school. But the child of today soon becomes the man of tomorrow and by the time Brahms, at the age of twenty-two, was copying out parts of *Die Meistersinger*, he himself was already recognized as another genius whose work showed endurable qualities. As the years rolled by and Brahms, like his famous contemporary, became more and more the mature artist, comparisons of style were inevitable. These soon ˌdeveloped into an acrimonious warfare of artistic creeds, and, much like the time, a century earlier, when the Gluck and Piccinni factions came to loggerheads, so did the partisans of Wagner and Brahms fall foul of each other.

In all many-sided quarrels desertion to the other side is not uncommon. Such a deserter was the philosopher Nietzsche. In his Selected Aphorisms contained in the volume *The Case of Wagner* (T. N. Foulis, 1911, translated by Anthony M. Ludovici) he attacked Wagner right and left.

" Wagner does not altogether trust *music*, he weaves kindred sensations into it in order to lend it the character of greatness. He measures himself on others ; he first of all gives his listeners intoxicating drinks in order to lead them into believing that it *was the music that intoxicated them.*" . . . " The arts should not always be dished up together, but we should imitate the moderation of the ancients which is truer to human nature." Elsewhere he wrote : " The most wholesome phenomenon is Brahms in whose music there is more German blood than in that of Wagner." [1]

Opinions on the relative qualities of Brahms and Wagner must always differ ; praise of the one carries with it, more often than not, dislike of the other. No composer has ever been so well hated as Wagner ; none other has aroused so much controversy, so much enthusiasm, so much critical condemnation. And perhaps none other has ever been so belittled as Brahms ; none so misunderstood, so praised for the iron discipline of his mind, so loved for his power to extract the greatest beauty from phrases most composers would have discarded as of no value. Yet between the two composers there is a common bond.

The vocabulary of musical sounds they both used to such purpose is the oldest, the only true musical speech in the world ; one that is founded on a natural phenomenon bound up in the laws of physics. That phenomenon is the inter-relation of sounds, more accurately known as the science of Natural Harmonics—the actuating force behind the

[1] All the same, Nietzsche was not by any means a follower of Brahms, as can be read in the second postscript to *The Case of Wagner.* He found him a " master in the art of copying . . . much too little of a personality, too little of a central figure. . . . The ' impersonal,' those who are not self-centred, love him for this. . . . People like to call Brahms Beethoven's heir." And again—" Brahms *or* Wagner . . . Brahms is *not* an actor.—A very great part of other musicians may be summed up in the concept Brahms," etc., etc. Nietzsche compared the two, it will be seen, much to the advantage of Brahms (he is contradictory at times), and the quotations given here were written before the composer's works had been thoroughly scrutinised through the microscope of the passing years. It is recognized generally that Brahms owed the origins of his music to the classical past. Brahms would have been the first to admit the fact and rejoice in it. Then he added his own individual touches to what was founded on Beethoven, Handel, Bach, etc., thereby forming his own extremely personal style. It would seem as if those traits were not recognized sufficiently at the time (Brahms was still among his critics in 1888) for the grafting of new shoots on old musical trees can be viewed only at a distance, after a lapse of time. Had Nietzsche lived today I feel sure that he too would have been as ardent a Brahmsian as anyone, especially as his horrified flight from the Wagnerian fold meant in itself a definite move in the direction of purer music of the classical type.

whole art of music.   Examined briefly, for the sake of those
not conversant with the principle, it means that when a
musical sound is created, other sounds are generated simultaneously with that sound.   These secondary (and very
much fainter) sounds vibrate in sympathy with the primary
note and are heard at definite and unalterable intervals of
pitch above it, falling into their places according to the laws
of natural sound.   Only those harmonics that are nearest in
pitch to the primary note (seven or eight of them) are
audible, the remainder gradually fading out of range of the ear.

Composers have always felt the presence of this series of
natural harmonics ; in fact, they have never been able to
avoid it, for the first five or six notes of the series in simultaneous combination form the basis of those common chords
and their inversions that are the root-matter of all music.
For they have fully realized from the earliest days that if these
sounds are used in sympathetic conjunction, music immediately becomes sonorous and satisfying to the ear.   Nature
places this extraordinary kaleidoscope at their disposal.

Therefore 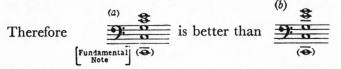 is better than

because it is more in vibrational sympathy with itself than
the less evenly distributed chord (b) which does not reinforce
the fourth note—middle C.

Wagner has one of the most outstanding examples of this
to his credit in the opening pages of *Das Rheingold*.   This is
nothing more nor less than a mighty development of the
natural harmonics, extending to a length of 136 bars through
a maze of *arpeggii* and chords of E flat, laid out with consummate skill and artistry and with a deep regard for the true
sonority of the music.   Here are examples taken therefrom.

Ex. 2
(a)

etc.

Brahms is equally dependent on this principle and his themes and harmonies are just as closely related to it as those of Wagner. Examples that will occur frequently in this book illustrate his implicit obedience to the laws of natural harmonics.

But at this point any arguable similarity between the two composers comes to an end. When they begin to speak, the difference between their methods is apparent at once. There is nothing, from the first æsthetic impulse down to the last turn of phrase, that can be identified as being common in style except the one fact that they both happen to speak the musical tongue of Germany. It is quite a mistaken idea to suppose that two composers are alike because one happens to arrive coincidently at a phrase, harmony, or rhythm that can be found in the other's work. Where would everyday speech be without the borrowings from Shakespeare, Chaucer and the others ? Yet an author has rarely to face the charges of plagiarism that are levelled so frequently at a composer.

The bigness of design of classical music often proves the stumbling-block to many listeners ; the average ear finds it difficult to piece everything together, a succession of complex harmonies being easier to grasp than an extended form. Common chords have gone out of favour and chromaticism reigns in their stead. Hence the appeal of Wagner to many. He searches the dark corners of the mind and expresses for them what is stored up there, often so dangerously. To many thousands Wagner's love-music acts as an outlet for the more worldly and erotic emotions, achieving not a little of its amazing popularity thereby. Those to whom the erotic appeal means much, experience less reaction to the older classical music. An ardent Wagnerite is rarely an ardent Brahmsian ; it is not easy for the lion to lie down with the lamb. Indeed, the whole question is well worth considering in the light of Sir Henry Hadow's words, when, in his *Studies in Modern Music* (Seeley & Co. Ltd., 1899) he gave expression to the following :—

" Either we are to hold that art gains by hysteria and extravagance, and that its highest climax is a delirium of unrestrained and riotous passion ; or, if this be impossible, we must accept the only alternative, and admit self-control as a necessary principle."

It is not my desire, nor is it the occasion, to make a partisan outcry against music of the merely sensuous kind. Such music is needed by all. It balances our appreciation of the art as a whole. Without it music would fail in its full message ; it would remain rooted to its scientific basis and afford us fewer opportunities for enjoying sound for sound's sake. Through it even Brahms indulged his fancy ; gave us the full rapture of romantic utterance—almost to the end of his days. Could anything be more sensuous to the ear (in the best meaning of the word) than those Pianoforte Intermezzi, Op. 116, 117 and 118, written in 1892 and 1893 ? They breathe throughout their lovely pages the spirit of true romance, not the hesitating and somewhat morbidly introspective kind of music found in the earlier works of like size. Brahms was certainly in the true succession of the Minnesingers, those mediæval precursors of the sixteenth-century Mastersingers. And like Francis Thompson's picture of Shelley, he could, between his symphonies and his greater works generally, still be at play, " save only that his play is such as manhood stops to watch, and his playthings are those which the gods give their children." Brahms " danced in and out of the gates of heaven : its floor is littered with his broken fancies." " He stands in the lap of patient Nature and twines her loosened tresses after a hundred wilful fashions, to see how she will look nicest in his song."[1]

And the hundred wilful fashions of Brahms's great genius found their expression in the many songs, instrumental music and other smaller pieces composed during a lifetime of endless variety. As a song writer he followed in the wake of Robert Schumann, capturing much of the general romantic style of the *Dichterliebe* and yet avoiding the sentimental extravagance which so often marred even the best of Schumann's compositions. Brahms's songs were of stronger calibre and altogether better made. In them we find the utmost regard for the value and effect of each note, whether in the vocal line or in the harmonic background. While at times Brahms may have transgressed the rules governing true verbal stresses, yet the onward sweep of the melodic line is never allowed to flag. There is indeed something almost symphonic about many of his vocal themes or melodies. Songs written prior to the First Symphony, songs such as the very early *Liebestreu* (1854), *Der Schmied* and *Von ewiger Liebe*, seem to contain more than a spice of that thematic vigour which was at long last to find its sublimation in the Four Symphonies.

It is through such experiences that a composer of the stature of Brahms learns to broaden his style. He sings constantly of the world, of a world of beauty and love, comedy and tragedy, laughter and tears. And when the cup of experience has been drained to the utmost, then, and only then, does he consider himself fitted to fashion the classical designs of a symphony. Now (to quote Francis Thompson again) : " the meteors nuzzle their noses in his hand," " he gets between the feet of the horses of the sun," " he chases the rolling world." He turns into abstract sound all the beauty he has seen in the many facets of life and nature. He subjugates the sensuous to the emotion of the intellect. So enduring is such music in its quality of

---

[1] *Shelley*, by Francis Thompson. (Burnes, Oates & Washburne Ltd., London.)

absoluteness that we can say truly that it is only tinged with, but not limited by the experiences that have gone to its making. We sense here and there that romantic feeling has played a part, however indirect, leaving its mark on the music in some curiously paradoxical way.

Brahms was indeed the most paradoxical of all composers. While at heart a romantic, turning again and again to those smaller forms of music wherein he could express himself as he never dared do in speech, yet his better judgment constantly reminded him that no enduring masterpieces lay that way, that romance must be forsworn or, at least, held firmly in check if the world of music were to be definitely enriched by his work. And so we find him always wavering between the two extremes ; one moment hot, the next cold ; now writing ardent love-songs because his feelings had been stirred that way ; now, as if ashamed, following them by an extended piece of chamber-music or a sonata, a Requiem or a set of variations in which bold design and a wholesome application of all his great contrapuntal skill gave the lie to any suggestion that romance was gaining the mastery.

His compositions, taken chronologically, are the story of a life caught in the toils of conflicting emotions. From a perusal of a list of his works we can almost reconstruct his story in detail, tracing the influence of the Schumanns and particularly Clara, the encouragement of Joachim, the ephemeral effect of those shy unspoken romances that came his way from time to time, the later middle-age contact with the Herzogenbergs, and, last but not least, his own artistic misgivings and those ever-renewed pledges of undying devotion to the cause of classical music.

His life was one continual battle royal between man and musician, with, as the years rolled by, victory resting more and more with the musician. The older he became the more did his mind turn towards the classical forms of composition. His major orchestral works—the four Symphonies, the Violin Concerto, the two Concert Overtures *Academic Festival* and *Tragic*, the Second Piano Concerto and the Double Concerto for Violin and 'Cello—are all gathered closely together between Op. 68 and Op. 102.

That the Symphonies are one of the major achievements in the world of musical composition can hardly be gainsaid. Their beauty of structure, the amazing fertility of their rhythmical devices, the strength and pliability of their themes (so conceived that they submit without strain or effort to the laws of invertible counterpoint), the restrained yet eloquent harmonies and their many other points of interest give them a balance of design and a precision of effect only to be found in the world's finest masterpieces.

While we know instinctively that certain of the Beethoven Symphonies strike deeper down into the rock of inspiration, yet for the sheer technique of the writing and for the amazing play and interplay of themes and counter-themes, we must yield the palm to Brahms for the four noble examples which are the subject of this book.

CHAPTER III

A MATTER OF KEYS

BEFORE proceeding to a more detailed analysis of Brahms's music we must not disregard an æsthetical matter of the utmost importance to every composer, for on it, more than all else, depends the general character and quality of the music being composed. This matter is the wide choice of tonalities available to every composer for the precise and colourful representation of all he desires to express.

A close examination of the Symphonies proves that Brahms was key-conscious to a remarkable degree and that no music could have been written by him that was not actuated, in its primary impulse, by an instinctive feeling for some particular pitch—a pitch suggesting to his mind a definite problem in sound that could only be solved at that pitch. And upon still closer examination it will be found that the keys chosen by Brahms for the various movements are in themselves (before ever a note was written) the outcome of a plan developed by Haydn, varied but little by Mozart and carried several stages further by Beethoven, Schubert and Mendelssohn. Brahms's concern over such matters brought about a new lease of life to the Symphony ; in fact it freshened to a remarkable degree a century-old form of music that was beginning to show signs of wear and tear because it had been for long the overworked servant of a too rigid pitch. Of the hundred and four symphonies by Haydn and the thirty-nine (complete) by Mozart, no less than twenty by the former and seven by the latter are pitched in the natural key. The few examples in other keys by Beethoven, Schubert and Mendelssohn—Schumann was least successful in this form—are insufficient to compensate us for all that C major energy displayed so lavishly and disproportionately by the two earlier composers of those many symphonies. So a new symphonist had to come to redress some of the balance, even if only to a comparatively small extent, and create anew what was needed in order that the symphonic form could spring once more into a new, flexible, unfettered life, unhindered by key-complexes of the rigid sort.

The opening of this chapter must therefore trace briefly those mid-eighteenth century events which proved to be such a turning-point in the art of musical composition.

There is hardly anything in music more difficult to explain than the extremely subtle differences existing between various tonalities. Even many accomplished musicians are insensitive to what is called Absolute Pitch. Hence the great difficulty in attempting to convince those not possessed of this instinct that such differences do actually exist in the composer's mind and that they are actually the life-blood of all music.[1] They do indeed represent those finer shades of musical expression, which, at any higher or lower pitch, would become distorted and meaningless.

There was a time, not two hundred years ago, when composers could not be accused of being too venturesome in the matter of the keys they employed. Handel's *Messiah*, for instance, never goes beyond a key-signature of four sharps and the bulk of his other works is written in keys much nearer to the white notes of the piano even than that.

But one composer did come along (and he was born in the same year as Handel, 1685) who was determined to exploit all the keys, both major and minor, and show the world that in them were differences most marked.

There is no need to recount in detail the qualities of the forty-eight Preludes and Fugues in the *Wohltemperirte Klavier*. When this " Bible " of music became known to

---

[1] Pitch has gone through many vicissitudes in its chequered career, and it has taken 200 years or more to get it definitely settled *near* what is known as Philosophical Pitch, i *.e.*, treble C = 512 vibrations per second.

musicians it must have been a revelation almost incredible
to the ears.   It must have set composers' minds working as
never before, spurring on the imagination to possibilities
of tone-colours almost without end.   The more remote keys
attracted Bach to some of his loveliest utterances, as witness
the moving elegiac Prelude in E flat minor in the First Book
of the *Forty-Eight* and the equally beautiful Prelude in
A flat major in the Second Book.   Transposed a full semitone either way they would lose their special quality and
become characterless and distorted.[1]

By the time Beethoven, in his Piano Sonatas, was indulging
his fancy for such extreme keys as A flat minor, F sharp
major, etc., music had been more or less liberated from the
sober restraint imposed upon it through the preceding
centuries and composers had profited fully by the examples
set them in the *Forty-Eight*.   And with a curious difference.

Solo instrumental and vocal music of the new romanticists
tended more and more towards the extreme keys, while
classical orchestral works, as exemplified, for instance, in
Beethoven's and Schubert's symphonies, preserved mainly
the simpler keys found in the earlier works of Haydn and
Mozart.   This is food for thought.

Extreme keys and coloured harmonies make excellent
companions.   Chopin would have found it difficult to pour
his love-lorn music into the cold philosophizing key of C
major.   Black notes on the piano are a *sine quâ non* for
lovers' vows and vain regrets.   It is interesting, in this
connection, to recall the fact that unhappy women in (or
out) of novels most often fly to Chopin for solace, finding
in the Nocturnes and Preludes that favour the remoter keys
an emotional substitute for those fond caresses discontinued
by their faithless lovers.

Now it has been shown in the last chapter how Brahms
in his general style steered a middle course, avoiding the

---

[1] In Bach's day, treble C equalled 515 vibrations per second or thereabouts,
as against our present-day new Philharmonic pitch of 522, a difference of little
account.

meretricious harmonies of the extreme romanticists, modelling himself on Bach, Handel and Beethoven for design and polyphonic treatment, and then adding something of himself. During those years of diligent study between the Ballades and the first Piano Concerto he must have pondered at great length over this burning question of keys and their relationships ; have noticed how simple were the changes of key used by Haydn and Mozart for the slow movements of their many symphonies ; have admired the freedom that came to Beethoven later when he so successfully broke down some of the established traditions set by the older men, and have realized, in his turn, that further developments were still possible. Mozart, Haydn, and then Beethoven in his earlier days, were content to remain more or less key-bound in their symphonies. Slow movements would be, in the main, in the keys of the subdominant or dominant, while minuets or third movements would invariably return to the key of the first movement. Which meant, since three movements out of the usual four were in the same key, that there was not much variety in the pitch of the notes employed nor much chance of escaping the monotony which was bound to result unless themes and rhythmical vitality were of the highest order. Haydn and Mozart did not altogether escape this failing. For this reason quite a number of their symphonies are rarely, if ever, played. On the other hand, Beethoven had the advantage of profiting from his knowledge of their more inspired symphonies and so by degrees became more venturesome. In his First, Second and Fourth Symphonies he is content to follow the beaten tracks of keys, using the subdominant and dominant for his slow movements and returning to the fold for the other movements following. And despite the extended scope of the music, his choice of the submediant key for the slow movement of the Third (*Eroica*) Symphony is no more out of the ordinary than Mozart's use of the key of E flat in his famous No. 40 in G minor. But with his Fifth Symphony Beethoven went much further. The pent-up feeling of the C minor third movement had to break through its *minor* bonds and then merge even more emphatically into C *major* for the finale. In the next Symphony, the *Pastoral* in F major, we get the tonic minor key for the thunderstorm[1] (was there ever a better thunderstorm written ?) and later, in the Seventh and Ninth, other extraordinary departures from the well-known key-sequences of the earlier symphonies.

Enough has been written here to indicate how determined Brahms was to break away still further from these traditional key-sequences by a series of experiments which was to prove the complete justification of his ideas.   And so, in the light of this knowledge, we can now proceed to examine the first skeleton structures of his Four Symphonies, analysing the keys of the various movements so that the sequence of thought, in the music itself can be the more easily followed.

Notwithstanding what has been stated about the number of symphonies that have the note C as their foundation it would appear that Brahms was predestined to start his symphonic life on this note, proceeding from alpha to omega by devious paths unexplored by the other great symphonists before him.   It may be that he felt unconsciously that the last word had not been spoken about this key ; that its qualities had been fringed too often yet not mastered completely except on such rare occasions as the Beethoven Fifth and Mozart *Jupiter* Symphonies.   Be that as it may, Brahms certainly invested the note C with a new significance when he made it the actuating force behind his First Symphony.   The message it conveys is one of such depths of feeling and at the same time one so elusive, that we never seem within reach of its full meaning.   The reiterations of that C are like the heart-beats of some metaphysical world dimly comprehensible and yet beyond our power of thought to analyse.   Beethoven, in his own

---

[1] If F major meant to Beethoven the green of the landscape, the trees, the flowers and birds, is not F minor the *only possible* key that can suggest the tempest enshrouding everything in its terrifying blackness?

way, solved this strange problem of the fundamental note C when Fate was no longer allowed to knock at the door in the triumphant closing major section of the Fifth Symphony. Yet the same problem in sound is back again sixty or seventy years later for Brahms to settle once more in much the same way.

In all this long struggle round the note C there must be some strange contact between music and philosophy, and it may be towards the solving of this sphinx-like riddle that the composer, a modern Œdipus, turns. If we examine the question of pitch in the light of what has been stated at the beginning of this chapter, certain conclusions immediately suggest themselves to the mind. For instance, if we take a theoretical note C that has *one* vibration per second and double the vibration number for each succeeding octave upwards (in accordance with the general laws of sound) we arrive at a Treble C that equals 512 vibrations per second. Round this Philosophical Pitch the finest masterpieces cluster like planets about some central orb. The great composers cannot get away from its influence ; they grope after the note C as after none other. The more classical the bent of their music the more they need it. Possibly the old modes were imagined by the ancient theoreticians near this pitch, although we are told that they were, as a rule, independent of any fixed tonality. The greater part of Wagner's opera *Die Meistersinger* is one of the most inspired illustrations ever written of the power of this note. Richard Strauss' Nietzschean tone-poem *Also sprach Zarathustra* sets its philosophic problem in this·key ; indeed, the contradiction at the very beginning between the major and minor chords is most eloquent, just as if the music were saying :—

> " Into this Universe and *why* not knowing
> Nor *whence*, like water willy-nilly flowing."

Numerous other examples, such as the great C major Symphony of Schubert, will readily spring to the minds of those well acquainted with the masterpieces of music. And, before resuming, I am fanciful enough to wonder whether there is more truth in the theories of old Pythagoras than is generally credited him in an unbelieving age.

It was not enough for Brahms, in his First Symphony, to recapture the combative spirit of the minor key of C and write the middle movements in some nearly related pitch such as is found in the slow movement of Beethoven's Fifth Symphony. Instead, he adopted a novel succession of keys for the various movements, which, for subtlety of thought and adroitness of effect, was far in advance of anything yet conceived in the symphonic form. Each movement is pitched a major third higher than the preceding one— C minor, E major, A flat major (G sharp), C minor (and, major).

The following table of keys illustrates the point.

The Symphony was first performed at Karlsruhe under Otto Dessoff on November 4th 1876, some three months after Wagner's *Ring of the Nibelungs* had been produced in its entirety at Bayreuth. 1876 was indeed an historic year.

One of the most fascinating things in all music of symphonic proportions is this correlation of keys, achieved either by the direct employment of at least one note carried forward from the triad of the previous key, or by means less direct, such as the inferential use of a note to suggest a new key, and of which the synonymous E flat—

D sharp in the above table (*a*)—is a most eloquent example. How far Brahms's working out of these problems was a subconscious matter actuated by instinct, or how far it was an analysed process of the intellect, no one can say. He kept but few sketches, destroying everything that showed a work in its early fragmentary stages.

In such matters Beethoven was often hard beset, and no better instance of this is afforded than the attempts made by him to define the key of the slow movement of the Fifth (*Emperor*) Piano Concerto. The first and third movements, as will be remembered, are pitched in E flat major. Beethoven's original sketch for the slow movement was in C.

Ex. 3   Tritone—B flat to E natural

Key of 1st movement   First sketch of slow movement

Could anything be more disagreeable to the ear than the *tritonish* effect produced by the juxtaposition of that E natural to the B flat in the chord which ends the first movement? Beethoven solved his problem by transposing the slow movement a semitone down, thereby turning his strong *E flat* of the first movement into a *D sharp* as romantic and beautiful as anything ever written. Brahms, one suspects, mastered these difficulties long before any notes were composed. To him they were fundamental matters of æsthetics, matters of design out of which would grow the thoughts to clothe and beautify the skeleton structure. They were the girders and crossbeams, more or less invisible to the eye, but vital to the architecture of his house of music and just as vital to the ear.

And so it can be reasonably inferred that Brahms did not experience Beethoven's initial difficulties. We have little evidence of that blind groping after keys and modulations which occasionally mars the work of the latter composer— more particularly in some early Piano Sonatas (but happily not in the Symphonies).

In the Second Symphony in D, Opus 73, produced under
Hans Richter's direction at a Vienna Philharmonic Society
concert on December 30th 1877, Brahms follows much the
same plan of key-sequences, allowing a predominant note in
one movement to become the basis of the next. F sharp
seems to control the first movement and indicates the key
of the second (B major). The B of this movement then
automatically becomes the major third of the key of the next
movement (G major) and we are then taken back to D major
for the finale—a simple transition from subdominant to
tonic that has the note D as the common factor.

It will be seen that the general scheme is again as simple as
in the First Symphony, all the keys being related by a
note common to two consecutive movements. Major-key
symphonies are much less subject to complexity of thought
than those cast in the minor, and so any drastic key changes
between the movements of this D major Symphony would
be out of keeping with the general character of the music.

The Third Symphony in F, Opus 90, was also produced in
Vienna on December 2nd 1883 under the same auspices
as the Second. Hans Richter again conducted. Couched
once more in the major key, it is of very different substance
to its predecessor. Lengthy excursions into minor keys (in
the third movement and most of the fourth) impart to it a
seriousness of purpose in marked contrast to the general
carefree character of the Second Symphony. The key-
sequences are as follows :—

Brahms seems to have become obsessed once again by the note C, which, it will be seen, is common to every movement. There are other features, too, that give the Symphony a character all its own. These are examined in later chapters. It is curious that out of the great feeling of optimism prevalent at the beginning of this Symphony there should grow an exceptional conflict with minor keys—a proceeding very rare indeed among symphonies that are written in a major key.[1]

Of the Fourth Symphony in E minor, Opus 98, it is difficult to write with moderation. There is so much grey matter in it that a full understanding of its qualities would seem to be an impossibility. We can only marvel at the strength of purpose which urged Brahms to the composition of such a remarkable piece of music. Here he seems to have banished for good and all every particle of that introspective mood against the danger of which he—the *thwarted romantic*, as I have seen him described somewhere—fought for the greater part of his life.

The Symphony was produced at Meiningen under the composer's direction on October 25th 1885. With the work as *cheval de bataille* and Brahms as conductor the Meiningen Orchestra toured Rhineland during the following month. Everywhere the Symphony was received with much enthusiasm. Even Spitta, greatest of Bach worshippers, stated that the slow movement had no equal anywhere in all symphonic music. That opinion, shared by others, was no doubt the result of a natural enthusiasm for a symphony born out of due time in an age of non-classical compositions.

The key sequences of this Symphony have again a common note (E) between them, as shown by the table.

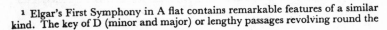

1st movement.   2nd   3rd   4th.

[1] Elgar's First Symphony in A flat contains remarkable features of a similar kind. The key of D (minor and major) or lengthy passages revolving round the

Many years before this work was written, Joachim had
suggested to Brahms that he should adopt the musical
motto F.A.E. (*Frei aber einsam—Free but lonely*). We have
seen how Brahms preferred the more optimistic F.A.F.
(*Free but glad*) and how this device, with variants, is found
scattered over the pages of his music. Yet in this, his last
great work for the orchestra alone, the insistence on the E
brings the *einsam* vividly to mind. When Brahms was
writing this symphony he was over fifty and becoming more
and more withdrawn into himself ; a man ploughing a lonely
furrow, looking into the beyond through the eyes of his
music ; still writing, like any student, his daily counterpoint with which to protect himself against the insidious
tendencies of the day. He was indeed a thwarted romantic,
repressing himself again and again as no composer before
or after him. Fanciful this all may sound. Nevertheless,
the spirit of *Einsamkeit* overshadows the whole work, the
boisterous third movement notwithstanding.   In this
Symphony we see Brahms as a man apart, returning to his
flat in the Karlsgasse or, maybe, seeking seclusion at
Mürzzuschlag in Styria (where he wrote most of the
work), tired of the glamour of public success, even perhaps
of the company of men in the Red Hedgehog smoke-room.
    Was the key of this Symphony preordained or was it a
matter of fortuitous chance ? We cannot say. We know,
however, that Kalbeck, despairing of the success of the work
implored Brahms not to perform it ; that even Hanslick (one
of the most discerning of Brahms's protagonists) looked
askance at its severe outlines and thought that this time the
composer had overshot the mark.   Yet today the work,
despite its brooding loneliness, holds the mind in thrall.   It
is undoubtedly one of the most impersonal masterpieces ever
penned, a fitting conclusion to the master's immortal
contributions to the world of the Symphony. It ends in
the stark minor, unredeemed by any concession to romance

note D, dominates the bulk of the music that is merely *framed* by the key of
A flat

or feminine influence.   What a picture we have here of this great musician-philosopher, doomed throughout his life to bachelordom, afraid to surrender to the call of the love that must have knocked at his heart many times ; shy, reserved, leaning on his shaky prop of Platonism, yet through or in spite of these things writing as his final symphonic message to the world, a work that sails among the stars and into the endless spaces of the universe.   It was fitting to end it thus, for the master had stretched out his arms towards the Absolute and the Infinite. A major ending would have limited it to the earth. We who know it so well (and yet so little) would have loved it the less for that.

CHAPTER IV

CHARACTERISTIC TOUCHES

IN his lifetime Robert Browning must have caught much of the fragrance of music and acquired more than an average knowledge of its technical terms. Here are some random lines from *A Toccata of Galuppi's* :—

"What ? Those lesser thirds so plaintive, sixths diminished,
    sigh on sigh,
Told them something ? Those suspensions, those solutions—
    'Must we die ? '
Those commiserating sevenths—'Life might last ! We can but
    try ! '

     ·   ·   ·   ·   ·   ·

Hark ! the dominant's persistence, till it must be answered to !

     ·   ·   ·   ·   ·   ·

So an octave struck the answer . . .
Brave Galuppi ! that was music ! " . . .

What a deep understanding the poet showed here of the many characteristics to be found in notes and intervals. His was a real musician's mind that could take in the quality of a sound and make its message clear through the medium of his own art. And similarly, if Brahms could write a succession of notes F.A.F., or something equivalent, reading into those notes a personal meaning intimately bound up with his own life, what could he not do with " those lesser thirds so plaintive," " the dominant's persistence " and all the thousand and one adventures in intervals that go to form such a large proportion of the composer's art ?

The strength of the dominant's persistence in music needs no comment here ; the plaintive cry of the minor (" lesser ") third is known to all and as easily understood.

But in much the same way as with the improper use of

harmonies, to which reference has already been made, so certain intervals or notes, if used too frequently in the wrong place, can weaken a melody and destroy its worth. And of this, as will be seen presently, Brahms was fully aware.

Now the strength of a composer's melodies is largely determined by his avoidance of a too frequent use of the *major* third of the primary triads (*i.e.*, those of the tonic, subdominant and dominant) on the *strong* beats of the bar. It is a curious and, upon examination, a most obvious fact that practically all the finest themes written obey this rule, not through deliberate conscious effort on the part of the composer but by reason of an intuitive process of the mind, functioning automatically. It has been shown already how the employment of the major common chord of the key brings with it a sense of completion, how the stress and conflict of music in the minor so often finds its solution in the major.[1] A palpable truism, no doubt, but one that I have never yet seen applied to the analysis of *melodies*.

Below are a few examples taken at random from familiar works by the great masters, in which the major thirds of the primary triads have been marked with an asterisk, and the harmonies roughly indicated.

1 See the tables of keys in the last chapter.

Ex.7

5th Symphony. Beethoven

[(*) Major 3rds, but not of primary triads.]

The last example is quoted to illustrate the romantic use of the major third. It is on this that our unconscious appreciation of the tender beauty of the music mainly depends.

That there are exceptions to the general rule above must of course be admitted, but all the same they are comparatively rare. The opening of Beethoven's *Waldstein* Pianoforte Sonata is a notable exception; yet the C major and B flat major chords (with their thirds uppermost) would lose their entire significance, robbed of their powerful rhythmic reiterations.

Pursuing this analysis still further we discover that, in melodies, strongly accented major thirds are used much more frequently in slow movements than elsewhere and (to narrow the issue down again) more frequently in second subjects of *Allegro* movements than in initial themes. We can therefore look upon the major third as a distinctly feminine thing in music, an ideal only to be realized on occasions; not to be squandered, but to be put aside the moment the music calls for stirring action. Mendelssohn, sentimental to a fault, succumbed to this major third influence far too often. I fancy that the secret of the cloying sweetness in so much of his music is to be found in the superabundance of this major third, as witness the following example (*Adagio !*).

Ex.8

Adagio   Symphony No.3. (the Scotch) Mendelssohn

Perhaps to such a cause can be traced the reason for the hesitant, qualified approval of much of his and Schumann's music, ar.d also the reason why the Brahms Ballade stagnates so painfully, despite its romantic atmosphere.[1]

Enough has been written on a technical matter of this kind to indicate that we shall discover all these forces at work in the Brahms Symphonies. We shall find the music very plaintive in its lesser thirds ; the dominant's persistence answered in resounding style, suspensions, (re)solutions, commiserating sevenths and all the other intervals taking their places to mix harmoniously with a discreet number of major thirds, whenever the composer needs the solace of romantic utterance.

Nietzsche and others of his time were exceedingly slow to recognize the individual style of Brahms's music. Opinions were so sharply divided that there was something like open warfare in the 'eighties between the Brahmsians on one side and the Brucknerites and Wagnerites on the other. Not that the adherents of the great Richard loved their " allies " ; they merely used Bruckner as a catspaw in order to show their contempt for the less sensuous music of Johannes Brahms—music that worshipped at the shrine of Athene, flouting Aphrodite, singing of Pierian meadows and never of the Venusberg.[2] Such music, especially when championed by eminent artists and critics like Joachim and Hanslick, was in itself a direct challenge to the methods of Wagner. Therein lay its fault. Beethoven was dead, praised to the skies by Wagner himself, who had of course the most profound admiration for the master's music and who interpreted

[1] See p. 21.

[2] Anton Bruckner (1824–1896) is little known in this country, but in Austria he is reverenced by many almost as much as Brahms. He wrote eight Symphonies and an incomplete ninth, works of great length and wealth of ideas. Bruckner had not the sureness of expression of Brahms (no less than five of the Symphonies required revision by the composer) and the religious and mystic element of much of his music has undoubtedly limited its popularity outside Southern Germany and Austria. There, *in situ*, he is regarded as a great classical composer. Brahms's most emphatic display of sarcasm— " Bruckner's Symphonies immortal ? It is ludicrous ! "—was the outcome of prejudice against the music, not against the man.

the Symphonies with consummate skill. But to the Wagnerites it was another matter to have in their midst a living reactionary, obviously a genius, one who disdained the school of realism by reverting to the methods of the dead Beethoven. This had to be stopped at all costs because it implied the falsity of all things Wagnerian.[1] Thus, for instance, the hisses that marred the conclusion of the Third Symphony's first performance at Vienna—hisses that were drowned in a storm of applause from the faithful who saw this work as yet another example of the composer's mastery over form and thematic material.

In those days, it will be seen, the individual style of Brahms's music had little chance of being recognized. There was too much thunder in the air. The atmosphere reverberated so noisily with the music of Wagner, Berlioz and Liszt that anything written in the old style was by many condemned at once, sentenced and summarily executed without any fair trial. But to continue.

There is a marked difference between the themes in the Beethoven Symphonies and those in the Brahms. Beethoven's are largely concordant, *i.e.*, the main notes of the themes belong to the harmony itself and, by comparison, rarely occur as *dissonant* auxiliary or passing notes needing resolution. One example from Beethoven and another from Brahms will suffice to illustrate these characteristic differences.

Ex. 9   Symphony No. 3. (the Eroica) Beethoven

[1] When, in 1883, Brahms sent a wreath to Wagner's funeral, Cosima, Wagner's widow, remarked—" Why should the wreath be acknowledged ? *I understand the man was no friend to Our Art.*" (See Ethel Smyth's *Impressions that Remained.* Longmans, Green & Co.) Again, my own mother, who, as a girl, used to play piano duets with Siegfried Ochs, a famous choral conductor and friend of Brahms, often told me in the early 'nineties of the bitter strife between the Brahms and Wagner camps. Later, to her regret, I became violently Wagnerian, the while she pointed out the beauty of her idol's music to an errant son. As recently as the early 'nineties the old feuds were still alive, it will be seen ; even disturbing the peace of a Worcestershire home.

It will be seen how the Beethoven theme agrees at all points with the harmony, whereas in the Brahms example, there are two notes (*) that require resolution. This is a marked characteristic of Brahms and also of his great contemporary Wagner. Notice, however, in the two following examples, the different methods of these two composers.

Brahms, despite the general semitone movement of the music, preserves his tonality by means of the C bass, while Wagner, in a similar yet (paradoxically) vastly different passage of rising semitones, gives us a series of chromatic chords that for many bars afterwards finds no secure home in any given tonality.

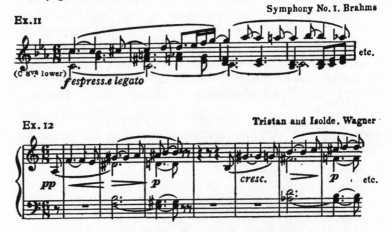

Was it through such superficial similarities that Liszt visualized Brahms as belonging to his party of realists? I doubt very much whether the radical differences between Brahms and Wagner were properly recognized in the composers' lifetime, for chromatic melodic movement was part of the general technique of the day and many composers came under its spell and influence. Partisans of one composer probably accused the other side of thunder stealing because they little realized that this general technique was not the personal property of anyone in particular, but merely the natural and long overdue development of old laws governing the harmonious combination of sounds.

In addition to his liking for melodic notes not immediately concordant with the harmony, Brahms invented or developed other individual characteristics that singled him out as a composer of great originality. Perhaps the most important of all these was the novel way in which he enlarged the accentual interest and vitality of music by what can be described as *softening the hard edges of the bar-line*. This, of course, had been done by other composers, and was a particularly notable feature of Elizabethan vocal music of the madrigal type, written by composers who preferred true verbal stresses and accents to an arbitrary use of bar-lines. Brahms did much the same thing in his orchestral music by using to a larger extent than ever before a device much exploited by Beethoven, namely, the transference of an accent either to the weak beats of the bar or off the beat altogether.

Ex.13

Such developments made the music flexible. They helped to prevent stagnation, to eliminate square-cut sections and, further, to give increased vitality all round. This, to Brahms, was the best way to maintain interest and ensure a logical development of his thematic material.

Besides all this fascinating play of rhythms between and over the bar-lines, Brahms, of all the great classical masters,

was the one who did most to break down the tyranny
of the four-bar phrase. While it is not necessary here
to trace more than briefly what is meant, it should be
remembered that the four-bar phrase and its double-length
companion of eight bars are to composers what quatrain and
octet stanzas are to the poet, namely, standard phrase-lengths
that must of necessity form the basis of the greater part of
their work. It matters not whether it be a song, a waltz, a
Beethoven sonata or a symphony, a Mozart minuet, a
Bach gavotte, a foxtrot or a tango; everything falls
naturally into that mould unless a composer has an extremely
fanciful or quixotic turn of mind—like the poet's that can
imagine ballades, triolets, rondeaus or other uncommon
forms—and can conceive phrases which are either longer or
shorter than those of standard length. Brahms, in his desire
to expand the design and forms of music rather than languish
in an opulence of harmony, must have pondered at length
over the possibilities of cheating these unadventurous phrase-
lengths by the use of others three, five and seven bars long.
We can imagine his joy when he discovered that manuscript
Chorale *St. Antoni* by Haydn, a melody constructed on
two five-bar phrases, followed by nineteen bars, grouped
4, 4, 4, 2, 2, 3.

Ex. 14

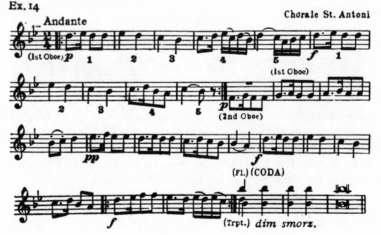

Around this lovely theme he composed those masterly variations, all of which, together with the finale, conform to the five-bar phraseology shown in the quotation above. The first variation begins backwards with a statement of the *coda* notes of the theme. How gratified Brahms must have been when he discovered this remarkably original opening, so unlike all others. The ingenuity displayed is entirely natural and the effect, coming where it does, takes one completely by surprise.

Later, in the First Symphony, we shall find a passage that is originally a five-bar phrase, expanded, as the movement progresses, into one of seven bars. And again in the third movement of the Second Symphony there are variations of similar rhythmical patterns, extraordinarily interesting to the ear and also to the eye of the score reader. Not content with all this freedom from conventional four-bar shackles (for Brahms was a great adventurer in his own classical way), there is even a theme with a double time-signature,

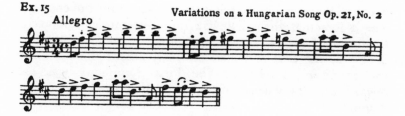

Ex. 15 Allegro Variations on a Hungarian Song Op. 21, No. 2

also treated to a series of variations. Here Brahms keeps the alternating time-signature going for eight variations out of the thirteen comprising the work.

His devotion to the variation form—he wrote no less than seven sets altogether—was the outcome of his studies in counterpoint. These were all written before the First Symphony and must have acted as a stimulating contributory cause toward the shaping of this and the other three symphonies that followed. And the last of all was

the *St. Anthony*, the only set that he wrote for orchestra.[1]
In most of Brahms's larger works we see a foreshadowing
of other compositions of similar style, and certainly in these
Variations fleeting glimpses of the First Symphony are
visible here and there. It should not be forgotten that
sketches of the Symphony were already in existence at the
time this work was written. Brahms always had the future
in view, and it is more than likely that these Variations, fine
as they are as music (even apart from their purely technical
excellence), were but another exercise in the forms of
counterpoint that were to stand the composer in such good
stead in the First Symphony.

By sheer industry Brahms had now overcome the limitations of his youth. First of all, as we have seen, there
was the suppression of romantic music of the false kind ;
then a further intensive course of counterpoint without
which no symphony could hope to be a symphony proper ;
studies and experiments in orchestration ; then the matter
of key-sequences, and finally the fusion of the thematic
material into an unified whole. It should also be remembered that the many exercises in phrases of unconventional
length loosened the whole fabric of his music, liberating
it from the overworked convention of the four-square.
Such was the task to which the master bent the whole of
his mind and intellect. The First Symphony was his
reward, and the writing of the other three made the easier
thereby.

We have seen how Brahms focused his attention on the
many technical points just mentioned, how he could not
have " created without hard work," and how he took the
threads of his music one by one to weave them into a pattern
woof on warp. " Music," he said to Henschel, " must be
perfect, but whether it is beautiful or not is another matter."
It would be foolish to deny that Brahms, in his search

---

[1] The *St. Anthony Variations* are in two forms, viz. (*a*) for Orchestra, and
(*b*) for Two Pianos.

for perfection, sometimes overlooked the creation of the beautiful. With a composer of such technique this was bound to happen on occasions. We are inclined to make too much of a cry over the dry formal patches that everyone knows can be found in the music here and there. And it is quite an everyday criticism to charge the composer with labouring over themes that have little intrinsic worth. In the end, Brahms comes in for a good deal of disapproval somewhat undeserved.

There is a great difference between the obvious and the inevitable, a fact not always recognized by those who are inclined to criticize harshly. "Great art," said a philosopher (was it Schopenhauer ?) " is the saying of uncommon things in the common language." All the great masters in music have relied on this simple aphorism. If it can be urged against Brahms, in his use of the common language, that he is dull at times, what shall be said of Bach, Beethoven, Mozart, Haydn and Schubert ? Homer also nodded. So let us leave the masters to their sleep when they need it and live with them only in their waking moments. We forgive Shakespeare *Timon of Athens* because of *Julius Cæsar.* Similarly, we can endure any uninspired moments in Brahms, Bach, Beethoven or Schubert because of the legacy of their imperishable masterpieces.

It is not an easy matter to detect the melodic shortcomings that may exist in the four Brahms Symphonies. Many of the themes are so simple, as, for example, those at the opening of the first movement of the Second Symphony and the second movement of the Third Symphony, that the tendency is to belittle them because of this patent quality. Because they are founded on the first three or four notes of the harmonic series they are often dismissed as being of no real significance. This view, however, is chiefly confined to those modern iconoclasts who disbelieve that music primarily depends on its obedience to certain basic laws. From simple beginnings Brahms builds up his music, knitting the fabric so closely together that its qualities will be obscured from the mind of the listener unless it be fully

understood what development is taking place. Even
Wagner, that great wizard of orchestral sounds—he who
understood so well what every instrument could do in
any particular register of its pitch, and how much it could be
relied on to add effectively to the general mass of the sound—
even Wagner knew the value of the modest beginning. The
Valhalla motif that originates so simply and serenely in the
second scene of *Rheingold* is nothing more than a melodic
illustration of the three primary triads—*tonic* (I), *dominant* (V)
subdominant (IV)—learnt by every student of elementary
harmony.

The godlike majesty of this theme depends on its simplicity.
Had Wagner commenced with a more complicated harmonic
scheme it is indeed doubtful whether he could have carried
this theme through to its logical conclusion at the end of
Götterdämmerung. There, amid the holocaust of Valhalla in
flaming ruin, he utilizes three or four other main themes in
conjunction with this motif, either by direct combination or
at cæsural points in the development of the main Valhalla
theme. And so, as befits the dramatic situation, themes
representing Valhalla, the Rhine, the Curse of the Ring,
Redemption through Love, etc., all find themselves cheek by
jowl in the last moments of that great pagan Odyssey of
sound.

It is difficult to appreciate the kind of reasoning that allows
such a plan in *dramatic* music and yet turns to criticism of a
condemnatory kind when the same methods are applied to
the construction of *absolute* music. The amazing synthesis
of Brahms's music is at once its glory and its tediousness,
according to the personal reactions of the listener. A symphony has its own drama ; its movements are the various

acts in that drama and everything builds up (or should do) to some inevitable climax very akin to what has just been described. Brahms takes all his simple material and develops it to a degree not found in any other symphonies, with the possible exception of the last movement of Mozart's *Jupiter*.[1] Herein lies the excellence of these four works. That they are also beautiful is the judgment of the world after nearly half a century's appreciation of their sheer musical worth and their technical skill.

The disarming simplicity of the music in many instances is indeed a trap to the unwary. When one of the smart critics of the 'seventies pointed out to Brahms the similarity between the "Ode to Joy" theme from Beethoven's Choral Symphony and Brahms's own gloriously-swinging theme in the finale of his First Symphony, the composer in all his gruffness replied, "Any fool can see that"—a riposte that admits of no further argument.

It is deeper down than this that we must look for the salient features of a composer's style and of his greatness. Critics of today are much more discerning than those of fifty years ago; superficial characteristics of style no longer act as a snare and delusion, blinding the eyes and closing the ears to a proper appreciation of the fundamental worth of the music.

It goes without saying that the first essential to a symphony is unity of thought between the movements. This cannot be achieved by hard work unless the themes themselves are actually worth fashioning and polishing. Many a symphony has been written by a cunning hand through clever cerebration. And, in this respect, it is interesting to recall the painstaking attempts made by Brahms's talented friend Heinrich von Herzogenberg[2] to achieve by workmanship

[1] Here there are five distinct themes used in astounding double and triple contrapuntal combinations—a feat without parallel anywhere. The themes are so constructed that over a hundred different combinations would have been possible. This movement is in fact an amazingly ingenious " cross-music " puzzle.

[2] Heinrich Picot de Peccaduc, Freiherr von Herzogenberg (to give him his

alone what Brahms himself could do only when primarily guided by the power of inspiration.

[Beethoven's Sketch Books are eloquent undecipherable proofs of the grim struggles that must have taken place in the composer's mind before artifice could hold inspiration long enough to give the music its true outward expression.]

If, then, this unity of thought is the acknowledged basis of all symphonies, how can it be detected? We tread on dangerous ground when the dissection of inspiration is attempted, for the intuitive processes of the mind defy analysis :—

> " Where neither ground is for the feet
> Nor any path to follow,
> No map there, no guide."

This unity of thought between movements must assuredly depend on something tangible, not merely on the elusive qualities bound up in these intuitive processes of the mind. There must be somewhere in the music some outward and visible signs of what has been conceived subconsciously. We can often sense from the Beethoven Sketch Books what the composer is attempting to express. Still, those fragments of themes in the raw state hardly tell us why the *second* movement of a symphony does in very truth grow out of the *first*. Everything depends on the impression created in the composer's mind during the outpouring of his first movement. What he has already written seems to indicate the germ of the music that follows. There may be the obsession of a single note ; there may be the strong pull of a certain sequence of notes or phrases driven into the

full name) and his wife Elizabet enjoyed the friendship of Brahms for many years from 1876 onwards—he till Brahms's death in 1897, she till her own in 1892. Brahms came to rely on Elizabet's judgment on his music to an extraordinary degree, even sending her part of the score of the Fourth Symphony before the work was completed—a most unusual practice for a composer who was very secretive about his unfinished works. The *Herzogenberg Letters*, of which Kalbeck edited no less than 281, are indeed among the most intimate records of Brahms we possess. To these letters references will occur later in this book.

composer's brain to come out again in subtly altered form in another movement.

The linking up of moods between the two movements of Schubert's *Unfinished* Symphony is a remarkable illustration of this. From the B minor conclusion of the first movement we are translated into that serenely, yet at times tempestuously beautiful slow movement in E major. It may be argued that B becomes the dominant of the key of the new movement, acting as an obvious link, and that there is nothing very extraordinary in the fact. But the link depends on more than that. Nineteen bars before the conclusion of the first movement we hear this progression.

Ex. 17

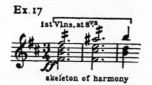

This is repeated much more forcefully with *fortissimo* detached chords five bars from the end of the movement. The initial thought, however, can be traced long before the nineteen bars from the end. At the ninety-second bar of the movement it puts in its first appearance thus :—

Ex. 18

It is vaguely suggested again four bars before the repeat of the first section, being divided between a *pizzicato* F sharp on the strings and the first Flute two bars later, where the latter instrument reinforces the A sharp, B of the first Oboe. Again, at the sixty-fifth, sixty-sixth and sixty-seventh bars of the second section, and also two bars before the *réprise* of the first section, there are further references to it.

Now it may be argued that a few coincident notes that are purely cadential in their character and thereby secondary in relation to the main subject-matter are, as tailpieces, insufficient in themselves to create a link between two movements. But after conducting many performances of this Symphony over a period of twenty-five or thirty years, I am convinced that in this *secondary* detail we find the *primary* creative impulse for the lovely opening of the slow movement.

Ex. 19

[Note the First Bassoon.]

Again, in Tchaikovsky's Fourth Symphony in F minor, there is a most interesting alliance between the four movements, caused through the fall of four notes—this time at the beginning of each main theme and not in cadences, with an additional chromatic B natural thrown in in the instance of the first movement).

Ex. 20

Brahms is much more subtle in his use of the abstract essence of themes or notes transferred from one movement to another. The whole tissue of his symphonic music is so closely knit that it is quite impossible to identify every family tie. Many of those ties that are demonstrated later in the analyses have become evident only through frequent conducting of the Symphonies. Each time there is a new discovery ; each time the feeling that there is still more to be revealed.

So far this chapter has dealt with an analysis of the main characteristics of the composer's style, and little reference has been made to Brahms's method of harmonization because it has been generally explained in Chapter II.

The glowing warmth of much of his harmony comes from the rich uses he makes of dissonant notes, either suspended from a previous harmony, or employed accentually on the *stronger* beats of the bar and resolved on the weaker beats. The general nature of this book prevents more than a brief reference to this fine characteristic, but the following example, taken from the opening of the Pianoforte *Intermezzi*, Op. 116, No. 6, is all the more eloquent when it is shown (in the following skeleton structure of the harmony) how diatonically simple the music is—actually only one note, A sharp, being chromatic to the triads or chords of the key of E major, the remaining accidentals merely indicating dissonant passing notes.[1]

Ex. 21

---

[1] Sir George Henschel tells how Brahms, with whom he was on terms of intimate friendship for over twenty years, once cautioned him on this very matter. " And then, my dear friend, let me counsel you : no heavy disso-

The richness of the harmony is all the more remarkable because in it we find none of that pandering to chromatic chords of the sensuous kind so beloved by modern composers. In such things lay the strength of Brahms's smaller romantic compositions, and, for that reason, even such music cannot but be enduring. It is founded throughout on the basis of diatonic harmony, which in its own turn has sprung from the well of natural sounds. That is why Brahms, great classicist as he was, could also afford to be the romanticist of the *Lieder* and the lesser pianoforte pieces. Through experiences of this kind, wherein everything was tempered with discretion, he gathered to himself more and more of the spirit of true music, music that was perfect in technique and masterly in effect.

nances on the unaccented parts of the bar, please ! That is weak. I am very fond of dissonances, you'll agree, but on the heavy, accented parts of the bar, and then let them be resolved easily and gently." (*Musings and Memories*, by Sir George Henschel. Macmillan and Co. Ltd., London.)

CHAPTER V

BRAHMS'S ORCHESTRATION

AS is well-known, opinions differ about Brahms's methods of orchestration, and even today there are those who see but little virtue in the composer in this respect. No other master of his reputation has encountered so much diverse and unflattering criticism. Adjectives like turgid, thick, monotonous, colourless, dull, uninteresting have clustered round his scoring like ivy round a tree because his stern suppression of all garish colouration was at complete variance with the accepted practices of his famous contemporaries. The growing tendency for the last hundred years to indulge in explosive orchestration and false conceptions in regard to the true sonority of sound—*sound* being on occasions merely a synonym for *noise*—has hindered to a large degree the true appreciation of Brahms the orchestrator.

It was unfortunate that Brahms should be born into the era of Liszt, Berlioz and Wagner. They were in their heyday, each with very individual ideas about the orchestra and how to write for it ; each piling Pelion on Ossa in attempts to press the last ounce of sonority into their large-scale works ; bent on giving the world quantity even if it meant less in the way of sheer quality. By these methods they had attracted the interest of the many who rejoiced in this new revolution in music ; Liszt by such extended works as his *Dante* and *Faust* Symphonies, Berlioz by his *Damnation de Faust*, Wagner by his *Rienzi, Flying Dutchman, Tannhäuser, Faust in Solitude*, etc. In those days Goethe was quite the standard dramatist for these revolutionary musicians. By following the sinister necromantic spirit of his *Faust* they soon found themselves inventing, out of sheer necessity, many new realistic touches and tricks in the orchestration. These essays revolving round Goethe were but characteristic examples of the forceful orchestration that had developed through the onward sweep of realism and romanticism in music. Every department in the orchestra had to be enlarged considerably to meet the demands of the moment. The customary double wood-wind (*i.e.*, two of each family of flutes, oboes, clarinets and bassoons), brass, and the (usually) solitary percussion instruments, the two timpani, were insufficient to express all the storm and stress that now gathered round music like the black clouds of an oncoming tempest.

In these circumstances Music was bound to attract her uncouth half-brother Noise ; bound, because of her willing or unwilling acceptance of the new school of thought, to turn to sounds of indeterminate pitch that often ran without rhyme or reason contrariwise to everything that the art had stood for previously. The parting of the ways had come. Gradually there appeared in the orchestra more and more percussive instruments, such as side, tenor and bass drums, cymbals, tambourine, triangle, etc., which were used, often with indiscriminate taste, as rhythmic pointers to the sounds of definite pitch.[1]

Round about this time, from 1820 onwards, Europe was rarely out of the throes of warfare or revolutions. A Miguelite dynastic struggle in Portugal and a similar civil war in Spain were but precursors to the overthrow of the monarchy of Louis-Philippe in France in 1848. During this year revolution also broke out in Vienna, while the Magyars defeated the Hapsburgs and the National Liberals of Germany endeavoured to form a constitutional empire, an attempt which failed owing to the autocratic obstinacy of

---

[1] I am conscious here of the great musical skill and discretion shown by Wagner in his later works, by Bizet in his immortal *Carmen*, etc., where the composers used the percussion department of the Orchestra as special rather than general effects. But, *per contra*, heaven preserve music from any more *Rienzis !*

Frederick William IV., King of Prussia.[1]   Europe was in the melting-pot once again, and when there is a clash of arms composers will indulge in many a clash of cymbals.

So in this period of national and political unrest and disturbances music could not avoid taking on some of the general characteristics of the day, especially when handled by artistic revolutionaries of the Berlioz and Wagner types. A composer would need a good deal of vision and common sense to realize that these ephemeral events, mighty in themselves at the time, were but a poor stimulating force for the creation of world-masterpieces which would outlive the memory of such events.   As already stated, Wagner had made himself the musical prototype of the new Germania that was arising.   But how far this aided the growth of that powerful military machine which wrought such havoc in Europe is beyond estimation.   It is enough to remember that the rhythm of the drums, the clash of cymbals, and the martial strains of brass instruments in full cry are potent means for precipitating a fevered nation into war.

Amid all this discontent, this noise, Brahms was unaffected by the events of the day.   In four symphonies he used what is to all intents and purposes the ordinary classical orchestra. Beyond that he did not care to go.   Except for one tiny triangle used in the third movement of the Fourth Symphony he nowhere used any other percussion instruments save the timpani.

For this fine and inherently musical characteristic of restraint he was much misunderstood.   He was regarded as some kind of musical monk, living in times long since dead, out of touch with the world and ignorant of all progress. Decidedly his orchestration was out of date ; it lacked modern attractiveness, for he only used his instruments in the manner of Beethoven or of Schubert.

He would adhere whenever it was possible to the old-

---

[1] Wagner was implicated in the Dresden riots of 1849. A warrant was issued for his arrest, he being described as a " politically dangerous individual," but through the good offices of Liszt he was able to escape from the country.

fashioned use of the " open " notes on the Horns and Trumpets because he knew that these instruments were at their best thus. He preferred the Waldhorn (Hand-Horn) to the Ventilhorn (Valve-Horn) and made of it a thing of beauty, a medium for the creation of some of his most wonderful melodies. Chromatic music (obtainable by means of the valves) on instruments designed primarily for diatonics was anathema to him : he would have none of it.[1]

Comparison between the diatonic Horn melodies in a Brahms symphony and their chromatic brassy brilliance in those by Elgar does not come amiss here, for it illustrates the difference between the classical and modern romantic schools. The first composer explores with much restraint the whole nature of the instrument, from its highest effective melodic notes down to the sustaining notes in the bass clef, and in such a comfortable and comforting way that variety is always present. The other composer, brilliant in the extreme, makes so much use of the higher registers of pitch and of chromatic notes that the instrument is apt to lose its especial identity and become merged into the general monotonous tension of the sound—a disturbing characteristic not confined to the works of our great English composer alone.

The Harp is not to be found in a Brahms Symphony because there is no place in the music where it can be introduced with effect. Brahms was throughout his life very chary of using this instrument, doubtless through fear of creating too sensuous an effect by its soft clinging tones.

Rarely, in fact, does the contrapuntal nature of his music (even apart from the æsthetic misgivings just mentioned) admit of a successful employment of the Harp. It can be found in the first two and final numbers of the *German Requiem*, used with great discretion, firstly and lastly to

[1] See p. 28 in respect to what is written about the series of natural harmonics.

convey an atmosphere of spirituality and, in the second number, to illustrate a text which says that " all flesh is as grass and the flowers of the field wither and fade away."

Brahms knew the quality and effect of the Harp very well indeed and through a chain of happy circumstances was able to use this instrument to great effect in his Op. 17—four Choruses for female voices, accompanied by two Horns (a real Brahms touch) and Harp.   In 1859, after the hostile reception given at Leipzig to the D minor Pianoforte Concerto, Brahms returned in bitter disappointment to Hamburg for the winter.   In St. Michael's Church he happened to hear a Ladies' Choir perform a motet by a local musician, one Graedener.   So struck was he with the beauty of their singing that he let them study three of his own sacred choruses, including the *Ave Maria*, Op. 12, and these were performed in the church in due course.   Out of these happy beginnings the Hamburg Ladies' Choir was soon formed, with Brahms as conductor, and the four choruses—*I hear a Harp, The Gardener, Come away, Death* and *The death of Trenar*—followed as a natural sequel.

Here was an occasion for inspiration, and Brahms, spurred on by affection for his bright-eyed enthusiastic young choir of twenty-eight voices—he was always susceptible to feminine charms in his own shy, almost passionless way—produced these lovely things in which the combination of voices and instruments is, in its way, a piece of perfect orchestration.

Of *I hear a Harp* Specht writes : " A magic horn, something of a Minnesinger's exultation, may be perceived in the prelude and postlude."   In *The Gardener* the Harp arpeggiates a simple accompaniment and the Horns play a two-part sustain to the harmony on simple natural harmonic notes only (with a hand-stopped B added) while the chorus sings a lovely melody redolent of the flowers expressed in Eichendorff's poem.   Did Brahms, in writing *Come away, Death,* have in mind the Illyrian Duke's words to Viola ?

" O fellow, come, the song we had last night :—
Mark it, Cesario, it is old and plain :
The spinsters and the knitters in the sun,
And the free maids that weave their thread with bones
Do use to chant it : it is silly sooth,
And dallies with the innocence of love
Like the old age."

(*Clown sings " Come away, Death "*)

Or was this composition (and perhaps *The Gardener* too)
prompted by platonic dalliance with the fair Agathe von
Siebold,[1] she who occupied so much of his thought at the
time.

Old and plain these choruses are in many ways and they
certainly dally " with the innocence of love like the old age,"
helped along by those highly original, almost terse accom-
paniments for Horns and Harp. *The Death of Trenar*[2] takes
us still further back. It possesses all the remoteness of the
Third Century, when, so we are told, the bard Ossian sang
the deeds of the mighty warrior Fingal to his Gaelic harp
in that misty ghostly land of Morven. The bardic sweep of
the Harp strings is a notable effect in the music and the
use of the Hand-Horns—this time with quite a number of
accidental notes that are produced, not by valves, but by
shifting the position of the hand inside the " bell " of the
instrument—suggests an empty dreariness and a ghostliness
of atmosphere that sends quite a shiver down the spine.

" Weep on the rocks of the winds that are roaring
Weep, O thou maiden of Inistore,
And over the waves let thy fair head bend,
Lovelier than the ghost of the mountains,[3]

---

[1] She was the beautiful, intellectual and highly musical daughter of a
Professor of Medicine at Göttingen, who was also a scientist. Brahms wrote
three Vocal Duets with Pianoforte accompaniment for her (Op. 20) and was,
no doubt influenced by like feelings when writing the B flat Sextet (Op. 18) and
the Five Songs (Op. 19).

[2] The text is from Book I. of Ossian's epic poem *Fingal*, translated (or
written, according to Dr. Johnson) by James MacPherson, and first published
in 1762. MacPherson died in 1796 and is buried in Westminster Abbey.

[3] " A blast came from the mountain, on its wings was the spirit of Loda "
(? Odin). *Carric-thura*. Ossian.

That which at noon, in the brightness of the sun
Over the silence of Morven moves."[1]

This brief digression from the main subject-matter of this book perhaps serves the general argument to some purpose, for in writing such harmonically simple passages for the Horns Brahms was once again paving his way to the First Symphony, which was not written until fifty other works had come from his pen. And in exploiting the Harp for romantic music, with the composer sometimes in the guise of bard or minnesinger, Brahms shows us clearly why this instrument never again appeared in his purely orchestral music. What he did was done deliberately, because, as we know already, vivid colours with him were secondary to the music itself.

It is almost a matter for regret that the Bass Tuba appears in the Second Symphony. While it must be admitted that it serves its purpose well in a work that is totally different in character from its three companions, one could have wished it otherwise. Brahms's thickening of the bass line of his harmony by the use of the Contra Bassoon in the other Symphonies is a remarkable piece of insight ; in fact it is impossible to imagine the Symphonies without this effect of expanded richness deep down in their foundations. Why was the Tuba substituted in No. 2 ? The work hardly gains by the change, for, although there are a few indispensable notes here and there (notably in the section commencing in D minor, seventy-seven bars before the close of the finale) there is not an effect in the music that could not have been obtained by the retention of the Contra Bassoon ; not an effect that would have suffered had we never known in the Second Symphony the sound of that strange and uncompanionable instrument. In the opinion of many, a single Tuba is hardly worth while, for the tone-colour dominates an orchestra most alarmingly owing to its lack of combinative quality.

[1] Translated by Rev. Dr. Troutbeck. Music published by Novello & Co. Ltd., London.

There are, apart from this solitary instance of the Bass Tuba, no other instruments employed in the Brahms Symphonies that cannot be found in Beethoven.   True, Brahms employs four Horns throughout instead of Beethoven's

PLAN OF ORCHESTRA.

	Brahms's Symphonies.	Wagner's *Ring*.	Elgar's 2nd Symphony.
Flutes } . .	2	3	} 3 (including
Piccolos } . .	1 [1]	2	Piccolo)
Oboes } .	2	4	2
Cor Anglais } .	—	1	1
Clarinets } .	2	3	3 [8]
Bass Clarinet } .	—	1	1
Bassoons . }	2	3	2
Contra Bassoon }	1	—	1
Horns . .	4	8	4
Trumpets .	2	4 [3]	3
Trombones .	3	4 [4]	3
Tubas . .	1 [2]	5 [5]	1
Timpani . .	2 [3] [1]	4	3
Percussion (extra)	1 [1]	4	4
Harps . .	—	6 [6]	2
Strings . .	(No particular number specified)	64 [7]	(No particular number specified)

[1] Third movement (and Fourth movement for Timpani only) of Fourth Symphony.
[2] Second Symphony only.
[3] Including a Bass Trumpet.
[4] Including a Contra-Bass Trombone.
[5] Two Tenor, two Bass and one Contra-Bass Tuba.
[6] Wagner might just as well have asked for the Moon !
[7] Sixteen 1st and sixteen 2nd Violins, twelve Violas, twelve Violoncellos, eight Basses.
[8] Including small Clarinet in E flat.

customary two, but the music demands it.[1]   The moods are more complex, the keys through which the music travels

[1] Beethoven uses three Horns in the *Eroica* (No. 3) Symphony and four in the *Choral* (No. 9) Symphony. In the other Symphonies there are only two. Many conductors now double the Horn parts, particularly in No. 5 in C minor and No. 7 in A—a practice that is not approved by many musicians.

more variable. And so Brahms, to preserve his cherished principle of using as far as possible only the unvalved (open) or hand-stopped notes on the Horns, had recourse to another pair out of sheer necessity.[1]

The list of the instruments (p. 72) used by Brahms in his Symphonies makes interesting reading when compared with that used by Wagner in the *Ring of the Nibelungs* and by Elgar in his Second Symphony. The comparison with Wagner demonstrates how Brahms kept aloof from the expansion of the orchestra in 1876—the year of his First Symphony and of the production of the complete *Ring* at Bayreuth. The comparison with Elgar is interesting in that it shows the expansion of the orchestra to meet the demands of twentieth-century symphonic music.

Wagner's formidable list, which would require at least 110 players, makes Brahms's orchestra look almost like a toy. But since the former needed his numbers for the sake of the presentation of his music-dramas on the stage, while the latter was only concerned in abstract problems in sound, no real comparison is possible. More is possible in the case of Elgar, for, if we exclude the Contra Bassoon that is used by both composers, we find that Brahms thinks in *twos* in the Wood-wind family while Elgar thinks in *threes*. [We must remember that the Cor Anglais is actually a member of the Oboe family. The Bass Clarinet explains itself.]

Herein lies the difference between the classical and the modern composer. The one is content with the use of a restricted number of instruments to give a straightforward, yet, when necessary, sufficiently coloured presentation of the music ; the other calls for mass sonority—double Wood-wind would prove utterly inadequate—so that the themes and counter-themes can all be plaited into an iridescent pattern

---

[1] It is really a technical question, outside the scope of this present book, involving the whole principle underlying what are called the *transposing instruments* of the Orchestra. But, for those interested, it is perhaps permissible to state here that Brahms's directions are rarely followed nowadays because Horn players, since the introduction of the Valve-Horn, have learnt to play practically everything on the F crook—transposing the music by means of the valves. Modern German rotary action Horns simplify matters still further.

having no loose ends anywhere.   Which school of thought
is the more satisfactory and satisfying is difficult to say, for
the whole matter is one of personal reactions.   But it does
involve a burning question—*whether colour is, or is not, a
detrimental adjunct to the symphony?*   Can our ears, our
minds, accept classical design and vivid colouration at one
and the same time?   Brahms thought otherwise and
expunged from his consciousness all thoughts of the opulent
orchestration he could obtain from Wood-wind in *threes*.
And the important fact stands out that not one of the great
classical symphonies depends for its success on colour obtainable through the use of extra wind instruments.   Works
like the César Franck Symphony in D minor pall on the
musical sense as much on account of excessive richness in
the Wood-wind scoring as on account of faulty construction
or redundant chromatic harmonies.

But to return to our old-fashioned Brahms ; old-fashioned
now for two reasons—his contemptuous disregard for the
sonorous orchestration of his illustrious compeers and his
preoccupation with the unvalved Brass instruments.   His
Symphonies, unaffected, unadorned, never fail to illustrate
the old argument about the plain and fancy keys of music.[1]
Straightforward themes in plain keys demand direct methods
of scoring, there is no doubt.   Equally, orchestral music in the
more remote keys will conjure forth romantic colouration
from the instruments.   Just as the great German-Austrian
composers begin, so to speak, in C major and make it the
philosophic basis of their music, so do the prolific French
composers (who do not show any uncontrollable desire to
turn to philosophy in music) avoid that key ninety-nine times
out of a hundred because the greatness of its quality eludes
their particular natures.[2]   That is why ornamental scoring of
the nebulously indirect kind, as found in many composers
like Debussy, Ravel, Dukas, etc., has caught the Frenchmen

---

[1] See p. 37.

[2] Debussy wrote his composition for Piano *Doctor Gradus ad Parnassum* in the
key of C.   Was this intended as a sly piece of anti-Teutonic humour ?

in its toils—much to the gain of colour but little to the gain of music apart from colour. To their many delightful fancies we surrender gladly, for such compositions are the lightly-sketched water-colours and *intermezzi* that help to balance our appreciation of what really matters in music. Then we return to the classical masters with our faith undiminished.

The various ways in which music can be scored nowadays are practically endless. A composer can take a chord of C major, orchestrate it differently a hundred thousand times and still have further devices up his sleeve. All this has been made possible since the orchestra became an increasingly flexible " instrument " in the hands of Haydn, Mozart, Beethoven, Wagner, Berlioz, Brahms, etc. As cohesion of tone-blending improved—through the introduction of the Clarinet, whose lyrical quality neutralized much of the hard-edged tone of the Oboe and Bassoon, and through the expansion of the Brass family to Trombones and valved Trumpets and Horns—composers indulged in far bolder experiments in orchestration. And, it is hardly necessary to add, further inventiveness in the music itself was bound to follow in the wake of this stream of new sounds. The nineteenth century saw the flood-gates opened ; it gave to composers[1] that perfectly balanced instrument the modern orchestra, wherein cohesion and blend of tones were perfected not only *in* the separate sections themselves—*i.e.*, the Wood-wind, Brass and Strings—but also *between* these different sections. The results were miraculous. Whereas orchestral effects had been restricted in variety of colour in the days of Bach and Handel—relying mainly on block formation of the Strings (even when used contrapuntally) a few Wood-wind instruments and tonic-dominant use of Horns and Trumpets—they now became extraordinarily resilient, romantically emotional and luxuriant. No longer could

[1] Excepting the noisier ones who out-brassed and out-percussioned the orchestra.

Dryden's soft complaining flute discover the woes of hapless lovers. It would require more than a pastoral *bergerette* touch of this kind to realize to the full the emotional drama of a Tchaikovsky or a Berlioz conception of *Romeo and Juliet*. Although this placid instrument might have proved excellent in effect for the Watteau-esque music of the seventeenth century and the early part of the eighteenth, yet the cold breath of its soft complaining tone could not warm to the love-stress of such works as Wagner's *Tristan and Isolde*[1] or Tchaikovsky's *Francesca da Rimini*. It was found that the Clarinet and Oboe served these ends far more effectively and with greater warmth of colour, especially when combined with modern writing for the Strings.

Elsewhere it has been shown how chromatic writing for the Horns in a high register of pitch tended to cancel the effect of variety in the orchestration and how it all melted into a monotonous tension of the sound. And, because of the frequency with which modern composers use a number of instruments to give the required tonal intensity to a theme, there is much the same danger of monotony throughout all their scoring. Notes are doubled, trebled, quadrupled, and added to even further to secure this effect of intensity. Thus we find in the opening bars of Wagner's Prelude to *Parsifal* an unharmonized theme that is scored for six different strands of sound,

Ex. 22

Muted 1st and 2nd Violins; muted Violoncellos
1st Clarinet; 1st Bassoon

and in Elgar's First Symphony in A flat similar treatment, but with harmony added.

[1] Wagner's employment of the Flutes in this music-drama is almost negligible.

Ex. 23 Andante, nobilmente e semplice
[Flute, 2 Clarinets, Bassoon and divided Violas]
[2nd and 3rd Flutes added]

Violoncellos, Basses

That both quotations are examples of masterly scoring
cannot be gainsaid, and their effect, coming where it does,
could not be bettered.   Yet after a while this very quality is
apt to become a defect because of the continual tension to
which the music is subjected.   The ear longs for simplicity,
longs to listen to single strands of sound rather than to the
endless interweavings of Wood-wind, Brass and Strings—
interweavings which, because of their frequency, tend to
neutralize every effect intended.   To my mind, there are,
because of this, many more tedious effects of orchestration
in a work like *Parsifal* than in any or all of the Brahms
Symphonies.   Superb as Wagner's orchestration is in its
dazzling radiance, we must not be led away by it and
because of its splendour condemn Brahms's without a fair
inquiry into his own methods.   Colour in itself should be
reckoned secondary to thematic inspiration, as has already
been argued, and so we must not arrive at any rash
assumptions about the general superiority of Wagner merely
because he sweeps us off our feet with his amazing mastery
over orchestral technique.   It should be remembered that
by the very nature of his work Wagner saddled himself with
thematic and tone-colour *clichés* not discoverable to any
extent in Brahms.   Plain direct scoring of the classical
kind is never at the mercy of any such *clichés*, for the effects
obtained by the composer lie more in the music itself than
in any particular feats of orchestration.   Brahms may have
lacked the spirit of adventure in his orchestration and have
been content to accept without demur the traditional type

of scoring associated with Beethoven and his contemporaries, turning the new paths of those early nineteenth century years into the well-worn yet serviceable tracks of his own period. But, at the same time, ought that to be urged against him in the final assessment of his worth as orchestrator? Scarcely. Had Brahms explored the possibilities of a richer type of orchestration, such as is found in all Wagner's works, there is little doubt but that the worth of the music, *quâ* music, would have suffered in the process. And, in this respect, it can well be argued that Sibelius, of all the symphonists since Brahms's day, must rank highest because he, too, has been content to follow the substance of his sheer musical invention rather than be lured away by fanciful pictorial orchestration, superimposed on the music after true invention in the act of composition has ceased.

The French composers have developed orchestration on much more piquant lines and have given us many compositions that are the musical counterpart of Monet, Manet, Cézanne, Renoir and other painters of similar type. These compositions are full of a vague impressionism that finds its orchestral outlet through the nebulous sounds usually associated with *tremolando* muted Strings divided into many parts, and through muted Brass and Wood-wind instruments used in somewhat topsy-turvy fashion—*e.g.*, Flutes in a low register of pitch against Bassoons in a high register, etc.

To conclude the argument. Orchestration falls into three distinct categories—the *Classical* as represented in the works of Mozart, Beethoven, Schubert, Mendelssohn, Brahms, etc. ; the *Realistic and Romantic* as represented by Liszt, Berlioz, Wagner, Elgar, Richard Strauss, Bizet, Rimsky-Korsakov, etc., and the *Decorative* as exemplified in the works of modern French composers, Ravel, Debussy, etc. It is with Brahms's choice of the first-named that we are now concerned.

CHAPTER VI

THE ORCHESTRATION OF THE SYMPHONIES

[*Note.*—Miniature Full Scores of the Symphonies are easily obtainable in the " Philharmonia " Edition at the cost of a few shillings.]

BY avoiding the rich sonority that characterized the Wagner school, Brahms was able to throw into bold relief not only each section of the orchestra but also each individual instrument. In this respect he relied on Beethoven's method of giving to each instrument a definite message in the music.[1] And so we find that the general massing of his (Brahms's) sounds in the *forte* and *fortissimo* passages contrasts vividly with his employment of the instruments sectionally or solo-wise ; it is as if the climaxes in the music grow naturally from a gradual weaving together of the separate strands of sound, and not from the bulk of the orchestra combined in a pre-climactic state of tension. And so from this point of view it is worth analysing the Four Symphonies in respect to the instruments employed in stating the main themes.

Passing over the magnificent introductory section of the First Symphony—where, amid the general throbbing of the sound, the Timpanist reiterates those challenging Cs,

and later on (at reference letter A in the full score) those mysterious lightly tapped Gs

---

[1] With the possible exception of the Trumpet in Beethoven's case.

79

it will be noticed that the orchestration at the opening of the first *Allegro* makes its effect by contrast of sections ; *i.e.*, Wood-wind and Horns against the agitated rejoinder on the First Violins.[1] And this rejoinder relies on no double strands of tone in the orchestration ; it is given to Violins alone.   Brahms could have yielded quite easily—and without *temporary* damage to the general type of the tone-colour needed here—to the impulse to add an Oboe, for this instrument combines most effectively with agitated String passages.   But, had he done so, he would have greatly weakened, through anticipation, the effect of the Oboes' first entry on this theme (two bars after reference letter B).

Ex. 24

and would have robbed the second subject—which grows so curiously, almost indefinitely, out of what has preceded it—of much of the effect of its characteristic plaintive quality.[2]   The orchestration of this movement varies but little and hardly calls for more than general comment. Two outstanding features deserve mention, however ; the fine use of the Violas on the C string—we are reminded of the early Serenade, Op. 11—and the arresting " boom " of the Contra Bassoon on those many deep notes in the development section (letter I in the score).

After the intense contrapuntal battle between Wood-wind and Strings in the first movement—with the Horns, Trumpets and Timpani stepping into the fray as occasion demands—the profoundly moving quality of the Strings at the beginning of the slow movement, where for some time

[1] See Ex. 84, p. 135.
[2] See Ex. 88, p. 138.

they are helped only in a small degree by Wood-wind and Horns, comes like a soothing dream of bygone days. When the solo Oboe is heard for the first time in this movement (10 bars before letter A) its melody comes straight from the fountain-head of inspiration. Further on (at letter E) we see how Brahms enhances the beauty of this melody by adding a Horn and solo Violin to the Oboe, thereby increasing the interest in a theme which originated on one instrument alone.

Brahms was far too great a craftsman to allow one type of tone to dominate his Symphony, even though he made the first movement practically all of one piece. As we have seen, the Oboe plays a very important part in the first and second movements; indeed its frequent use is pre-ordained in the first movement by the serious nature of music that demands few excursions into the lyrical speech of solo Clarinet or Horn. These two instruments act momentarily as balsam to the sorrowful spirit of the symphony, but do not affect it for long, for the return of the music to a state of conflict that cannot be stayed until the final movement is inevitable. But in the second movement the Clarinet begins to play a more important rôle, even ousting the Oboe from one of its sadly plaintive themes[1] and investing this theme with a ray of hope which so far has been absent from the music. We can hear in the upward phrase that terminates this passage the gentle persuasion of the Clarinet heralding the way to a happier issue in the music in contrast to the marked dejection of the Oboe four bars previously.

Ex. 25   Clarinet

Ex. 26   Oboe

From here onwards the Clarinet is more and more in evidence. And so it is not surprising to find that by the

[1] See Ex. 96, p. 146.

time the third movement is reached it has taken control
of the music in emphatic style.   Here this instrument gives
out a serenely beautiful melody marked *Un poco Allegretto e
grazioso*, the rhythmic scheme of which is analysed in detail
later.[1]   The five-bar length of the phrase is a striking
characteristic needing no comment here.   Of greater
importance at the moment is the introduction of the Clarinet
on this main theme.   For the first time in the Symphony we
feel, through this instrument, that the clouds are beginning
to lift, if only temporarily.   This cannot be said of the
second movement, where the music, despite its character,
comes only as a soothing and romantically beautiful interlude, prior to the resumption of the conflict in the sinister
opening to the last movement.   And in this third movement
Brahms returns to the Clarinet again and again for his main
tone-colour, the Oboe being relegated to a comparatively
unimportant position.   Only twice does the Oboe attempt
to recreate a mood of unrest and discontent in the music,[2]
(3rd bar after B in the full score), but the remainder of the
Wood-wind disallows the plaint and answers it on both
occasions with a cheery *forte*.   Towards the end of the
movement the two Oboes indulge in a serene and lovely duet
of a few bars that no longer suggests any of the previous mood
of melancholic inertia.   But the movement belongs to the
Clarinets ; they bear the message of hope.

The music is now obscured by gloom, by a veritable
Stygian blackness that suggests most eerily the darkest hour
before the dawn.   The orchestration, in the opening *Adagio*
to this last movement, takes on a sombre colour that has no
equal anywhere in symphonic music.   Its sense of deepest
mystery, its ominous presageful character, hinting darkly at
something we cannot fathom, leave us completely nonplussed
as to what is to emerge when the clouds have rolled away.

Being concerned here with the chief points in the orchestration of the Symphony more than with the substance of

[1] See Ex. 99, p. 151.
[2] See Ex. 101, p. 151.

the music itself (which is analysed in another chapter) it
should be noticed how Brahms achieves, by the simplest
orchestral devices, this sense of mystery and gloom.   The
Strings are " played off " against the rest of the orchestra—
less the Trombones who, so far, have not been heard in the
Symphony—in what can be described as Brahms's usual
penny plain style.   There is as yet no attempt to rouse the
music to decisive action ; we are not even sure whether
all this heavy foreboding presages good or evil ; whether the
music is to remain permanently in the minor mood of
the first movement (to which it has returned) or whether
it will break its bonds and burst asunder into another C
major apotheosis as glorious as the finale of Beethoven's
Fifth Symphony.   We wait on the event for nearly five
(common time) bars of crotchets, played *adagio*.   And then
the sluggish minor-key anticipations of the great major
theme are twice broken by strange convulsive *pizzicati* from
the whole of the Strings.   The music is now being slowly
aroused from its deathlike slumber.   The Oboe returns to
its plaintive character ; in fact the entire Wood-wind are
affected by the unearthly mood as the music mounts
higher and higher in pitch (reference letter A in the full
score) towards a succession of upheavals that suggest a
whole universe in travail.   Here is cumulative classical
scoring of the noblest kind, wherein each instrument contributes something, both tonally and rhythmically, to the
onward sweep of the sound.   There is a devastating clap of
thunder on the C drum and then occurs a series of
miracles in the orchestration which are without parallel
anywhere in music—*i.e.*, if we accept the principle that
orchestration should be the servant of thematic design.
The 1st Horn enters *forte sempre e passionato* with a theme as
simple as it is beautiful[1]—a theme constructed round the
main notes of the harmonic series.   If ever Brahms needed
justification, on musical grounds, for his devotion to the
principle of the old-fashioned Hand-Horn, here it is.   Until

[1] See Ex. 108, p. 159.

the moment of the entry of this theme, the four Horns have
been kept, throughout the Symphony, in the background ;
strengthening the fabric when needed, reinforcing the quieter
harmonies and adding a melodic strip here and there, yet
only in a secondary capacity. The moment the gloom is
dispelled, the 1st Horn becomes the most important instrument in the whole Symphony. The lovely romance of the
slow movement, the lyrical Clarinet of the third, have gone
beyond recall ; instead, the golden-toned Horn strikes
a note of victory that shatters for ever the forces of darkness
and despair. And in this moment (reference letter B) the
Trombones enter for the first time in the Symphony, with
pianissimo tonic and dominant accompanying chords, which,
together with the veiled undulations of the Violins (muted)
and Violas, constitute the main essentials of the harmonic
background to this arresting theme. Nearly every
instrument, with the notable exceptions of the Oboes and
Contra Bassoon, has its own part in the seventeen bars that
follow, the Flutes taking up the Horn theme two octaves
higher. Then (at reference letter C) the 1st Trombone,
assisted in the harmony by the other Trombones, two Horns,
two Bassoons and the booming foundation-deep notes of the
Contra Bassoon, chants a solemn hymn of faith which is
eventually to become the culminating point of the whole
Symphony.[1] The Horn theme returns and is joined at
intervals by the Wood-wind—yet another example of compound tone-colours that are developed from a single instrument. The mood is hushed to a held chord of the dominant seventh, distant and expectant,

and we know instinctively that nothing but a song of
triumph can follow in its wake, nothing short of a pæan

[1] See Ex. 109, p. 161.

can celebrate the delivery of the music from its long bondage.

Massed orchestration, yet with infinite variety, is the general feature of this last movement. It could not be otherwise. For a few phrases the Oboe is doubtful of the coming triumph ; it lingers regretfully on this (5th bar after F in full score) :

and on this (28th bar after F), which should be compared with Ex. 105 on page 158,

but each time it is answered by the remainder of the orchestra (less the Trombones, who are again being kept in reserve) with a new emphatic expression of triumph (31st bar after F).

There comes a moment when the sky is overcast (letter I in the full score) and we hear once again the convulsive *pizzicati* of the gloomy introduction. But neither they nor the doubting Oboe can stay the course of the music, which now mounts up and up like the lark at heaven's gate to a superb and overwhelming climax (letter N in the score).

Here the sharp-edged tones of the 1st Violins give all the power they have to the first phrase of the Horn melody.

Ex. 30

Two things are noticeable here ; (a) the intensely dramatic silence of one beat (*) before this moment of climax, and (b) the inability of the 1st Violins to cope with the great weight of the full orchestra on the thunderous accompanying chord. [I recommend for the consideration of those who conduct this work the following rearrangement of four bars of the score—a rearrangement that will enhance the ecstasy of the music beyond all belief.

Ex. 31

Any reduction of the tone in the Wood-wind, Brass and Timpani would completely ruin the grandeur of the climax, and so it is necessary to build the Violins up to this *fortissimo*. Brahms undoubtedly made a miscalculation here.]

The music now hurries along without further misgivings to its appointed triumph, and the 1st Trombone's hymn of faith, stated previously with such quiet confidence, is thundered out with great emphasis of tone just before the rapturous carefree close of the Symphony. The orchestration is masterly in its cumulative effect. It brings us once again face to face with the knowledge that its superb quality is its innate simplicity—a simplicity that concedes nothing to colour when the essential features of the music are at stake.   When it is realized that the Trombones play for only 83 bars out of a total of 1,262 and that the 1st Horn has no *principal* theme until the last movement (to state just two instances) it will be seen that the quality of Brahms's orchestration is not as monotonous as some critics aver. Brahms used his instruments with great judgment, aided by a far-seeing vision that realized the supreme virtue of holding in reserve certain tone-colours until the moment they could make their full effect.   In that respect he was very akin to Beethoven, who used no more instruments than the contra-puntal texture of his music would allow.

Brahms had a sense of quiet homely fun enjoyed at the expense of others.   And so, after the grim struggle heard in the music of the First Symphony, it is hardly surprising to find him playfully misdescribing his Second in several letters to his friend Elizabet von Herzogenberg.

She and her husband had met Brahms for the first time during the year of the First Symphony (1876) and friend-ship between the three had quickly ripened.   By November 1877 references to the newly finished Symphony are frequent and Brahms deludes his friends into the belief that the Symphony is in F minor, forceful in character, and as stern in the mood as the opening of its predecessor.   " You have only to sit down to the Piano," he writes to Elizabet, " put your small feet on the two pedals in turn, and strike the chord of F minor several times in succession, first in the treble, then in the bass ($f\!f$ and pp) and you will gradually gain a vivid impression of my latest."   And again on the day before its first performance under Richter (December 30th, 1877) : " The Orchestra here play my new Symphony with crape bands on their sleeves because of its dirge-like effect.   It is to be printed with a black edge, too."

The Second Symphony in D major is commonly described as genial, pastoral, singing of sunlit meadows, the most easily understood, Brahms at his happiest, etc.   No wonder that the composer felt in a jocular frame of mind, for the writing of this, his most " singable " Symphony, must have come from a great joy of spirit. Sunshine is there in plenty. Perhaps the spring of that year in Vienna was particularly lovely and Brahms was able to enjoy to the full his morning walks in the Prater where so much of his music must have come to him, later on to be translated into graphic form at beautiful Pörtschach in Carinthia.

The change of mood in the Symphony is extraordinary. Brahms does not keep us waiting until the last movement for the sun to break through the clouds ; it shines at once. Needless to say, an artless opening of this kind—one preludial (but importantly melodic) bar on the 'Cellos and Basses and we plunge at once into the principal theme on the Horns and Wood-wind—would require equally artless orchestration. Notes are very sparse in these first pages, the absence of any complexity of mood accounting for what is often described as *thinness* of orchestration. But in that sparseness lies the beauty of the instrumental writing ; it suggests the spring buds of the music gradually blossoming into fulness of flower.

Had Brahms any pictures of nature in his mind when he wrote his Symphonies ? If the First Symphony with its sombre orchestral colours—Violas, Bassoons, Oboes, etc.— represents a conflict of abstract forces in darkness, a conflict that ends with the break of day, is it not possible to imagine the Second, because of the genial nature of its melodies, as an early morning picture of apple orchards in blossom, the purple haze of bluebells, the yellow of the primrose and cowslip, all under a seven-o'clock sun ? And, further, may we not imagine the Third as sinking to a sunset with *chiaroscuro* effects of the greatest beauty, and the Fourth as steely-blue as the realm of the infinite to which it belongs ?

The springlike nature of the first movement of the Second Symphony calls for the straightforward orchestration it contains. The doubling of melodic lines through the super-imposition of Wood-wind on Strings is comparatively rare,

each section of the orchestra having its independent movement most of the time and only coalescing with the other
sections when the music approaches its joyous climaxes.
By itself the Wood-wind is used largely in what can best
be described as *choral* style (for it suggests singing) ; *i.e.*,
there are doublings of the melody and harmony in two and
sometimes more octaves, as the following example, taken
from the opening page of the Symphony, will show.

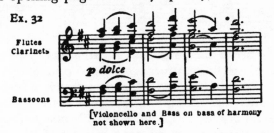

This effect is common to all Brahms's orchestral works ;
it is another of those very individual points in his scoring
derived from Beethoven which often eludes the listener
because of its simplicity. For it is regarded by many
musicians as a dry effect, dull and colourless ; for what
reason one cannot say. Given good Wood-wind players, the
effect is beatiful and utterly right to the type of music.
Luscious or even moderately rich orchestration would be
entirely foreign to the spirit of what is written and would rob
the Symphony of its clear-cut outlines.

Brahms was continually at pains to achieve interplay
between sections of the orchestra ; it was part of his contrapuntal creed. His frequent use of the Wood-wind in this
manner is like a stream of pure mountain water trickling
through the music. He knew better than to combine
these instruments for many bars together with the more
sensuous String tone. Hence the infinite variety of his
scoring in the greater part of this Symphony ; never hot,
never cold, but alternating deliciously between the genial
warmth of the early sun and the invigorating snap of the cool
morning air.

And just as Brahms's muse in this Symphony is much more rhapsodic than elsewhere, so do we find a free careless unconcern about the general lay-out of the orchestration. The first movement introduces the Trombones and the Bass Tuba quite near the beginning, in sleepy chords that suggest a waking, limb-stretching world.

It is not beside the point here to call attention to Brahms's sparing, masterly treatment of the Trombones throughout his Symphonies. We have already noticed their very limited use in the First Symphony; how they were held in reserve for an especial moment and how immensely effective they became because of this. Examination of the full scores of the other Symphonies will show how rarely Brahms used the Trombones in melodic passages. He was content, in the main, to point the harmony of a few climaxes with their noble dignified tone, adding their weight to the mass sonority only when the urgency of the mood swept away the previous restraint imposed on the orchestration. Hence the sheer exuberance of spirits found in the *Allegro* movements of this Second Symphony—in the 'seventies sometimes called the " gay Vienna " Symphony—demanded a more frequent recourse to the Trombones than can be found elsewhere. It is quite in the natural order of things that the passage quoted above should seem like the slow rousing to action

of four stalwarts who are soon, in strenuous cross-rhythm, to play about most energetically with the suave Horn theme of the opening (see Ex. 34).

There are two instances in this first movement where Brahms seems hoist with his own petard of a Tuba, the spread of the harmony over this instrument and the three Trombones being anything but happy.

In the first example (17th bar after letter E) the heavy D in the Bass Trombone part is a cumbersome effect, even on what is called a G Trombone,[1] more particularly as the E above this note is on the less noticeable 1st Bassoon alone. The second example is altogether too highly pitched to be happy, the four Horns that cluster so noisily round the 2nd and 3rd Trombones adding to the general discomfort of the sound. As if to make amends for his uncouth effect here, Brahms, in the very next passage for these instruments, forty-three bars later (5th bar after reference letter M), gives us a few moments of rare tenderness —a most soothing prelude to the wonderful Horn passage that is quoted on p. 186.

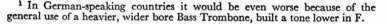

[1] In German-speaking countries it would be even worse because of the general use of a heavier, wider bore Bass Trombone, built a tone lower in F.

More than ever in this movement did Brahms fashion beautiful phrases for the Horns out of his simple natural harmonic material, putting us under an everlasting debt of gratitude to him for his preservation of the inherently lovely quality of this instrument. And throughout the Symphonies he used his four Horns as a middle-pitched " spine " to the general balance of the sounds, thereby releasing the Clarinets for use in the upper registers of their pitch, a very marked characteristic of Brahms's general style of orchestration.

We cannot leave consideration of the scoring of this movement without reference to the singing quality of the 'Cellos in the second subject.[1] The lambent nature of the music that has preceded this theme calls for just such an emotional response and, as might be expected, Brahms does not fail us. The coda (letter M onwards) is almost unsurpassed for beauty of colour. The combined tones of the Strings and Horns as they relapse into an atmosphere of serene contentment is a piece of orchestration completely in accord with the mood of this lovely movement, while the later use of the Wood-wind in delicately-tongued effects against the remarkable *pizzicato* passage on the Strings is a miracle of contrast and ingenuity—to say nothing of the intrinsic worth of the music itself.

The 'Cellos resume their singing at the very outset of the slow movement in a fine broad melody twelve bars long,[2] accompanied by the soft tones of Tuba and Trombones in addition to other instruments. This use of quiet Brass is a very significant feature here, for it colours the music with a new richness that seems to have originated in the mellow mood of the first movement. And also the prevailing atmosphere of contentment in the music is further enhanced by the *grazioso* colloquy between Wood-wind and Strings, where the Clarinets, in particular, have a most fragrant passage (2nd bar after B).

[1] See Ex. 123, p. 179
[2] See Ex. 133, p. 188.

Ex. 37

The interchange of thought between these sections of the orchestra twice becomes embittered, and the orchestration (at letter C and at the 19th bar after E) turns to a dark mood indeed, wherein the hitherto peace-loving Trombones and Tuba are now heard in stressful chords of ominous character. This leaves its mark on the music, which, after the second outburst, never fully regains its *grazioso* singing quality. In the final five bars the Strings contradict the general mood of the movement by a series of emotional *nuances* on notes that are foreign to the B major key—an unlooked-for outbreak of pessimism that can be traced to the mournful Bassoon G natural (reinforced by Horns) in the second bar of the movement.

Ex. 38   *(a)*

Strings

etc.

(pizz. Bass)

(b)

Bassoons 1 & 2 (bar 2)

Brahms was too good a musical psychologist to be affected for long by this temporary setback in the mood. So in the third movement we find him resuscitating the light-hearted character of the first, but in daintier style. The music is so slight in comparison with what has gone

before, that it is in reality almost chamber-music ; indeed
it is called by Specht a " rather unimportant scherzo "—
a criticism which seems not a little unfair. The light
pastoral touch of the Wood-wind at the beginning, followed
by the *Presto* Variations (based on the first theme) on
staccato Strings, contrasts in happy style with the clouds that
gathered over the final bars of the slow movement. We are
taken back to the apple-blossom and the lilacs ; to Vienna
in springtime and the Prater under the morning sun ; to
Johannes Brahms singing to himself of the joy of living.
Most of the heavy instruments disappear from the score of
this movement ; a single Horn in G is used for graceful
cantabile passages, while two others help to maintain the
spirit of the strongly-marked *forte* music that occurs momentarily in the two *Presto ma non assai* sections. For simplicity
of design the score is again a model of its kind. The tossing
of the musical fancies to and fro between Wood-wind and
Strings in battledore and shuttlecock style brings vividly to
mind Elizabet von Herzogenberg's letter to Brahms (May
6th, 1879) in which she refers to the D major Symphony as
being " as beautiful as any foam-born goddess." It is
Brahms at his simplest. Nowhere else in the Symphonies
do we find such ingenuous scoring ; nowhere else do we find
such a complete cessation of everything that suggests a
problem yet to be solved.

   In such a happy-go-lucky Symphony, where three-quarters
or more of the music is idyllic and almost static in
mood, it is quite certain that the finale will contain a
great amount of massed orchestration to point the happy
moral. And Brahms does not disappoint us. From the
moment the music has shaken off its somewhat slothful
beginning, it sounds, with few interruptions, as merry as a
marriage bell. Consequently the orchestration loses something of the individuality that characterizes that of the other
three movements. We feel that we are past the time for any
marked changes of colour and that Brahms realized this. In
fact, we sense that he was at times at a loss for the next

best thing to do to maintain interest in a Symphony which so far had basked in over half an hour's spring sunshine. If only a threatening cloud or two could have swept right across the face of the music as in the slow movement, all would have been well.   But the infectious light-heartedness of everything prevents this, and the clouds that do pass are only billowy-white cumulus or filmy cirrus shadowing the music just for an instant.   Certain thematic weaknesses are analysed in another chapter.   It may be on their account that the orchestration seems to hang fire.   Brahms must have done a little head-scratching here, and have felt very anxious as he committed himself to this and that expedient in order to jog along his scheme of colour variation and yet retain the customary classical scoring.   The ineffective use of *pizzicati* in the Strings against the flabby combination of Flutes and Clarinets (at letter E in the full score) is one example of several such doubtful moments.

Ex. 39

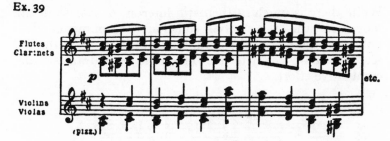

When a shadow does fall on the gay music Brahms responds at once with many an individual touch.   The section of fifty-eight bars from letter I to the twelfth bar after L, commencing

Ex. 40

is a fine piece of interest alternating between Wood-wind and Strings, with mysterious *pp* Trombones and Tuba later on contributing a cold shiver to the sound by a passage in descending fourths, which, curiously enough, owes its origin to the simple inoffensive 9th and 10th bars of the movement.

Ex.41

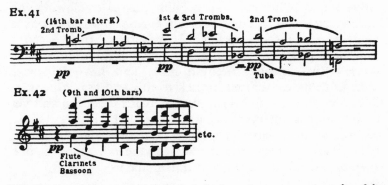

Ex.42   (9th and 10th bars)

While there is much of thematic interest to analyse in this movement, the orchestration calls for few comments. It is only near the end of the Symphony (at letter O in the full score) that we begin to feel there is to be a dramatic and cumulative effort.

Ex.43

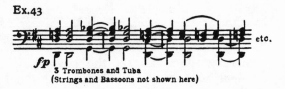

Once again, this section starts " under a cloud," a feature that seems to imply that Brahms was wearying of the prolonged major mood of this forty-minute work and needed a strong minor-key impulse to get him out of the rut. Admittedly the good honest scoring of much of the preceding matter tries the patience of the acute listener considerably ; we have too little of the minor key, and tire even of the spring buds and the soft balmy air.

But from the moment when this final building up begins, the music gains in power and interest and forces us once more to the conclusion that Brahms was indeed a master of classical orchestration who could be relied upon to redeem even his own weaknesses, which, in this finale, seem to have arisen from the limited range of the thematic material.

Brahms, with all his ingenuity, could not hide the bare moments in the music. Being a designer first and a colourist afterwards he failed just where we should have expected. He was true to himself even in defeat ; he foisted on us no ill-advised experiments in the orchestration, fighting a lone battle with the difficulties he set himself when he chose such a happy theme for this Symphony. We must assume that he preferred to find the way to happiness rather than have it disclosed to him at the outset. If at times in the finale he struggled to little purpose we must remember that the work contains page after page of the rarest orchestral beauty.

CHAPTER VII

THE ORCHESTRATION OF THE SYMPHONIES
(*continued*)

SPRING has gone. In its place, not high summer, but the rich gold of the harvest ; the trees still heavy in leaf but turned to those colours that are the glory of autumn. If ever a symphony could suggest Keats's " Season of mists and mellow fruitfulness," then Brahms's Third does so more than any other. The music seems to alternate between retrospection and introspection, between happy memories of springtime and unhappy fears at the approach of winter. It is, in fact, a symphony of the equinox, and because of this is splendid in its changing moods and yet more splendid in its mellowed orchestration.

> " Where are the songs of Spring ? Ay, where are they ?
> Think not of them, thou hast thy music too—
> While barrèd clouds bloom the soft-dying day,
> And touch the stubble-plains with rosy hue ;
> Then in a wailful choir the small gnats mourn
> Among the river sallows, borne aloft
> Or sinking as the light wind lives or dies."

But of the character of the music itself, more presently ; here we are concerned with the orchestral expression, difficult though it may be to disentangle the one from the other.

"Frei aber Froh"—F, A flat, F.

serves as the general motto for the Symphony, the Wood-wind, Horns and Trumpets giving it out at the start of the first movement in such a convincing *forte* that we know instinctively that it will re-echo throughout the work, even if it is not actually the main theme. Not a section of the orchestra escapes its persistent attention. In the first thirty bars of the music it is found no less than nine times, its entries being spread over every Wood-wind and Brass instrument (with the exception of the 1st and 2nd Trombones) and also over every String instrument, either by direct, or (in the case of the 2nd Violins and 'Cellos) by indirect utterance. Even the Timpanist helps to hammer out its rhythm in several bars. Such prolific use of a sign-manual of this kind is quite unique among the symphonies, and our amazement at the technique shown is all the greater when we realize that the motto acts mainly as a background to another primary theme of passionately stressful character, played on the Violins.[1] It should be noticed particularly what a richness is imparted to the orchestration here by this F.A.F. undercurrent, coupled to the syncopated intensity of Brahms's rarely forgotten Violas. The following is a quotation from bar 7 onwards.

Ex. 44   (Theme on Violins not shown here)

Clarinets
Bassoons
Horns
(in 8ves)

Violas

(Bass of Harmony)

Like the 1st symphony

Once again Brahms, at the second subject, brings forward his Clarinet for a lyrical melody of great beauty.[2] And, in this respect, it is perhaps interesting to remember that he had met the Meiningen Orchestra Clarinettist, Richard Mühlfeld, some little time before he began scoring the Third Symphony in 1883. Later on Mühlfeld was to become a great friend. It was for him that Brahms wrote his Op. 114

[1] See Ex. 157, p. 214.
[2] See Ex. 162, p. 218.

Trio in A minor for Piano, Clarinet (or Viola) and 'Cello, his two Op. 120 Sonatas for Clarinet (or Viola) and Piano, and his famous and very lovely Op. 115 Quintet for Clarinet and String Quartet.   In the postscript of a letter to Brahms dated March 15th 1882, Elizabet von Herzogenberg writes : " the Meininger Clarinettist is great " ; a fact that would not have escaped Brahms when he reached Meiningen on a concert tour in February 1883, where, incidentally, he found the conductor Hans von Bülow overwhelmed with grief at the death of Wagner (February 13th).

When Brahms is past this exquisite Clarinet melody he is soon busy again on the motto phrase, which is flung all over the orchestra, either in simple form, as on the 1st Oboe (6th bar after letter C), or in a more halting rhythm, on the Horn, accompanied by yet another form of it in *stretto* on 'Cellos.

Ex. 45

(Harmony omitted here)

The orchestration now reaches a fulness that needs no comment, for it is the usual type of clear-cut scoring consistently employed by Brahms in all his climaxes.   Wood-wind, with Horns added at times, alternate with the Strings.   And it is worthy of mention that in all the stress of mood found here the Trumpets have but a few bars of notes to point this climax and the Trombones are content with two strong ejaculatory *staccato* chords (10th bar after letter D onwards). A tranquil mood is reached, bringing with it a *cantabile* Horn version of the motto (this time in E flat) which is one of the really great moments in classical music :

"Think of us to-morrow," writes Elizabet (February 11th 1884) to Brahms from Leipzig, "when the famous E flat comes in in the first movement."[1]

And when the Horn does come in (letter G in the score) attention should be paid also to the Contra Bassoon with its sunken foundation notes—for all the world just like great 32-foot Organ pipes. No Tuba could have made such an effect,[2] and so it is most gratifying to find Brahms's old and trusted friend restored to the Symphonies, never to be ousted again. A little further on (letter H) this instrument, in company with the other Wood-wind, makes a mysterious *pp* allusion or two to the vigorous first subject, the stressful Violin theme. Here it touches the lowest C flat possible—a difficult note for the instrument—and conjures up a menace of the dark storms ahead in the finale of the Symphony.

With the arrival of the recapitulation section of the first movement (9th bar after H), there is little else to comment upon in regard to the orchestration ; it is much as it was before. But when the coda arrives (16th bar after K) the whole orchestra is in a state of excited agitation, and the peak of the great climax here (13th bar after L) is another

---

[1] She meant, of course, the *key* of the music at this point, for the Horn is crooked in C and does not reach the note E flat until the fourth bar of the melody.

[2] I am indebted to Professor Sir Donald Tovey for the information that when Brahms could not get a Contra Bassoon for some performances of the *St. Anthony Variations*, he substituted a Bass Tuba. The effect must have been strange.

proof of the extremely simple means employed by Brahms when achieving his sublimest moments. Here the Wood-wind, Horns and Basses sustain the harmonies in the plainest manner possible against the descending Strings. The gradual attenuation of the sound during the succeeding sixteen bars again shows the touch of a master-hand. Out of this grows the golden F major close to the movement.

The tranquil beauty of the opening of the second move-ment finds its complete justification in Rimsky-Korsakov's interesting book on Orchestration.[1]

" The art of orchestration demands a beautiful and well-balanced distribution of chords forming the harmonic texture. Moreover, transparence, accuracy and purity in the movement of each part are essential conditions if satisfactory resonance is to be obtained. No perfection in resonance can accrue from faulty progression of parts."

Examination of this movement shows what loveliness of utterance Brahms could produce from an ordinary quartet of Wood-wind instruments, viz., two Clarinets and two Bassoons, playing in four-part harmony,[2] aided by a few cadential notes on the Flutes and a heart-felt strip of melody on the 1st Oboe. And when all this unadorned beauty has echoing phrases (founded on the motto) on Violas and 'Cellos, also in four-part harmony, the total effect is so beautiful that surely the angels must stop to listen. The whole movement is instinct with noble-minded feeling that increases as the music develops. Brahms employs a small orchestra here (he always does in his middle movements) but retains the three Trombones for chord effects of great yet simple beauty. The usual antiphonal phrases between Wood-wind and Strings occur again and again ; yet the ear never wearies of them, for they come straight from the heart of the music.

It is especially a movement for Clarinets and Bassoons,

---

[1] *Principles of Orchestration* (2 Vols.) by Nicolas Rimsky-Korsakov, translated by Edward Agate. (Russian Music Agency, 34 Percy Street, London, W.1.)
[2] See Ex. 173, p. 228.

the writing for the latter instrument deserving particular mention.   Passages such as at letter D in the score,

Ex. 47

and at the seventh bar after G

Ex. 48

are extremely individual in their effect, coming where they do.   In Example 48 the Bassoons, with the Clarinet melody above them, create a remote atmosphere, like the clouded memories of long ago.   The three Trombones at the end of the movement more than justify their inclusion by their quiet cadential chords—chords that enrich the philosophic calm of this C major conclusion.

In this movement, if we can except the momentary emotional outburst of the 'Cellos at letter D in the score, there is hardly a passage that calls for sensuous expression ; the beauty of the music (and what a high level it touches !) is more of the intellectual order.   Hence the unadorned, even austere orchestration.   Simple Wood-wind and Brass combinations are only half ornamented by equally simple *arpeggio* treatment of the Strings (see more particularly letters E to G in score), and nothing orchestral in this movement suggests that Brahms was trying to break away from the golden serenity that possesses the very soul of the music.

It is therefore nothing less than what we should have expected, to find Brahms deserting his beloved Wood-wind at the commencement of the third movement and scoring mainly for Strings, placing the lovely *cantabile* melody

in this intermezzo,[1] firstly on 'Cellos and then on Violins.
Note what a contrast to the slow movement is obtained by
this easy transition to the simplest of all orchestral media,
the Strings. When the Horn, in company with Flute and
Oboe, takes up the melody later, what a new richness is here,
what a sense of something added that burnishes the melody
to a brighter gold. The delicate tracery of the accompanying Violin and Viola *arpeggii* should not escape notice
either here or at the beginning of the movement. The
middle section (letter C onwards) is a quiet conversation
between Wood-wind and Strings used chordally, with
syncopated interjections from the Strings (the 'Cellos more
particularly) adding to the greyness of effect. The return
of the opening music leads to variations in the orchestration,
the Horn and the Oboe paving the way to a richer version
of the theme on Strings—a reversal of the previous order of
things. Then at letter G the Bassoons and Clarinets have
an especial piece to themselves founded on the 'Cello and
Violin duet that appears first at letter A.[2] Altogether the
movement is remarkable for the consistency of its colour,
so suggestive of a dark uneventful autumn day.

From this pensive minor close it is not a far cry to the
gloom that enshrouds the opening of the finale. Strings
and Bassoons,[3] joined later by Flutes and Clarinets, make a
sombre picture indeed. A strange uneasiness heralds the
approach of some great crisis in the music. The Trombones
strike a solemn note of warning three times (letter A in
score)

Ex. 49

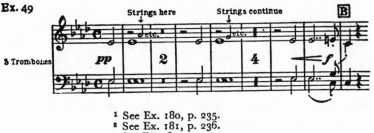

1 See Ex. 180, p. 235.
2 See Ex. 181, p. 236.
3 See Ex. 185, p. 241.

against a theme on the Strings that is soon to break out into
fierce rebellion before it sinks finally to its rest. And then
these forces, so surreptitiously at work at the beginning,
are lashed into a fury on the full orchestra (letter B in the
score), but, once again, without the Trombones. As in
many other like instances the orchestration hereabouts
follows Brahms's consistent plan and therefore calls for no
further comment. We can pass the second subject on the
'Cellos and Horn for consideration elsewhere since its
interest lies in the theme itself rather than in its presentation.[1]
But at the third bar after letter D in the score we begin to
see daylight, the stressful character of the music notwithstanding. " Frei aber froh "[2] makes a disguised reappearance on the Wood-wind and Trombones—the latter
instruments having been purposely kept in reserve for this
moment.

Ex. 50

The purpose of the Symphony is here made manifest ;
we now know what is eventually to happen. There is, from
this point onwards, a fine burst of cumulative scoring which
again relies only on the Trombones for a few stray chords.
Brahms is never in danger of yielding to the temptation of
maltreating his Trombones, however urgent the mood of the
music. Hence the great effectiveness of the writing when
these instruments enter. The climax having subsided, we
reach a point (letter G to letter K) where the orchestration
seems mysteriously to conjure forth the spirits of long ago.

[1] See Ex. 190, p. 245.
[2] It should be borne in mind that this motto-phrase does not always occur
with the actual notes F.A.F. It is frequently used more in the spirit than in the
letter, as befits its symphonic character.

First of all, Flute, Clarinet and Bassoon run along, in three registers of pitch, on the first theme against *pizzicato* octaves on the Strings—in itself a mysterious effect.

Ex. 51

Better still is to come when the theme is resumed on Oboe and Bassoon against the hollow jerky whispers of the accompanying Strings (17th bar after letter G), played *pp* and *staccato*.

Ex. 52

At letter H a cold shiver runs through the music when the 1st Violins and Violas, followed by 'Cellos and Basses, give out a broken version of the first subject against sustained Wood-wind.

Ex. 53

Out of this the full orchestra suddenly takes up the dynamic surge of the music, while the warning notes of the Trombones and Strings (Ex. 49) become the basis of a truly great climax (letters I to L), again scored in the straightforward manner we have learnt to associate with Brahms's finest moments. The Strings here break out into new figuration,

Ex. 54

sweeping along with great intensity until the music relapses into the recapitulation section of the movement (letter K). From this point until letter N there is nothing in the orchestration but what has been heard already.

But at the seventh bar after N a complete and miraculous change happens to the music and orchestration. The fiery and impatient *fortissimo* phrases disappear almost in the twinkling of an eye—something like that sudden *macabre* scurrying away of spectres before the first streak of dawn in Saint-Saëns's picturesque work. A mist descends. An invisible friendly spirit seems to breathe a blessing through the muted Violins and Violas. We hear fragments of the first theme here and there in a softened rhythm ; the bitter sting has been taken out of the music and the whole orchestration sinks to rest in a sunset of peerless beauty. The semiquaver movement of the Strings against the sustained Wood-wind and Brass—employed in a gradual forsaking of the first theme for the motto-phrase F.A.F.—constitutes one of the finest examples of orchestration ever penned by any composer. And the soft glow of the chords on the Brass instruments (one bar before letter P)—as they, with Oboes, Bassoons and Contra Bassoon, make their final references to the solemn theme near the beginning—

Ex. 55

is nothing short of a miracle of loveliness.   F.A.F., heard on
Flutes, Oboes and 3rd Horn, resolves all lingering doubts·in
the music of the final thirteen bars.   On the last F of the
motto (9th bar from the end) the Violins make a veiled
allusion to the main theme of the 1st movement (Ex. 157).

Ex. 56

The last sheaves are gathered and the red ball of the sun dips
below the horizon on those unforgettable chords of F.

Were it possible to make any real distinction between four
symphonies that all sprang from the maturity of Brahms's
style we could say that the Fourth has the greatest claim to
symmetry of design and the smallest claim to colour variation
in the orchestra.   That is, at the same time, not to deny
the beauty of the orchestral writing, but merely to point
out that Brahms spared no pains in his endeavours to perfect
the musical detail of this Symphony, choosing only such
colours as would not interfere with the clear presentation of
his ideas.   But since the themes are so beautiful in themselves,
we cannot nowadays imagine the orchestration anything
but what it is.   Whether we have got used to its plain
outlines or whether it is *perfect* orchestration remains an
æsthetical question impossible to answer.

Some musicians feel that the prevalence of the E minor key for the greater part of two long movements brings with it such a touch of winter that they are tempted to turn up their coat collars to keep out the cold. And apart from this matter of key-consciousness, it is not certain that all listeners respond to the remote atmosphere of the music ; nor does the reticent orchestration help them to an understanding of this quality. There is no doubt that our appreciation of this Symphony largely depends on the amount of pleasure we can derive from the amazing interplay of counterpoints between Wood-wind, Horns and Strings. To arrive at a full appreciation seems impossible ; there is a new revelation at each hearing, a new discovery each time we open the score.

Yet, its austere outlines notwithstanding, it contains the aptest orchestration of any of the Symphonies. Brahms could not have done more with his instruments to bring out the quality of the music ; their discreet use is a perfect match for the themes. And even if the orchestration doubles back on itself so often, is not this all to the good ? Does it not demonstrate to the full Brahms's unshaken belief in music first and colour afterwards ? The language of this Symphony is Miltonic. Keats and Shelley we find forsworn. And so a desultory acquaintance with the music can only result in disappointment at its colour scheme.

There are, as with the First Symphony, but few outstanding points to look for in the orchestration of the first movement. At the beginning, the shadowing of the Strings by the Wood-wind is a very simple but extremely effective device ; a piece of musical synthesis of a high order.

At letter A the remarkable antiphony between the 1st and 2nd Violins, engaged in a decorated version of the opening theme, is made all the more interesting by a similar display between Violas and Wood-wind against it.

Ex. 58

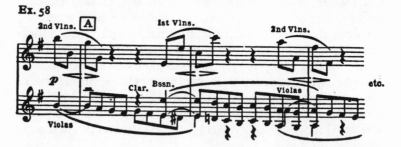

" The fiddles " writes Elizabet to Brahms—in a very lengthy enclosure to an equally lengthy letter dated September 31st (*sic*) 1885—" are given this scrappy version of the subject. It sounds very complicated, because the essential is made to appear accessory to the non-essential, the principal subject an accompaniment to the new figure introduced by the Wood-wind and Violas." Such criticism, coming from one whose judgment Brahms had every reason to respect, had resulted from a hasty perusal of the manuscript of the movement, received from the composer on September 5th 1885 and acknowledged three days later in the enclosure to the letter referred to above. But in the actual letter enclosing this three-weeks-old criticism there is a note of almost childlike contrition as Elizabet confesses that she kept it back " because I felt I was quite unqualified to criticise the Symphony after such a woefully brief acquaintance. . . . I can now trace the hills and valleys so clearly that I have lost the impression of its being a complicated movement."

A cold and forbidding effect (ninth bar after B) occasioned by the use of the isolated Wood-wind and Horns prepares the way admirably for the warmer atmosphere of the second subject, given to two Horns in unison with the 'Cellos (letter C).[1] From here onwards the orchestration keeps to the accepted path for some time. At the fifth bar after H the Wood-wind instruments again have four bars to themselves—an icy-cold *sotto voce* passage that has a touch of drifting snow about it. Note the disposition of the instruments and the absence of the Oboes.

Ex. 59

The compelling intensity of the high-pitched Horns (3rd and 4th) at the fifth bar after letter I deserves particular mention. Nor must the *pizzicato* Violins and Violas escape notice ten bars later, when they imitate the Wood-wind shadowing the opening theme (Ex. 57).

Ex. 60

This takes us immediately to one of the most remarkable passages ever written by Brahms, where (from letter K) the Wood-wind together with the Horns alternate with the Strings in sixteen one-bar phrases, founded on the ninth and tenth bars of the movement.

[1] See Ex. 202, p. 265.

Ex. 61

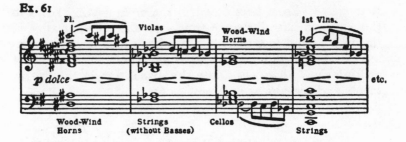

The shifting harmonies and alternating orchestration produce a sense of irreality beyond all analysis. We are borne
away from every earthly circumstance, beyond time and
space.

After this passage the orchestration repeats much of
what has already been stated ; alterations are few. At
letter Q the 'Cellos and Basses, aided by Horns, mass
together in a mighty *ff* presentation of the opening theme.
From here to the end the music is as hard as granite,
boulder on boulder being piled high on one another to form
a marvellous natural temple of sound. And, be it noted, to
achieve this result Brahms uses a small classical orchestra.
There are no Trombones—could any other composer have
resisted the temptation here ?—no shrieking Piccolo and
only fourteen bars of tonic-dominant Timpani out of the
forty-seven that conclude the movement from this point
(letter Q).

The Horns (3rd and 4th) enter with such challenging
emphasis[1] at the beginning of the second movement
that they sound just like Blake's " terrific porter " of
the eternal gate. We feel we are soon to learn something
of " the secrets of the land unknown."[2] This challenge is
reinforced by Oboes, Bassoons and Flutes, and within four
bars has faded away so as to introduce the 1st Clarinet on a
ghostly echo of the music—pitched a major third higher.
Brahms, to make the mood still more mysterious, adds

[1] See Ex. 210, p. 275.
[2] *The Book of Thel.*

pp pizzicato Strings to the Wood-wind harmony, thereby clothing the theme (*legato* on the Wood-wind, it should be noted) with a completely new touch of orchestration.

Ex. 62

Strings

Who can say whether there is to be found anywhere a more dramatic use of *pizzicato* Strings ? The effect continues for no less than twenty-five bars of music, during which the Wood-wind and Horns are occupied unfolding the theme ; at first tenderly, and then (letter A) in more emphatic style. And again, the lovely strip of melody found in this section (11th bar after A)

Ex. 63

must surely rejoice the heart of every Clarinettist and remind him of the famous Richard Mühlfeld, who was the first to give it life at Meiningen. In recalling Spitta's opinion that this movement, as *music*, has no equal anywhere in symphonic music, we must not forget the claims of the orchestration. The dual nature of the first theme, with its sombre challenge and then its tender mood, is in itself an incentive to variety of orchestration, and of this advantage Brahms availed himself to the full, investing the music with a hundred points of rare colouration.

The Violins make use of their bows for the first time at

letter B in a *cantabile* development of the earlier theme, the other Strings still playing *pizzicato*.

Ex. 64

The note of quiet ecstasy is enhanced here by the fact that the bows have not been used previously. The orchestral treatment of this passage is curiously akin to the exquisite moment or two in the second movement of the First Symphony (from the 7th bar after letter A onwards), but is actually more developed in the mood. Out of its heightened feeling grows yet another of those strong rhythmical exchanges between sections of the orchestra,

Ex. 65

which, six bars later, is to form the basis of the lovely 'Cello melody (Ex. 213). Bassoons and Violas make an admirable but slightly unconventional bass to the harmony of this melody, against which the 1st Violins contribute a delicately embroidered counterpoint. Further on, at the recapitulation (letter D), the Violas take up in their darker colour the opening Clarinet theme. The mysterious *pizzicati* on the other Strings have returned, while the remainder of the orchestra decorate the theme by a succession of neat touches that look to the eye of the score-reader as interesting as they sound to the ear of the listener. Shortly afterwards the whole orchestra (without Trombones of course) is roused to one of those great climaxes wherein Brahms exploits his entire forces to fine effect, everything being developed from the challenging phrase on the Horns and from the driving force of the figure quoted as Ex. 65. Eventually a point is reached (5th bar after F) where all is now lost in an extraordinary haze. Wisps of the lovely melody (Ex. 63) float about on the two Clarinets and 1st Oboe against veiled undulations on the Violins and Violas, sustained harmonies on the Bassoons and Horns and pulsations on the Timpani, all marked *ppp*.[1] The music seems to disintegrate into spirit matter to await the final challenge on the Horns that rings out six bars from the end. The unexpected and quickly-dying convulsion of the orchestra at this point brings a veritable shudder before the music finally sinks to its rest.

Three guests : a Piccolo, Triangle and another Kettledrum arrive to join the merry-making orchestra in the third movement. Boisterous in the mood and roughly bucolic as most of the music is, what else could Brahms do but surrender to its noisy spell and make it wholeheartedly gay for many bars together ? And so he lets himself go in the orchestration, permitting himself the shrill cry of the Piccolo, the merry ting-a-ling of the Triangle and that extra Drum that enjoys so much the thunder of the low F.

Ex. 66   (Bars 5–9)

What a movement of concentrated orchestral energy this is in every way ! So much of the music is glad of heart, fresh and buoyant, suggesting the mad pranks of a practical joker. The very frequent roll of the *fortissimo* F on the third Drum (5th bar after letter D, etc.) alternating with the Triangle

[1] Only here, thrice again in this Symphony and once in the slow movement of the First Symphony do we find Brahms making use of this extreme *nuance*.

Ex. 67

seems in itself to call up happy memories of the past.
" Frei " and perhaps even " Froh " it reiterates again and
again. On this note of gladness, despite the dark shadows
that at times chasten the spirit of the music, the movement
sweeps along with volcanic energy. Nothing can stay it
for long ; the F Drum is master of the situation.

At the tenth bar after F there is a veiled suggestion of
F.A(flat).F. which may be just coincidental. This leads,
four bars later, to three phrases for the Horns and Bassoons
which are very beautiful indeed and which evoke an
exquisite response from the Oboe in a fourth.

Ex. 68

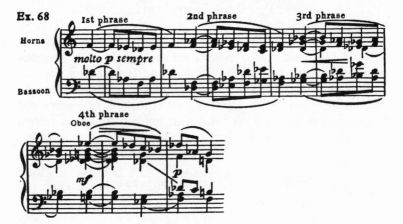

Clarinets and *pizzicato* Strings accompany these phrases.
Such lyrical touches are, however, merely brief interludes
which are soon brushed aside in a return to the general gaiety.
Unflaggingly the music drives its way along to the conclusion
of the movement, dressed in the usual orchestral clothes we
find in all Brahms's vigorous passages. The F Drum still
rings in our ears long after the movement has ended.

Brahms's borrowings from other composers became a stock joke among his contemporaries, a taunt that never failed to elicit a withering rejoinder whenever anyone was rash enough to give him an instance. A fine ground-bass [1] (how our own Purcell loved them !) was sufficient to set his imagination going. "Here is a suitable site" we can imagine his thoughts—"here is my foundation in the hard granite ; on this rock I will build a new temple of sound, a structure to outlast the centuries." Bach would have been the first to approve his taking the ground-bass of the choral chaconne from the 150th Church Cantata

Ex.69

and using it as the basis of this mighty fourth movement written in passacaglia form. [There is a bond of brother-hood between the classical composers not found elsewhere. We can almost hear a chorus of " What is mine is yours " resounding across the centuries.] Brahms tried to interest Bülow in the instrumental possibilities to be found in this *basso ostinato*, both of them admitting that its breadth of style called for a more powerful expression than could be obtained from voices and Bach's restricted orchestration. Dark hints of a future appropriation of this *ostinato* fell from Brahms's lips. " What would you say to a symphonic movement written on this theme some day ? But it is too lumpish, too straightforward. It would have to be chroma-tically altered in some way."[2]

And alter it chromatically he did, and to some purpose. Avoiding the repetitions of notes as shown in Ex. 69 and adding one chromatic A sharp, he combined with it many

[1] See, for example, the finale of the St. Anthony Variations.
[2] See Specht, p. 270. Brahms's version is seen in Ex. 70.

new themes and melodies, details of which are found in a later chapter.

In combined Wood-wind and Brass scoring Brahms made the opening a thing of wonder, the Trombones—with the Contra Bassoon enriching the Bass Trombone an octave lower—entering with the greatest possible effect.

Ex. 70

The outward spread of the harmony at the beginning has a solemnity and a dignity of mood foreshadowing the character of the whole movement. The absence of *bowed* Violins and Violas until the thirty-third bar should be noted; the hard-plucked *pizzicati* at the ninth bar of the movement—*i.e.*, at the second entry of the passacaglia theme (Ex. 70)—staving off any suggestion of the unwanted romance that could so easily slip into the presentation of the theme were the composer not continually on his guard against such influences. When the Strings enter with their bowed phrases (9th bar after A) they do so uncompromisingly; there is nothing sensuous about them. They seem to take on the hard, almost rough-edged manner and mood of the Wood-wind and Brass, set so relentlessly in the preceding thirty-two bars. Nor is there any concession to a softer mood when they commence (at letter B) the more ornate variations leading to that remarkable exchange of chords between Wood-wind and Strings (letter D). There, by the simplest orchestration, Brahms reaches a point of expression that seems to stretch far beyond anything terrestrial. Compare it with Example 61, noting the similarity of treatment and the same ethereal mood.

Ex.71

[Note the disposition of the *ostinato*.]
Everything is hushed to a whisper as the music takes us more
and more into the realm of abstract thought. Nothing in
the Symphonies heard so far achieves such pure distilled
essence of beauty, such spiritual ecstasy ; we are translated
we know not where, leaving the world far behind. After
the two variations commencing at this point, the Flute has
a new wistful melody that might have come straight from
Bach, despite its typical Brahmsian cross-rhythm.

Ex.72

The sparse sufficiency of the accompaniment for thirty-two
bars here—an accompaniment consisting either of plain
chords or of simple *arpeggii*—is an inspiring example of what
Brahms could achieve orchestrally by the most ordinary
devices. When the Trombones enter *pianissimo* (letter E) in
an E major version of the theme [1] and after a long rest of
seventy-nine bars, the effect is almost beyond belief—an effect
further enhanced by the use of the Bassoons on the lowest
notes of the harmony. Horns, Trumpets and Wood-wind
(except the Flutes) are soon added to the score to produce
a mood of serene grandeur that can only be likened to the
splendour of the heavens on a starry night. The melodic
strip that appears successively on Oboe, Horn and Flute
(the last-named abbreviates it) is a touch of instrumental

[1] See Ex 235, p. 301.

colour that must not be overlooked in these glamorous
moments, for here we find beauty in fullest measure, each
instrument demanding our rapt attention.

(8ᵛᵃ lower in instance of Horn)

Reference was made on page 68 to the fine use Brahms made
of the low notes of the Horns, of which there is a notable
example at the close of this section (16th bar after E).

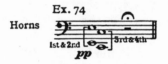

Horns

In conjunction with the low notes of the Bassoons the effect
is one of quiet contemplation, preparing the way for the
forceful, almost strident return of the Trombones and Wood-
wind (17th bar after letter E) in music momentarily similar
to the opening of the movement. From here onwards the
sheer strength of the orchestration is nothing short of amazing. It is all so straightforward that little analysis is required,
although the individual instruments have a series of technical
displays that infuse great vitality into the music. There is
no stagnation here. Even the E Drum has a turn at the
rhythm of the passacaglia theme (9th bar after H) and
helps to augment the effect of what is perhaps the most
stirring climax of the movement. It should be noticed that
in addition to the usual tonic-dominant Timpani notes—E
and B in this movement—Brahms uses a third Drum tuned
to low G. The effect of this note on a hard *staccato* crotchet
in two instances (one bar before letter A and one bar before
letter I) is a point that should not escape the ear ; nor should
the isolated *fortissimo* roll on this note (17th bar after L).
Apart from these three effects there is no further employment

of this Drum—a significant piece of restraint characteristic of the composer.

Finally, the Trombones come to the fore in a noble piece of writing (letter M), where also the 1st Violins have a remarkable headline plunge of three octaves certainly worth quoting here.

Ex. 75

(Remainder of orchestration omitted here)

No new adventure comes the way of the orchestration after this point. Everything in the coda is interwoven to such a degree that our ears must of necessity follow the counterpoints if we are fully to appreciate the music's great worth. It was impossible for Brahms to discolour this remarkable close to his symphonic life by the inclusion of anything false in the orchestration. He sailed among the stars with this Symphony, leaving all earthly dross far behind. There was no desire for sensuous colouration.

CHAPTER VIII

CO-ORDINATION OF DETAIL IN THE SYMPHONIES

" . . . the present, like a note in music,
is nothing but as it appertains to what
is past and what is to come."
(W. S. LANDOR.)

IN a letter to Joseph Joachim, dated February 26th,
1856, Brahms wrote :—

" And then I want to remind you of what we have so
often discussed, and beg you to let us carry it out, namely,
to send one another exercises in counterpoint. Each should
send the other's work back every fortnight (in a week's time
therefore) with remarks and his own work, this to continue
for a good long time, until we have both become really
clever.

" Why should not two sensible, earnest people like ourselves be able to teach one another far better than any
Pf. (? Professor) could ?

" . . . Send me your first study in a fortnight. . . . I am
looking forward hopefully to the first batch. Let us take
it seriously ! It would be very pleasant and useful. I think
it is a delightful idea.

" Always yours

JOHANNES." [1]

It is easy to imagine how the two composers, in the
enthusiasm of their early twenties, would throw themselves
heart and soul into these lessons by correspondence, how
each would " pick the other's brains " and would wrestle

[1] *Letters from and to Joseph Joachim*, translated by Nora Bickley. (Macmillan,
London.)

with problems in canon and fugue or invertible counterpoint, the one learning much from the other and, doubtless, applying the extra knowledge gained to whatever composition might be in hand at the moment. And Joseph Joachim would be by no means an unworthy rival in those days [1]; indeed, he was greatly respected, even envied by Brahms, who saw in the other's music strong, firm outlines that, he sometimes felt, were less in evidence in his own. Although Brahms's distrust of his own contrapuntal powers now seems quite inexplicable, there is no doubt that this sense or modest suggestion of inferiority at the time caused him to redouble his efforts to beat his rival, and so strengthened the fabric of his own music to an untold degree.

Unfortunately, Brahms's plan for these exercises " to continue for a good long time " was soon frustrated by Schumann's death (July 29th, 1856). We know already that this tragic event considerably changed Brahms's outlook and caused a cessation of his creative faculties for a while. And so it is not surprising to find Clara Schumann, two months after her husband's death, begging Joachim to resume the pleasant and instructive exchange of counterpoints. " And Johannes would like so much to recommence the delightful musical correspondence. Do send him some studies again and that will make him work." Work again he did, and always at his exercises, even if Joachim soon tired of the game because he was now so busy with his concerts, his visits abroad, and his musical duties at King George's Court at Hanover.

Possibly the failure of the plan taught Brahms to be entirely self-reliant; to turn, when need arose, to the masterpieces of the classical composers rather than indulge in pleasant healthy rivalry with a contemporary almost as young as himself. Stimulating the latter might be, but yet it could not serve Brahms's purpose so well as the intensive

---

[1] Some two or three years before he completed his Hungarian Concerto, a work somewhat unjustly neglected by violinists nowadays. It is a work of many beautiful melodies, and possesses great vivacity.

study of all that great imperishable music which was always to hand for the seeking and wherein could be found the very best examples of counterpoint, canon or fugue.

And thus it was that Brahms during these years settled once and for all the kind of music he was to write, music that was instinct with organic life because each note appertained logically to what was past and what was to come. " It is as true of Brahms as of Beethoven," says Sir Henry Hadow in his erudite analysis of Brahms's music, " that there is in him no redundant phrase, no digression, no parenthesis, nothing that does not bear some intimate relation either to its immediate context, or, with more subtlety, to a remoter part of the subsequent issue." [1]

To achieve these results Brahms took great pains. Counterpoint was not enough. Many a good contrapuntist had proved to be an indifferent symphonist, and *vice versâ*.[2] The combination of the two was Brahms's ideal. What value could any counterpoint have unless it informed the spirit of the music being composed? Therefore counterpoint became the necessary means to the end. Without it there could be no true symphony ; with it at full command the composer's imagination would set free the boundless possibilities stored up in the general welter of sounds, would co-ordinate those sounds and harness them into patterns of the greatest beauty. And that is why Brahms could delay for so long the completion of his First Symphony. He was mastering his counterpoint to make it the servant that would do his bidding on the instant.

Once that problem was solved all those dry-as-dust technical feats were transmuted into the living fibre of the music itself. Rarely in the Symphonies do we feel the creak of the machinery ; whatever contrapuntal feats are there (and they seem endless) pass the listener by because they are

---

[1] *Studies in Modern Music.* Second Series. (Seeley Service & Co. London.)
[2] On his death-bed, Schubert bewailed the paucity of true counterpoint in his own music, feeling that his larger works, such as the Symphonies, might have been so much better had he been versed more deeply in the laws of true counterpoint and polyphonic writing generally.

clothed with the warm spirit of the music, seldom sounding like the calculated effects of a clever theoretician.

In the creation of all great works of art a genius is little conscious of his technical skill ; he is concerned only with the vital expression of what he has in mind, driving along with a dæmonic energy that sees the end of the journey without having to count the miles. To that end Brahms devoted his technique for five or six years from 1856, ridding himself of his weak romanticism and emulating the styles of his great classical predecessors. The somewhat uninspired Serenades (Op. 11 and Op. 16) and the great Pianoforte Concerto in D minor (Op. 15) were the main products of this transitional period. The Serenades are not of much account, as has been suggested elsewhere. The themes lack distinction, their style is artificial ; inspiration is in fits and starts, and even the counterpoint uninteresting for its own sake. But the Pianoforte Concerto, unequal as it is, shows in no uncertain manner that in most of its part-writing there is that dæmonic spirit which is at the root of all true music, be it polyphonic or merely homophonic. The counterpoints are driven into place by the fiery steeds of inspiration. The music itself possesses a living soul and is at the same time unconscious of the structure of its own body or the functioning of its limbs.

And so it was not (nor could it have been) a far cry from the end of this great work to the beginning of a Symphony that proved to be more advanced in style than anything yet written in that form. In fact this Concerto and the First Symphony overlap one another in a remarkable way, for Albert Dietrich had seen sketches of the Symphony some time before the Concerto was produced at Leipzig in 1859. Again in 1862, Clara Schumann, in a long letter to Joachim, quotes, in full harmonies, the first phrase of the 6–8 *Allegro* of the Symphony.[1] " That is rather tough," she writes, " but I soon got used to it. The movement is full of wonderfully beautiful passages, and the motives are handled in the

[1] See Ex. 84, p. 135.

masterly fashion which he is making more and more his own. It is all interwoven in such an interesting way, and yet it goes with such a swing that it might have all been poured forth in the first moment of inspiration ; *one can enjoy every note of it without being reminded of the work there is in it."* [1] Such an interesting description tells us vividly what a labour of love those contrapuntal exercises must have been to Brahms, and with what joy he continued to serve his apprenticeship to his art—an apprenticeship that ceased only with his death.

Nor did his concern for detail end with his counterpoint. We have already seen, in another chapter, the meticulous attention Brahms paid to matters of fundamental æsthetic importance, such as the choice of interesting key-sequences [2] and the rightly-balanced use of instruments, either in a primary or secondary capacity. [3] Everything seems to have developed simultaneously with him, inventiveness and a properly controlled technique of expression going hand in hand towards the appointed goal. Even the nuances and marking of dynamics were matters of extreme importance. Extravagant hysterical outbursts such as are found in many modern scores from Tchaikovsky onwards—were anathema to him. Never do we encounter a *fortissimo* when a *forte* serves the full purpose of the music. In the Third Symphony, for instance, the Trombones do not reach a *ff* until they are well advanced in the finale, and even in this movement they play less than a dozen bars at this high pressure of tone. Nowhere in the Symphonies is *fff* to be found, the nearest approaches to it being the *crescendo* after *ff* just before letter P in the first movement of the C minor Symphony and a similar effect (indicated for the Strings alone) at letter G in the passacaglia of the E minor Symphony. [4]

---

[1] The italics are mine.—J. H.
[2] Chapter III., pp. 39–42.
[3] Chapter VI., pp. 79–87.
[4] See footnote on p. 115 with reference to *ppp*. Schubert makes a great effect with two examples of *fff* in the first movement of the great C major Symphony.

And, even more important than such detail, Brahms never forgot the many claims of melody. It was not enough for him to state a melody and accompany it with appropriate harmonies ; his melodies had to be of much more service to the general scheme. With him there could be no by-products, no residue, no " shavings " left over to be secreted in some out-of-the-way corner of his scores ; " no digression, no parenthesis," as Sir Henry Hadow points out. Every scrap of melody must justify itself by its ability to act in an accompanying capacity if called upon. In such a synthe-sized art as a symphony it was Brahms's creed that every particle of theme or rhythm, or even of *expression*, had to grow in logical fashion out of what had preceded it ; no loose ends were permissible ; only as many notes as would be required to give the music its perfect expression were allowed and no more.

Because of this, his Symphonies contain example after example of melodies used frequently as part of an accom-paniment to other melodies. His counterpoints remind us of a happy family wherein each individual member pulls his weight to the common harmonious good, or, better still, of that genus of flowers, called by botanists *compositæ*, where within the flower itself are found hundreds of florets, each one an integral part of the whole bloom.

No composer developed these matters with more care than Brahms. That, however, is not to imply that his counterpoint excelled that of Bach, Handel or other great classical composers. But it was more ingenious, command-ing immediate attention because of its rare flights of imagina-tion. If we once again except the finale to Mozart's *Jupiter* Symphony[1] we come to the inevitable conclusion that Brahms wove the fabric of his music more closely than any other classical symphonist. For instance, the three notes—D, C sharp, D—that occur at the opening of the Second Symphony are present in some form or other throughout the greater part of the movement, reappearing

[1] See footnote 1, p. 59,

in rhythmically altered form at the beginning of the finale, to become, eventually, the nucleus of the flowing quaver movement that supports the broad melodic second subject.[1]

Ex.76

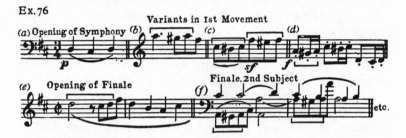

Or again, what could be more ingenious and yet at the same time more beautiful than the use Brahms makes of the melody of the slow movement of the First Symphony as a bass to the *continuation* of the Oboe theme (see * Strings).

Ex. 77

These and many other examples bear eloquent witness to the care taken by Brahms to perfect his detail. He who had studied so assiduously the works of the great masters trans-

[1] It will repay the interested reader to study the full score in regard to this detail. All the instances cannot conveniently be given here.

lated his own words into action. Music must be perfect even if it could not always be beautiful. Brahms strove for perfection and achieved much beauty of utterance because his mind was set above the fume and fret of a vain world. And that beauty of utterance manifested itself in a thousand different ways. He took simple themes and adorned them with counterpoints and other melodies as free as they were natural, reaching a sublimity of expression given to few. Not everyone can recognize his greatness ; to many his themes lack intrinsic worth. Hence the frequent criticism that his music is compounded of pinchbeck stuff, simulating the gold it is not. I fear such criticism arises from the fact that Brahms is too simple for many sophisticated musicians of today. Such musicians cannot recognize with what logic, with what mastery, he took his material and wove it into patterns of sheer beauty ; they do not examine with sufficient care the thousand and one points of detail that are co-ordinated to a degree not found in any other works of their kind. That Brahms tried his utmost to perfect his Symphonies by taking thought of this kind we know already through his own words.[1] And if genius is the capacity for taking pains, then Brahms proved his own case and the rightness of his methods of work. Inspiration he left alone. That could take care of itself, coming to his aid whenever needed and illuminating all that had been created by deep concentration of purpose.

[1] See p. 18.

CHAPTER IX

THE FIRST SYMPHONY ANALYSED

BRAHMS employs an introductory section in his Symphonies in this one instance only. The other three Symphonies plunge immediately into the main *Allegro ;* there is no " long preamble of a tale," as is often the case with Beethoven.[1] And the difference between this opening and those by Beethoven is most marked, for Brahms uses a compound time—time with subdivisions of three notes to a beat—whereas Beethoven concerns himself only with introductory sections set in simple time.

In fact, Brahms shows also a marked preference in his earlier movements for time-signatures of the triple kind. His incorporation of few of the Beethoven traditions in regard to these matters deserves more than passing mention. It suggests that his plan of architecture in the Symphonies was to build up his music *through* less imposing time-signatures to the monumental grandeur associated with all great music set in common or *alla breve* times.[2]

---

[1] Symphonies 1, 2, 4 and 7.

[2] It does not overstate the argument to mention here that our æsthetic appreciation of all great music is largely influenced by such considerations. Bach's *Sanctus* from the *B minor ·Mass*, Wagner's Overture to *Die Meistersinger*, Handel's " Hallelujah " Chorus and countless other instances will spring to the mind to suggest that music in quadruple time (and its derivatives) surpasses in the total effect any written in time-signatures dependent on three beats to a bar or three pulses to a beat. Many examples suggest themselves. A march stirs our feelings more than a waltz, its strength of rhythm being of higher value than the sensuous sway of the other ; the most effective and affecting parts of Schubert's great song *Der Wanderer* are those written in common time ; the Overture to *Die Meistersinger* (4–4 time) is more profoundly moving than the *Preislied* (3–4 time) from the same work, wonderful as the latter is as a piece of lyrical music. It is a palpable fact that common time, with its derivatives or variations, " boxes the compass " of all music in a manner not approached by any other time-signatures. While the sensuous beauty of Wagner's *Preislied* may mean more to some than the great dignity of the Overture, yet the argument here advanced is unaffected by such a predilection. On the other

That Brahms was conscious of the value of such a general scheme of time-signatures is borne out in emphatic style by reference to the four Symphonies.

TABLE OF TIME-SIGNATURES

SYMPHONY.	1st Movement.	2nd Movement.	3rd Movement.	4th Movement.
No. 1	$\frac{6}{8}$	$\frac{3}{4}$	$\frac{2}{4}, \frac{6}{8}$	$\mathbf{C}, \mathbf{\phi}$
No. 2	$\frac{3}{4}$	$\mathbf{C}, \frac{12}{8}$	$\frac{3}{4}, \frac{2}{4}, \frac{3}{8}$	$\mathbf{\phi}$
No. 3	$\frac{6}{4}, \frac{9}{4}$	$\mathbf{C}$	$\frac{3}{8}$	$\mathbf{\phi}$
No. 4	$\mathbf{\phi}$	$\frac{6}{8}$	$\frac{2}{4}$	$\frac{3}{4}, \frac{3}{2}$

The preponderance of triple or compound time-signatures in the earlier movements is a significant and interesting feature, particularly in this First Symphony. Such movements lead inevitably to a more expanded type of music in the finales. Yet in this respect we must not forget that even in the exceptional 3–4 finale to the Fourth Symphony there is a great breadth of phrase far exceeding anything heard previously in that work. Here Brahms's rhythmic scheme was determined by another mind, and so he seems to have reversed the usual order of things by opening the Symphony with an *alla breve* movement in order to create the necessary contrast.

Earlier in this book it was pointed out that Brahms must

hand, had Wagner given us in his *Lohengrin* more music in *triple* time, the whole work would have gained immeasurably in the total effect. Only the Prayer in Act I. is written to this time, the remainder of the Opera being set in quadruple or duple times—an error of æsthetic judgment that reduces the effect of the whole work to the point of frequent rhythmical monotony, more particularly in the choral ensembles. Here the redundancy of square *tempi* defeats its own ends ; we long instinctively for variety in the pulse, for something that will make the duple and quadruple times more effective by way of contrast.

have determined the inter-relationship of keys long before he made any actual sketches. He seems to have taken just as much care in the variation of his rhythmic schemes.

Whereas the homogeneity of Beethoven depends more on the spirit than on the letter of the music, that of Brahms depends on both. Beethoven stumbled on many of his greatest moments, the angel of inspiration often catching him unawares. Brahms, on the other hand, worked with patient zeal towards the appointed goal, aided by a technique that met inspiration halfway. Because of this we can regard Brahms as the superior technician, even though he falls short of the depths of inspiration manifest in such music as the Funeral March in the *Eroica* Symphony, the slow movement of the Seventh, or the First movement of the Choral Symphony.

In the introduction of the First Symphony Brahms sets his problem, much in the same way as chess players might decide on a King's pawn and Sicilian Defence opening. Unlike Beethoven, whose slow introductions contain little or no reference to the subject-matter of the subsequent *Allegro* until the change of *tempo* is almost upon us, Brahms makes his solitary introduction a most important feature of the whole Symphony, for it contains the nuclear matter of all that follows. Themes that are used in a diversity of ways in the *Allegro* make their appearance here in such forceful style that we are soon aware that no half measures will suffice with Brahms in his determination to solve once again the elusive quality of that philosophic C. In fact it is doubtful whether there is any other large-scale musical composition extant, with the possible exception of Wagner's *Das Rheingold* (which develops from an E flat), that owes more to a one-note beginning than this Symphony.

From this single note Brahms evolves his music. It plays its part at the beginning as if it were some hypothetical question not immediately answerable ; some quest for truth, the road to which is but dimly visible ; some great endeavour to achieve the simplicity of the sublime through the tortuous complexities of problems difficult to solve. In these matters the plan of the Symphony is similar to Beethoven's Ninth, where doubts and despairs are flung aside one by one as the massive choral finale mounts to its noble climax.

In his introduction—*Un poco sostenuto*—Brahms states the bulk of the thematic material that constitutes the first movement, though, in the *Allegro* that follows, its form is changed into shapes more virile and compact.   The problem is set in the introduction.   The *Allegro* grapples with it, seeking the solution with great impatience (hence the shorter phrases) ; is baffled time and again, and finally sinks exhausted without getting perceptibily nearer the truth.

From the opening C the music spreads outwards like a fan, as can be seen from the following illustration—

a feature that persists to a remarkable extent throughout the movement.   If ever music tried to burst its bonds, this does. It struggles again and again to reach the light, to win release from darkness and despair, to find the freedom that is constantly denied it.   And, in addition to the threefold character of the opening—wherein the soaring aspirations of the Violins and 'Cellos are in direct conflict with the dispirited downward pull of the Wood-wind and other instruments, above the pulsing Cs on the Timpani, Contra Bassoon and Basses—there are other embryonic themes no less important to the general scheme of the movement. These are : (*a*) the figure

Ex.79

Strings in 8ᵛᵉˢ

which, in the second bar quoted, is darkly reminiscent of the motto F.A.F.—a musical suggestion not without meaning here when we consider the general character of the Symphony—and which, at letter A, takes on a still more definite shape

Ex.80

Strings in 8ᵛᵉˢ

before its rebellious outburst in the *Allegro ;*

Ex. 81

1st Vlns

(*b*) the plaintive phrases that commence thus at the ninth bar of the introduction,

Ex.82ᵃ   Ex. 82ᵇ

p Wood-Wind in 8ᵛᵉˢ   *ff* Strings in 8ᵛᵉˢ
Pizzicato Strings

phrases that are soon given passionate rhetorical utterance in the *Allegro* (Ex. 82*b*). Other phrases are called into being, such as the deeply expressive Oboe theme

Ex. 83

p espr.

which originates in the downward passage for 1st Violins, Flute and Bassoon (heard two bars before letter A in the score) and which finds its eloquent echo on the 'Cellos five bars before the *Allegro*.   But such phrases, arising from the general texture of the music, have not the significance of the other quotations, except as melodic strips evolved from the descending phrase found in the opening bars of the Symphony.[1]

After the thirty-seven bars of introduction, wherein (at the 5th bar after letter A) the *ff* reassertion of the opening phrases forecasts more than all else the general stressful character of the music to come, it is inevitable that a momentous C (given to Oboes, Clarinets, Bassoons, two Horns, Trumpets, Timpani and *pizzicato* 'Cellos) should introduce the main theme of an *Allegro* movement that is founded on the opening bars of the Symphony.

Ex. 84

The above example is characteristically Brahmsian in the choice of themes of a dual nature that will submit to contrapuntal treatment of the invertible kind.   These themes are transferred from the treble to the bass and *vice versâ* without apparent effort.   Because of this we sense no gaps in the music ; everything seems to flow on uninterruptedly like a river to the sea.

Of the utmost importance are the first three melodic notes of the *Allegro*—C, C sharp, D (Ex. 84)—which, in the fifth, sixth and seventh bars are transferred from Flute, Oboe and

[1] Consult the Horn, Bassoon and Clarinet parts from the ninth bar after letter A onwards.

Clarinet to Bassoons and 'Cellos. It would seem, from what is to be explained later, that this aspiring phrase, this *Sursum corda*, governs the development of the Symphony more than anything else, however important other themes may be because of their passionate intensity. Its appearance, either in treble or bass, should not escape notice ; nor the frequent use of its descending opposite (Ex. 84, inner parts) which phrase, from letter B onwards, acquires some significance, firstly on the 'Cellos and Basses, and then on other instruments. Its length is varied, becoming this, at the thir-

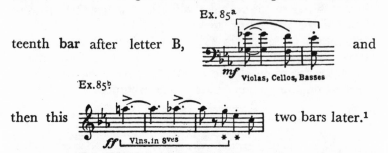

teenth bar after letter B, and

then this two bars later.[1]

To attempt a full description of the skilful treatment of these several themes in the opening of the *Allegro* movement is impossible. Nothing goes to waste. The score is tightly packed with endless detail, and yet all is presented in an amazingly clear and convincing manner. As it is equally impossible to give entire chapter and verse without prolonging this book out of all reason, I hope the reader will find sufficient to interest him in the following delineation of the main themes quoted above.

The theme of the three ascending notes, C, C sharp, D (Ex. 84), seems to suggest the lofty desire of the mind to triumph over sinister forces that hinder its progress, while the downward harmonies (against the theme) represent those forces themselves. Next in order of appearance comes what can be described as the theme of " action " (Ex. 81), a theme suggesting the resolute will of a man determined

---

[1] Compare the two notes * * with Ex. 86.

to conquer, whatever may be in store.   Incidentally, this theme's apparent relationship to the motto F.A.F. gives it every right to this description.

It becomes exigent when inverted (letter E onwards),

Ex. 86

and even violent just before the repeat of the first section of the movement, where (and elsewhere later on) its first two notes are hammered out with the greatest possible emphasis.

A new version in B major occurs at the opening of the development section.   Hope soars on buoyant wings once again as the theme recovers its original shape for a brief spell.   But actually its spirit is crushed (letter F) and it soon becomes despondent and rhythmless, affecting the whole mood of the music which fades into sombre contemplation and dismay.

Ex. 87

In its virile form we find this theme combining with the three ascending notes[1] (can it mean that lofty aspirations coupled to an indomitable will will overcome all obstacles ?) and with the more ominous descending harmonies,[2] which in their turn remind us that victory can only be won after a prolonged struggle.   Nine bars from the end of the movement, in the *Poco sostenuto* coda, the theme of action is a spent force.   The battle ceases for a while ; victory is by

[1] See Ex. 84 and the full score at letter D and at letter L (the recapitulation), etc.
[2] See the 'Cello and Bass parts at letter B and examine the structure of the middle parts in Ex. 84.

no means in sight.   And for that we must hold this theme
responsible.   Its many inverted appearances—from letter O
onwards, and particularly from seventeen bars before P—
have by now completely crushed the element of hope that
up to this point was continually present in the music.   Here
we must leave the reader to his own further analysis of a
remarkable theme that begins so courageously and ends in
such dismay, fighting a losing rather than a winning battle
(see Exs. 86 and 81).

Next in order of importance comes the beautiful episodical
melody for Oboe that is usually identified as the second
subject (10th bar after letter D), though, judging by its shy
emergence from the context, it barely justifies its title.

Ex. 88

p dolce.

Nevertheless, both here in the exposition and then in the
recapitulation it is of great importance, for its last four notes
form the basis of two fine climaxes, with the Horns much
in evidence on a development of these notes.[1]   And before
these climaxes are reached, variants of the four notes are also
heard in an exquisitely lyrical codetta to the second subject,
where, in particular, the first Clarinet and a Horn have
responding phrases of rare beauty.

The dark-hued Violas break this mood with three important notes on the C string, which quickly develop into a new
agitated four-note figure of much significance (letter E in
the exposition : O in the recapitulation).

Ex. 89ᵃ   Ex. 89ᵇ

---

[1] See the full score, 17th bar after letter E onwards and 17th bar after
letter O onwards.

Against this figure—which is often inverted later on, in
conformity with the general character of all the motifs in
this movement—Ex. 86 and also the climax notes for the
Horns derived from Ex. 88 are heard in emphatic style.
At letter G, Ex. 89*b* reappears and alternates with a new
theme of noble character, of which the first phrase is given
here.

Ex. 90

Was it for this that the music, forty-three bars previously,
made its glad and buoyant excursion into B major ? It must
be remembered that the key of this extract (Ex. 90) is closely
related to B major.   If the chord of G flat is changed to its
synonymous F sharp the relationship is apparent at once.
In fact it is almost unnecessary to point out that the two
chords of C flat major (marked with asterisks) are the actual
equivalent of B major.   The point is stressed, however,
because there seems to be a very definite æsthetic relationship
throughout the Symphony between the *E flat* of the C minor
triad and the *D sharp* that acts as leading note to the E major
slow movement.[1]   In all the music that occurs from the
beginning of the development section (eight bars before F)
to the point now being analysed there is an undoubted
struggle for mastery between the lyrical romantic element
in the music, as represented by the B major section (with its
D sharp), and the more forceful and austere phrases that
constantly return to the key of C minor (with its E flat).

[1] See p. 41.

When Ex. 90 appears, it is strong and resolute, carried along on giant steps in the bass and modulating with great confidence through various keys until it reaches C major. There it seems to hesitate in rich antiphony between Strings and Wood-wind, and is soon silenced by Ex. 89*b* and by the reappearance of the ascending three-note phrase shown in Ex. 84. It never returns, and with it vanishes for the remainder of the movement any ray of hope the music ever held. The romantic D sharp cannot hold its own against the powerful influence of the E flat and the music relapses into profound gloom.

The three ascending notes (Ex. 84) now take charge of the music, entering *ff* on 'Cellos and Basses twelve bars before H, only to fade away by degrees to a *pp* reached at I. Here the mood is very sombre and oppressive, especially when the three notes themselves adventure no longer and gradually lose their pitch through palindromic inversion of the phrase.

Ex. 91

Underneath all this melancholy is heard the sinister and distant tap of the G Drum, reinforced by 'Cellos.

The music reaches its nadir at letter I. From there onwards it begins to regain confidence through a gradual upward movement. The three notes still control the situation, but into them there enters a fresh vital spark that once more sets the music alight.

Until this moment the three-note group has only moved by semitones. Now, at letter I, it takes on a new significance, leaping a *minor third* between its second and third notes.

Ex. 92

In this secondary thematic detail, transient in character, but arresting to the ear because of the new interval involved, Brahms undoubtedly foreshadows the main theme of the slow movement.[1] This new device creates a great impression on the mind of the listener; it is not soon forgotten. Brahms must have sensed its possibilities in an instant; once he had found it there could be no mistaking the direction of the music. Soon the interval of the minor third itself becomes inadequate to the rising climax. A bigger leap is demanded, for the emotional content of the music increases rapidly to a point of great intensity.

Ex. 93

The close *stretto* in the bass is a remarkable feature here, creating a very importunate mood that breaks through all reserve in the magnificent climax at letter K. This climax leads through twenty-two bars of feverishly excited music of the *compositæ* type (for most of the main motives, even including the Timpani rhythm, are intermingled here most effectively) to a passionate restatement of the opening of the *Allegro* (Ex. 84). Hitherto Brahms has made but little use of the semiquaver figure found in the third and fourth bars of the *Allegro* (Ex. 84). In this climax it becomes the central figure, driving the music along with dæmonic energy to the recapitulation.

[1] See Ex. 94, p. 144.

It has been stated elsewhere how the music of this move-ment is " all of one piece." [1] Most of it revolves round the keynote, even the greater part of the development section. Its character seems to be dominated by many parent ideas and more particularly by the C Drum.[2] In the coda (17 bars before letter P onwards) this Drum reiterates the rhythm of the music with most dramatic effect. And the rhythm conveys its import with all the more eloquence when we realize that it imitates the exigent spirit shown in the first two notes of Ex. 86.

· From letter P the music speaks for itself. It sinks morosely to its quiet ending, with the three aspiring notes weak and failing (" where those yearning chords come on the B flat minor beats "—writes Elizabet von Herzogenberg to Brahms in 1881) and the two-note rhythm of Ex. 86 also a spent force. The final *Poco sostenuto*,[3] languidly reminiscent of the brave opening of the Symphony, sounds like an admission of defeat, while the C *major* close is no more than a temporary respite from the struggle.

It is difficult to say whether this tragic storm-driven music illustrates anything personal in Brahms's life at the time it was sketched and written. It may be partly autobio-graphical. On the other hand, since all great music of the absolute kind must express either the grave or the gay, the contemplative or the robustly happy, it does not follow that we need attach to such a masterpiece as this first movement any local explanation or read into it anything but our own personal reactions to its changing moods. Whatever programme of abstract ideas there may be in its deeply emotional phrases, the absolute quality of the music is not affected, for the movement speaks with an universal tongue.

·   ·   ·   ·   ·   ·

When Brahms completed the first movement of this

[1] For that reason it has not been possible to analyse all the music in true sequential order.
[2] See p. 39.
[3] Marked *Meno Allegro* in Philharmonic Miniature Score.

Symphony in 1862, Joachim optimistically jumped to the conclusion that the whole work was all but ready for performance. " I am delighted with what you tell me of his Symphony," he wrote to Clara Schumann from London on July 18th of that year. " If I could only see it, but I am afraid he would hardly like to send it over here. . . . But I will try and persuade him. When I think of the pleasure it would give me to rehearse Johannes' Symphony and to be the first to produce it. . . ." And again, in another letter to her, dated August 26th—" Perhaps I shall be able to invite you to Hanover for Brahms's Symphony at the end of October."

During the following month Joachim wrote to Brahms from Hastings, where he had gone for a holiday, inviting him to conduct the Symphony in Hanover. But, to Joachim's surprise and annoyance, no reply was received.

Subsequent events supplied the reason. Twelve years were to elapse before Brahms resumed work on the Symphony. The success that had attended the first performance of the *St. Anthony Variations* in 1874 determined him to complete it. How much of the first movement was altered we do not know. Possibly very little, for Brahms had long since arrived at the maturity of his style. Yet one can imagine that the music of this first movement must have been his constant companion throughout that long intervening period ; by 1874 it must have become part and parcel of his being, an *alter ego*, dogging his footsteps at every turn, begging for completion. Many sketches for other Symphonies had come and gone in the meantime. None had escaped destruction save what had been drafted for No. 1.

And so it is not difficult to believe that the romantically beautiful and long melody of the slow movement—*Andante sostenuto* (Ex. 94, p. 144)—owes its happy birth to the three-note phrase quoted in Ex. 92.

The melody is of great interest, even apart from its beauty. It begins on the romantic major third of the chord—a device common to Mendelssohn and Schumann (as has been

Ex.94

pointed out on pp. 49 and 50), but used more sparingly by Brahms. And as if Brahms were somewhat ashamed of his outburst, this major third is almost immediately contradicted by a series of G naturals (minor thirds) that give the music a greater and more serious beauty than could have been obtained by a sentimental loyalty to the G sharp.[1] No wonder that Elizabet von Herzogenberg writes to Brahms (January 23rd, 1877) in her usual homely way : " . . . and please have the symphony printed soon ; for we are all symphony-sick, and weary of straining to grasp the beloved, elusive melodies." It is that very elusive quality, those adventures into the unexpected that give this movement its somewhat wonderful character. A bare minimum of melodic major thirds has sufficed for the rugged first movement, and even amid all the tender romance of this slow movement Brahms instinctively avoids the cloying sweetness that is associated with a redundancy of this kind.

The melody itself stretches a long way. It is not until the seventeenth bar that there is anything like a real break, and even that is only a halfway cadence into the dominant, ushering in the lovely continuation of the melody on the Oboe.[2] The subtle introduction of the first bars of the opening melody as an accompaniment to the Oboe has been shown in the last chapter. This harking back to the opening bars seems the most natural accompaniment possible. The Oboe melody creates such a mood of ineffable beauty as it

[1] Note Ex. 8, p. 49.
[2] See Ex. 77, p. 128.

mounts to its highest note that it is only right that another melody of equal loveliness should be mated with it, rather than some ordinary accompaniment having no special merit in itself.

The Oboe melody remains uncompleted. "Just when one expects it to be finished by some cadential figure"—says Mr. Fuller Maitland very aptly (in the May 1933 issue of the *Musical Times*)—"it stops as if at the bidding of a little phrase of warning, which has already appeared in the third bar of the movement." In this way the first section of the movement is rounded off in E major by a return to the simple character of the opening, the orchestration—Strings, Bassoons and Horns—also being identical.

So far the music has remained in the parent key of the movement and round a middle pitch. But now the time for adventure has arrived (letter A). Consequently the Strings forsake the serenity of mood that has characterized the movement up to this point, to indulge in thirteen bars of emotional music founded mainly on the following phrase.

Ex. 95

The contrast obtained is most effective in every way. Not only do the Violins and Violas explore a much higher range of pitch, but the whole character of the music is altered completely. Syncopation, cross-phrasing and close imitative writing are much in evidence. Further, the tug of these syncopations in the third and fourth bars must have affected Brahms in no small measure, for this impatient soaring figure suddenly comes to life again in the *Adagio* section of the finale.[1]

Of great interest is the new melody on the Oboe that appears at the conclusion of this emotional outburst (letter B).

[1] See Ex. 105, p. 158.

Ex.96

Violins, Violas

In it I hear most distinctly the embryo of the third move-ment.[1] By the time that movement is reached, dark alchemic forces (typically Brahmsian) will have done their work and transmuted this secondary but important theme into something entirely different.

How important this theme is can be judged by the treat-ment accorded to it. Before its full length is run the Clarinet has already entered with a variant. Then, in their turn, the 'Cellos and Basses steal it from the Clarinet in like manner. After its syncopated accompaniment also has undergone development against various fragments of Ex. 96, the music is taken along to a fine climax. Here the theme is stated vigorously by full Strings in octaves, and for the last time in the movement.

Brahms quickly rids himself of the agitation in the music by dropping the semiquaver figuration; then, within the limits of a few bars, dovetails the end of this section with a return to the main theme (Ex. 94).

The recapitulation section is much more extended than the opening, both in actual length and in fulness of orches-tration. What it was originally it would be interesting to know. Brahms made cuts both here and in the third move-ment. Writing to Otto Dessoff, who conducted the first performance of the Symphony, he expresses the hope that these " violent " cuts will not be too apparent.

There is undoubtedly a feeling of incoherence for four bars from letter C onwards, where the running semiquavers—

[1] See Ex. 99, p. 151.

playing about with the group of four notes marked with an asterisk in Ex. 96—end abruptly and for no obvious reason. It seems as if Brahms were full of misgivings, feeling the urgent need of a speedy return to the original melody, for there are signs of laboured effort here which not even his skilled workmanship could hide.   Was it at this point that some excision was made ?

Three bars before letter D Brahms becomes involved in a lengthy excursion into the dominant key of B major.   This determines the course of the music in a totally unexpected manner, for we have been led to expect that the *tonic* key of E will be firmly established for some time.   But Brahms here commits himself to no less than eighteen bars [1] in the *dominant* and by such prolongation of the melodic line freshens up the music at once.   If the following quotations be compared it will be seen how, by the alteration of one chord (Ex. 97^b, bar 2), the phrase is given a new life, for

Ex. 97^a (6th bar of the movement)

Ex. 97^b (3rd bar before D)

---

[1] Three bars before letter D to letter E.

the raised pitch brings about a sense of buoyant freedom
not found in the earlier version, where the G naturals recall
tristfully to mind Browning's "lesser thirds so plaintive."
It is to this revivified phrase that the lengthy passage in
the dominant owes its existence. And it is strange, yet
fascinatingly beautiful at this juncture, to hear all this music
played a perfect fifth higher, since in most symphonic
recapitulations we learn to expect the lower (and duller)
pitch of the tonic. Had Brahms conformed to an academic
repetition in the tonic the coda following would have failed
in its effect through a redundancy of E major chords.

At the close of this section—wherein it should be noted
there is much embellishment of the phrases—a solo Violin
joins with Oboe and Horn in a lovely ecstatic version of
Ex. 77. Again this theme is left as uncompleted as it
was at its first hearing on the Oboe, for the counter-theme
(*i.e.*, the first melody) enters as before to take charge of the
eventual cadence into E major.

This cadence has been delayed for thirty-two bars while
the music has been adventuring elsewhere, as shown above.
Its belated appearance (10th bar after letter E) gives the
1st Horn the opportunity of consolidating the movement
with an exquisite moment or two of the Oboe melody
(Ex. 77). Round it the solo Violin weaves a beautiful
semiquaver pattern founded on the first four notes of the
Horn phrase, whilst the triple-quaver accompaniment on
various instruments, in conjunction with the prolonged pedal
E in the bass, gives to the music a breathless rapture that is
beyond analysis.

Ex. 98

The next ten bars (from letter F onwards) are exquisitely wrought.   An amalgam of phrases founded on the combination of Oboe and Strings shown in Ex. 77 continues what has once again been left incomplete by the Horn and solo Violin.   The music drops to a whisper, followed by an impressive silence.   Out of this the Bassoons attempt the cadence which we know is not far away, but withdraw shyly after one bar (Ex. 94, bar 3), leaving its completion to the other Wood-wind and the four Horns.   The Violins and Violas now enter with a less *legato* version of the rhythmic figure that first occurs at letter A.   This device seems to prolong the movement somewhat unnecessarily, since it fans the dying embers of the music into a fitful flame or two, producing what always sounds to me like two unwanted cadences.[1]   Up to this point Brahms has avoided monotony of key with such skill that it comes as a great surprise here to find him indulging in redundant phrase-making of the sentimental kind.   More particularly is this noticeable in the somewhat plagal effect of the final cadence.   Perhaps the pruning-knife had done other duty here and had done it none too well.

.   .   .   .   .   .

A boisterous Scherzo was never much in Brahms's line. His serious nature would not let him indulge in the robustious mad pranks that are heard in a Beethoven third movement.   Even the early Piano Scherzo in E flat minor, written in 1853, is black-edged.   And if music were such a serious business to a youth of twenty, is it likely that his style could or would change with advancing years ?   The irresistible one-in-a-bar drive of an orchestral Scherzo as we know it in Beethoven was not his choice ; he could not shake off for any length of time that minor-key feeling once described by Nietzsche as " the melancholy of impotence."   Unfair as this criticism is on the whole, yet it has a certain justification when we consider the amount of dark brooding

[1] 16th and 20th bars after letter F.

music composed by Brahms.   His strength lay in a different direction to the Scherzo ; what symphonic music of his found its outlet in a major key was rhetorical rather than boisterous ; dignified, rarely exuberant, and devoid of all rodomontade.

And the more we examine the lineal descent of his compositions the more we see that Brahms was bound by nature to rule out any idea of a Beethovenish third movement whenever a symphony should materialize.   It may have been through choice ; on the other hand it may have been that the peculiar turn of his mind left him no option but to discard what he knew would but fail in effect.   In all his orchestral compositions he comes near the feeling of a Scherzo but once, namely, in the fifth variation of the *St. Anthony* set.   This variation has much of the spirit of the Scherzo in Beethoven's *Eroica* Symphony and has animation enough to make us regret the absence of other examples of its kind.

But in place of a Scherzo Brahms has substituted in three of his Symphonies movements of elegant reposeful character that serve as admirable links in the chain of musical thought. They are in the nature of an interlude—a night-time bivouac during which the events of the day are gathered to the mind in retrospect before the onward march of the music is resumed on the morrow.

And nowhere is this mood suggested more than in the third movement of the First Symphony.   Hans Bülow thought so much of the music that on one occasion (March 14th, 1882) he repeated the movement to a Leipzig Gewandhaus audience before proceeding to the finale ; he felt that it had received insufficient applause,[1] and was therefore not clearly understood.

The opening theme on the Clarinet is most unusual in that it consists of two five-bar phrases,[2] the second

---

[1] Nowadays we in Great Britain have advanced beyond this.   A discerning audience applauds at the *end* of a symphony only.—J. H.

[2] See pp. 53–55.   At letter A it becomes a seven-bar phrase.

of which (not shown in Ex. 99 for lack of space) is a remarkable inversion of the first.

Ex. 99

How this was derived has already been shown in the analysis of the slow movement.   Its plastic nature, with the delightful *pizzicato* 'Cello accompaniment, and the charming response in descending thirds—so typical of the composer—

Ex. 100

gave Brahms another opportunity of indulging his fancy for music of the Intermezzo type wherein pictorial phrases and a lighter mood are substituted for the complex emotions and bitter-sweet romance heard so far.   But even then it is a quiet and restrained atmosphere that we find here.   The Scherzo has been sacrificed, so why attempt anything exuberant, says Brahms in effect.   This *un poco allegretto e grazioso* movement has all the quiet joy of a man browsing among his favourite books.   It touches lightly on things around ; it creeps within the covers of the volumes and even surveys a tragic or sorrowful story here and there, but only with a mildly pitying eye.

Ex. 101

Nowhere is it drawn into the vortex of deep soul-searing emotions ; had it been, Brahms could scarcely have conveyed the effect of that glorious finale which epitomizes everything heard previously, including this restful, modestly-wrought interlude.

The many points of decoration in the music are worthy of mention. Eight bars before letter A and elsewhere, the Strings have imitative *arpeggii* that are as ingenious as they are effective. From letter B they provide a light chattering background and then the 'Cellos and Basses play with a continuation of Ex. 101 as a bass to the plaint of the Oboe referred to on page 82.

At the sixth (see Ex. 101) and fourteenth bars after B the return of the Clarinet melody is heralded by a *forte* suggestion of its first bar on the Wood-wind. When the melody actually returns, running semiquavers on 1st Violins and Violas are added to the accompaniment, adding materially to the beauty of effect. Here Brahms leaves the melody at its first phrase on a half-close, the E flat of which he once again turns into an enharmonic D sharp in the space of a bar or two, modulating thereby into the key of B for the middle section.

Of sterner stuff, this section is constructed on the well-worn Brahmsian plan of playing off combined Wood-wind, Horns and Trumpets against Strings. The time-signature has changed to 6–8 and with it there is created a more restless mood, particularly as the music is founded throughout on two short phrases of three notes each, phrases that answer one another in rapid cross-fire.

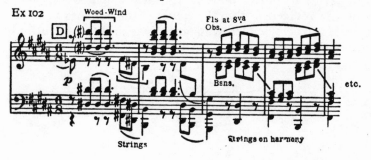

Ex 102

Everything here is so straightforward and methodical that there is little call for comment. The music explains itself, rising to a sudden *ff* climax of considerable vigour, at which point the Violins and Wood-w'nd momentarily exchange rôles—the former taking charge of the reiterated notes, while the three descending notes are transferred to the Wood-wind. Trumpets and Horns then combine with the others to make a fine, forceful B major ending to this middle section of the movement.

After a short repeat the music reverts to the Clarinet music of the opening through a bridge passage of six bars (before letter E). This is not only interesting because the synonymous D sharp–E flat is again pressed into service as, a link, but also very beautiful indeed by reason of the A flat minor cadence that resolves most unexpectedly into the major key of the opening (letter E). In this link the Strings give brief warnings of the return of the Clarinet melody, while the Wood-wind, Horns and Trumpets are concerned with the three reiterated notes that are so characteristic of the middle section. With these three notes, and a variant of the third and fourth bars of Ex. 102, the Flute and Oboe overlap the return of the Clarinet melody. After the first strain of this melody has been heard, its continuation is transferred to the 1st Violins in an exquisite variation from the original. Here the five-bar phrase is extended into one of six and the notes themselves are embellished with semi-quaver arabesques of rare beauty. This new interest at once enlivens the music to a small climax, Ex. 100 on Wood-wind being accompanied by more insistent *arpeggio* treatment of the Strings. And it is then that the two Oboes give out the beautiful *duettino* to which reference was made on page 82.

From the *forte* climax (24th bar after E) the music suddenly becomes sadly retrospective. Elongated shadows of the opening themes are thrown across this wistful coda, which sinks finally to its tranquil ending on allusions to the phrases of the middle section (Ex. 102).

This movement is so perfect in its structure that it is impossible to detect the cut (or cuts) made by the composer prior to the first performance of the Symphony under Otto Dessoff in 1876. It has been urged at times that, as with the third movements in the Second and Third Symphonies, it is too nearly related to chamber-music and cannot be considered truly symphonic. This view is one not easy to accept, for the music acts as a serene and most desirable interlude before the grave opening of the finale. It leaves us completely in the dark as to the nature of what is to follow. And while it is immediately effective in its own right by reason of the originality of its ideas, it also renders great service to the Symphony with its piquant orchestration. The whole movement, in fact, is set in a reverie far removed from the realities of life, a reverie in which thoughts are only half formed and where the imagination tries in vain to maintain contact with the unreal and elusive. Few movements by Brahms have such swiftly moving harmonies as are found here ; the ever-changing colours are kaleidoscopic in character ; we are left with the impression of having passed through some phase of twilight fancies belonging to a dream-world out of all reach. And this twilight mood is enhanced when we realize that the Timpani have been silent throughout the movement. But their glory is to come, when in the introduction of the finale the veil of the music is rent asunder with a C loud enough to wake the dead.

.   .   .   .   .   .

The first performance of the Symphony at Karlsruhe in 1876 was quickly followed by many others all over Germany, so famous had Johannes Brahms become. By now even the Leipzigers were less recalcitrant in their attitude, for a new generation was beginning to think somewhat differently about the master's music. Those " die-hards " of 1859 who had reviled the Piano Concerto in D minor were thinning out rapidly ; many were gathered to their fathers, unrepentant to the last. Happily some of those still alive were young enough to be converted to the music, young enough to enjoy the stirring events of this extraordinary year, yet old enough to advance argument against argument in the bitter warfare between the Brahms and Wagner camps now beginning to divide musical Germany.

But even then all was not plain sailing for the Symphony. A projected repetition of the Leipzig performance—Brahms himself conducted the Symphony there for the first time on January 18th, 1877—met with certain opposition, one unconverted member of the Gewandhaus committee being particularly loud in his protestations. " He could not face the terrific strain of deciding whether the finale led to heaven or hell " wrote Elizabet von Herzogenberg to Brahms a few days after the first performance.

Where the finale leads to has long since been decided. It is one of the most noble conceptions the mind of a composer has ever held. It consolidates a multitude of abstract thoughts and feelings quite beyond technical analysis, and does it so completely that we get the satisfaction of grasping the inner spirit of the music without being quite able to explain why. That quality bespeaks its greatness. At each hearing there is a new revelation ; at no time does it pall on the senses by the constant repetition of its familiar phrases. We recognize its rightful place in the whole Symphony and at the same time realize that not one note of it could have been born into the world of sound but for the three movements preceding it. We can hazard guess after guess as to its meaning, explaining its themes in a thousand different ways, yet even then we feel that we have only touched the hem of the music, so transcendent is its quality.

And that is why we can always hear it without tedium. Let it represent what it will, the triumph of man over fate, his soul " equal, equipt at last," or the struggle of Brahms himself for nobler self-expression ; let it deal with such abstractions as the awe-inspiring magnitude of space or the victory of good over evil, it matters not. We hear it primarily as music, and as music we enjoy it. If, incidentally, we detach our consciousness from the " life and death " programme contained in Liszt's *Les Préludes*, the music at once falls to the ground ; if, on the other hand, we desymbolize Brahms's First Symphony, not one phrase loses its value.

The note C, that central orb of the music, is the quinessential feature of the *Adagio* introduction. What themes cluster round it, and they are many, but serve to demonstrate its omnipotence. Whatever modulations occur are shortlived, the music being drawn back to the C as if by some centripetal force. And one cannot say this of all symphonies, despite their allegiance to a pre-determined tonality. In many the themes function by fortuitous chance, while often the key of the work is merely the " peg to hang the coat on." But with Brahms that is not so. His First Symphony is more than the co-ordination of themes and movements ; it is the exultant progress of a single note, the triumph of a musical philosophy founded as much on a scientific principle as on any artistic endeavour. It reveals the note C as the underlying principle from which all accepted music springs.[1] By obedience to the natural laws of sound it links a science and an art together in perfect accord, yet without detriment to the rhapsodic beauty of the music itself. Only to a few of the great masters has this perfect adjustment been possible.

The *Adagio* introduction of the finale is well described by Specht. " We receive the impression that a higher power is at work, one so great and mysterious as even Brahms was but rarely able to summon." That higher power is manifest in the very opening, where the descending notes in the bass usher in the black-shrouded hint of the great theme to come (Ex. 110).

[1] See p. 40.

Ex. 103

It will be seen that this is only an embryonic fragment,
bearing but an inverted likeness to the great theme itself.[1]
Whereas the full statement of the theme will eventually move
with great confidence from the dominant note G to the tonic
C, here the reverse is the case.   The C is at present obscured
by the gloomy shadows of the minor key ; we are in touch
with it only indirectly.   But after the first *pizzicato* passage[2]—
that rousing from death-like slumber—a first streak of light
breaks across the music, and the C is definitely established in
its rightful place in the theme, though the harmonies are still
in the minor.

Ex. 104

Another convulsive *pizzicato* interruption of four bars,
ending in an even more dramatic *ff* than its predecessor,
stirs the introduction to a climax of unearthly character
and power.   It sounds as if all the elements in the music
were being summoned one by one to some supernatural
court, there to assist in the apotheosis of that great C major
chord.

The Violas and 'Cellos are the first to move, their demi-

---

[1] Compare the inner harmonies with those at the opening of the Symphony,
etc.

[2] See p. 83.

semiquavers breaking in on fragments of the opening (on Oboe and Clarinet, two bars before A). But it should be noted that in all this activity no further allusions are made to the great theme itself. After its second abbreviated appearance (Ex. 104) it disappears until that moment when, released from bondage and free from all perplexing doubts, it shines forth in the full radiance of its major key.

But strange events are happening in these moments. Ghosts of the past stalk around in barely recognizable shapes. At letter A a distorted version of part of a theme from the slow movement[1] makes a surprising entry on Wood-wind and Horns against greatly agitated upward demisemiquavers on the Strings.

Ex. 105

(in 8ves) *cresc. poco a poco*

And now (3rd bar after letter A) the Violins break out into rapid figurations which, taken with their context, form a remarkable epitome of all the black despairing moods that have haunted the Symphony from its very first C.

Ex.106

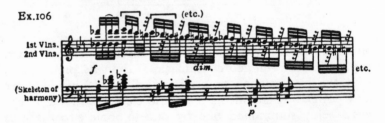

It is impossible adequately to describe the effect of these few bars as they rush headlong to the thunderclap of the C Drum. I cannot remember any other music that creates such an overwhelming impression of some imminent

[1] Compare the following Ex. 105 with the latter part of Ex. 95, p. 145.

cataclysm, of some instantaneous rending of the veil which will disclose to astonished eyes and ears a new spiritual kingdom of unutterable beauty and oneness.

And in this instant Brahms makes us understand that these last convulsive efforts are not so much the death-pangs of evil spirits as the struggle of positive forces breaking through darkness to the refulgence of a never-ending day.   Such is the extraordinary course of the music in a brief bar or two.

It is therefore interesting to trace the rapid growth of the lovely Horn melody in C major that is now close upon us.   After being vaguely prophetic on the 1st Violins—see the bracketed notes (⌐⌐) in Ex. 106—its initial notes cry out in great impatience on the Wood-wind, three bars later.

Ex. 107

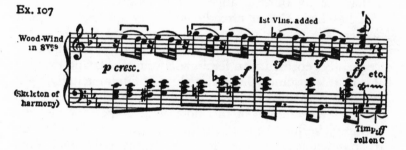

The overwhelming *ff* roll on the C Drum now banishes all doubt and prepares the mind for the entry of this sublime melody.

Ex. 108 (Incomplete sketch)

The oft-quoted similarity of this theme to the celebrated

chimes, the " Cambridge Quarters,"[1] is one of those happy
coincidences that make for the better amity of nations.
That the Symphony's first performance in England should
have been at Cambridge (March 8th, 1877, Joachim conducting) makes the coincidence all the more remarkable.
But, as with so many of Brahms's Horn melodies, the main
interest here lies in the employment of the harmonic series
of notes, to form, with a hand-stopped F sharp in the fifth
bar, a theme of outstanding loveliness. And so, because
of this, it can be said that both the " Cambridge Quarters "
and Brahms's great theme come of the same parentage.

The music now definitely establishes the C major key
when from the Horn is heard as firm and convincing a
melodic major third as anyone could desire.

It has been shown already how very sparing the great
masters are in the use of strongly-accented *melodic* major
thirds belonging to the primary triads of a key, for such notes,
frequently repeated, can feminize music to a trying extent.[2]
But in this instance the major third is fundamentally right
from every point of view. Up to now Brahms had given
us but few examples of this note as an important melodic
feature ; he had kept it in the background, dwelling on
it conspicuously in the slow movement only, and even
then using it with the utmost discretion. Now this note E
(*i.e.*, the major third) is made the most important feature in
the Symphony so far, for no other note, not even the C and
G that complete its own triad, could have defined the major
key with quite the same address. All doubts are set at rest
by this one note ; none other could have convinced us.
The ideal has been attained and the final song of triumph
cannot now be far away.

But before the triumph comes, we listen to a solemn
service that begins with the Horn theme now under discussion. This theme, marked *f sempre e passionato*—the
passionato surely connotes a far finer meaning here than we

[1] More commonly called the " Westminster Quarters."
[2] See pp. 48–50.

usually accord to it ?—is repeated on the Flute two octaves higher, and is then followed by a noble hymn of faith (letter C in score).

Ex. 109

1st & 2nd Trombones

3rd Trombone Contra Bsn.

p dolce

[Bassoons and Horns omitted here]

Timp. roll

etc.

No other title seems appropriate to this theme whose harmonies modulate with such freedom through various keys without once detaching the theme itself from its anchorage to the C major tonality.

Five bars later the 1st Horn re-enters with a briefer version of its own theme, and, in close imitation with the 2nd Horn and various Wood-wind instruments, completes this long complex introduction on the dominant chord described elsewhere. From this chord at last springs the long-promised song of triumph (Ex. 110).

Before proceeding to the *Allegro non troppo, ma con brio* section which forms the bulk of the finale, it must not be forgotten that the long *Adagio* introduction contains themes and phrases—*e.g.*, Exs. 107, 108, 109 and the interposed *pizzicato* passages—which will assume great importance at a later stage. Actually the hymn of faith constitutes the thematic climax of the whole movement and Symphony, shining forth in dazzling splendour in the final *alla breve* coda. The equally inspired treatment of Ex. 108 has already been described on page 86.

Taking the finale as a whole, we have, therefore, a very elaborate structure in which there is a perfect fusion of elements, both musical and psychological. A long conflict is ended at the Horn theme with the appearance of the C major chord (Ex. 108), to which the solemn hymn

(Ex. 109) acts as a natural and mystical corollary. From this music arises a great song of jubilation (Ex. 110), one that might well express the joy of a man whose soul is loosed from bondage. Then, when this song has soared to its zenith, a spiritually ecstatic version of the Horn theme (Ex. 30, p. 86) reaffirms the victory of light over darkness, of order over chaos. And, to conclude all and to bring the C major full circle, there is added the transcendent version of the hymn of faith, in which we catch more than a glimpse of some divine cosmic principle outshining everything, even man's jubilant song of deliverance.

The remainder of the story is one of musical analysis.

The theme of the *Allegro* is of such importance that it needs must be quoted in full, despite its length.

Ex. 110

Its cousinly likeness to the " Ode to Joy " theme in the finale of Beethoven's Ninth (Choral) Symphony is more in the spirit than in the letter of the music, though indeed much has been, and still is, made of their similarity. Both themes are of the same stock ; both are expressions of " this world's joie," and, as such, must inevitably spring from a common parentage.

The length of the theme is perhaps its finest feature. Its outlines stand in bold relief against the curtailed phrases characterizing so much of the earlier part of the Symphony. All hesitancy is thrust aside and replacing it are great melodic curves that fill the remainder of the movement with ever-increasing grandeur.

Examined in detail the theme shows a great partiality for the accented major third of the *subdominant* chord (F), a feature that gives it its unique character.[1] And because of the insistence of this note A rather than a redundancy of the major third (E) of the *tonic* chord, a contented manly vigour is imparted to the music, unspoilt by anything of a sentimental nature.

We have seen in the Horn theme (Ex. 108) how the E defined the major key of C at a given moment as no other melodic note could have done. But now, in this exultant song of freedom, the *note* C is of even greater importance. Here it dominates the theme as strongly as the E had defined the nature of the Horn theme, establishing itself as the axis about which all else must now rotate. And with this note in its rightful melodic place (*i.e.*, at the most important accentual points) comes complete justification of all instances of the C *tonality* occurring ·in the introduction. Each instance has its own particular meaning and its own intimate relationship with the Symphony as a whole. And because Brahms varies his themes with such wonderful skill, selecting at one time the *third* of the triad and at another the *fifth* or the *keynote* as the theme's most essential feature, there is never a moment where any redundancy of a fixed tonality is felt. Of how many Symphonies can this be said ?

After its initial statement on the 1st Violins, aided here and there by the 2nds, the great theme is transferred to Wood-wind and Horns against a *pizzicato* and Timpani accompaniment. At this repetition it again runs its complete course, the penultimate bar being imitated at close range by Violins and ·Violas, now playing *arco* in an eager *forte*. This serves to introduce the rousing *animato* section (letter D). Here Brahms shows his mettle in a magnificent development of the thematic content. Taking the first five notes he turns them by diminution into a splendid *stretto*

---

[1] See the notes in Ex. 110 marked with an asterisk.

in quavers, one that gives an exhilarating impetus to the
music.

Ex. 111

While it is not possible to quote each detail, the score
deserves the closest attention here, for the music is profuse
in points of interest. Upward syncopations on Bassoons,
'Cellos and Basses serve as a bass for a bold descending figure
on the Violins, while many *sforzando* effects produce a more
intense mood. Such virile movement inevitably leads to
a further contraction of the note-values, and so within a
few bars the music leaps into semiquavers which soon
become an integral part of the music (13th bar after D).

Ex. 112

Through this sane and healthy music, sounding as fresh as
if it had been washed clean by the rains of heaven, Brahms
takes us past a transposed strip of the Horn melody (Ex. 108)
to the second main theme of the *Allegro*.

Ex. 113

It will be seen that this happy melody is founded on a ground-bass of four descending notes. This bass is derived unmistakably from the first bar of the finale, the C and B[1] springing to life again after being hidden away in Brahms's mind during the more recent development of the music. With such a background Brahms presses the music onwards with great dexterity, developing the counterpoints in many unexpected ways, yet building everything in logical fashion on what has been heard already.

In this respect it is extremely interesting to trace the growth of the music hereabouts, especially if we remember that Brahms was constantly under the sway of what can be described as the *agitated four-note group*.[2] In Ex. 111 this feature makes its first appearance in the *Allegro*, both in the foreshortening of the theme and in the bass of the harmony. From this particular bass (which, on its first appearance, looks scarcely worthy of such attention) Brahms develops his music in most unexpected places. Like some ubiquitous traveller of whom it is said " You never know where he is going to turn up next," these four notes appear and reappear in many different guises. And it should not be forgotten that the parent thought to this four-note group is contained in the C,B,C,A of the great theme itself.[3] The following illustrations will make this point clear to the reader.

Ex. 114

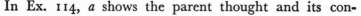

In Ex. 114, *a* shows the parent thought and its con-

---

[1] B *flat* in the introduction.
[2] Not only in this Symphony, but everywhere.
[3] And even in the opening of the introduction.

tracted version ; *b* and *c* are two consecutive bars from
the continuation of Ex. 113 ; *d* and *e* are respectively the
third and fifth bars after letter F in the same section,[1] and
f acts as the resumption of the agitated *Allegro* after the long
Oboe melody *e*.[2] The evolution of each new idea is shown
in Ex. 114 by the bracketing of the four notes concerned.

From the Viola phrase *f* there now arises a fine climax
that owes its freshness to the introduction of new figuration
in triple quavers. This figuration traces its origin to a
humble idea of three notes heard on the Violas as an acom-
paniment to the Oboe melody quoted on page 85 as Ex. 28.
Within a bar or two the Violins have appropriated this new
figuration in a vigorous *forte* (10th bar before G). Then
the Wood-wind and the Horns join in with merry chatter
to produce a great climax that rouses even the Trombones
to action for the first time since their *pp* chords in the introductory section (Ex. 108).

The play of rhythms, syncopations and invertible counterpoints here (*e.g.*, Ex. 29, p. 85) is far too involved to admit of
separate analysis. Every section of the orchestra is busily
engaged making sounds that produce, by combination, music
of extraordinary sonority yet of transparent simplicity.
Brahms delighted in complex patterns of this kind, but
however involved the counterpoints might be, he never gave
us any congestion in the total quantity of the sound.

Although the music at this point of climax has only
completed what is called the *exposition,* no development
section intervenes between it and the recapitulation. This
very exceptional omission is justified in every way. Had
there been any prolonged development section, Brahms
could scarcely have avoided considerable tedium, for the
exposition is one continual development within itself,
requiring no further elaboration of themes at its conclusion.
And so (at letter H) Brahms modulates back to the recapitulation in the space of three bars.

[1] See Ex. 27, p. 85.
[2] A more detailed description of the Oboe melody and its companion is to
be found on p. 85.

But to compensate us for our possible loss, he extends the recapitulation very considerably, making of it a further development which balances the long exposition in highly satisfactory style. There is no particle of the music here, however small, that does not assume remarkable significance. After the 'Cellos have joined the Violins in a richer presentation of Ex. 110 than was the case at its first hearing, the music modulates almost without warning—at least it seems so, so inspired is the effect—into the key of E flat (letter I). The immediate result of this is to darken the general colour of the sounds. And so, through the reappearance of the three flats, Brahms's never-failing imagination fastens in a flash on to the moods and music of the introduction. He must have seen the possibilities here in some moment of preternatural inspiration. The effect is dramatic in the extreme. The sinister *pizzicato* passages creep out of the E flat version of Ex. 110 (5th bar after I) like ghosts from a cupboard. Then, after another similar passage in B major and minor, the great theme (Ex. 110) suddenly recovers all the majesty and sunshine of its C major key (letter K), and follows for twelve bars the same course as in the *animato* section of the exposition (Ex. 111).

From this point (13th bar after K) the Strings begin a new section which extends to no less than fifty-three bars of contrapuntal music of amazing skill and workmanship. It all speeds along with the greatest confidence and vigour, founded on various phrases that have already appeared in some shape or other, and which now find themselves cheek by jowl in this unstemmed flood of counterpoints. First of all there appears in strongly accented crotchets a figure that has so far appeared only in a secondary capacity [1]—almost unnoticed, one might say—and which is now heard as follows. :—

[1] Fourth and fifth bars after D. 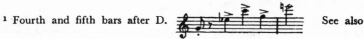 See also ninth bar after D.

Ex. 115

Strings

To this is added, at the third bar, a new version of the semiquaver figuration found on Bassoons, 'Cellos and Basses at the thirteenth bar after D.[1] This new version appears only in the inverted form shown in Ex. 115, and, for thirty-eight bars of this section, is used not only in conjunction with the crotchet phrase but in close *stretto* with itself and, from letter L onwards, also in combination with the four quavers derived from the great theme (Ex. 114*a*).

Ex.116

(Skeleton only)

Once again it is not possible, for lack of space, to demonstrate further the many convolutions of this section of the music. But it must be added that the eleven bars preceding letter M in the score, and more especially the last five bars, deserve the closest study, for they contain feats of counterpoint almost unparalleled for sheer strength and independence of movement. Brahms's fecund imagination intertwines everything with such great skill and with such intrepid mastery over the part-writing that we get the impression of some colossus at play, striding across the world like the Gigantes of old.

[1] For a skeleton framework of this, see Ex. 112, and, for the probable origin of this new version, the groups of demisemiquavers that are divided between 1st and 2nd Violins in Ex. 106.

Needless to say, the music is pressing onward to some great event. At letter M a *point d'appui* is reached with a reaffirmation of the key of C major, in which the Timpani play a big part on the G and C, while the agitated four-note phrase (Ex. 116) now takes charge of the situation and drives everything along to a phrenetic *stretto* between Stings and Wood-wind (7th to 11th bars after M). Out of all this excitement there leaps a most dramatic and extended version of Ex. 107. This renders the return of the Horn theme (Ex. 108) inevitable ; so urgent a challenge cannot be ignored. For six bars during these exciting moments nothing is heard on either the first or third beat of each bar, the tumultuous syncopated phrases leaping in, one quaver late, like some irresistible force out of control.

And then, at letter N, the majestic breadth of the music is restored by the 1st Violins with their ecstatic version of the Horn theme (Ex. 30, p. 86) and the whole meaning of this long and complex finale is made convincingly clear.

The 1st Horn resumes with a continuation of its own theme and is then joined by various Wood-wind instruments and the Violins in a tranquil and beautiful codetta founded on the same music. Then a return is made to the second subject (Ex. 113), now in the key of C and varied in style. The ground-bass is no longer continuous in the lower Strings, but is shared between them and various Wood-wind instruments—a touch of variety that is very acceptable here. And since Brahms now gives us a long and formal repetition of the whole of this second-subject section, amounting in all to sixty-six bars (*i.e.*, from the 17th bar after N to Q), we can be grateful for any such variety, however small.

This lengthy formal repetition is perhaps the least interesting feature of the movement. While it contains all the many points of interest heard previously (*e.g.*, Exs. 113, 114, 27, 28, etc.), and while it gives us many a thrill for its own sake, it all sounds somewhat mechanical, and, after the wonderful climax just heard, psychologically unconvincng. Admittedly, much of what is included is needed to complete the symmetrical design of the movement, yet the great length of the section seems to delay the approach to the final coda to an unconscionable extent. One wishes Brahms could have curtailed it somewhere, despite its magnificent periods.

And so, through an ingenious modulation (10th and 11th bars after O)[1] the music finds itself once more in the key of C minor (Q). Here the final summing up begins with one of those dramatic changes of mood so characteristic of Brahms.

As if some black cloud had suddenly robbed us of the sun, the music deserts the C tonality as soon as it is established there. It then wanders through a rapid succession of keys—E flat minor, F major, D flat minor and then to E flat major. Established in this tonality, the Contra Bassoon, 3rd Trombone, 'Cellos and Basses give out a modulatory version of the first notes of the great theme (Ex. 110), which is imitated at a bar's distance by the Wood-wind, while the Violins add to the growing excitement with widespread variants of the Viola figure found in Ex. 114f. And as if to keep the music rooted to the spot, Horns, Trumpets, 2nd Trombone, Drum and Violas engage at this point in reiterated Gs. These for sixteen bars proclaim with ever-increasing enthusiasm " the dominant's persistence, till it must be answered to." By such superb feats of imagination and technique Brahms reaches his final *Più allegro* coda.

The C is now apotheosized ; nothing can cloud its glory for an instant. There only remains a climax of rejoicing in which everything shall join. And so Brahms makes this final coda one great shout of joy in which will be recognized (on the Strings) three notes of Ex. 110 in new rhythmical formation and the A, G of the same theme (bars 12 and 13) on Wood-wind and Brass.

---

[1] To appreciate this point, compare with 14th and 15th bars after letter F. Had Brahms not made this particular modulation at O he would have " landed himself " in the key o A minor at Q.

Ex. 117

(incomplete
framework)

Finally, after sixteen bars, the music reaches its most triumphant expression when the hymn of faith (Ex. 109) is thundered out in rapturous exultation. Everything is enfolded within its arms ; everything resolved into perfect harmony.

The remainder of the coda is one long rejoicing round the note C, with the Timpani much in evidence on the tonic and dominant. Each instrument becomes an expression of complete joy, while the 1st Violins mount higher and higher until they finally reach the topmost C for the first time in the Symphony (41st bar of the *Più Allegro* section). At this dizzy height they reiterate, eight bars from the end, the C, B, C shown in Ex. 117—a last tribute to the mighty theme from which this figure sprang to life, and a still greater tribute to the omnipotent power of that note C on which Brahms constructed his masterly Symphony. There I must conclude an analysis which, even at some length, only plumbs the middle depths of the work.

CHAPTER X

THE SECOND SYMPHONY ANALYSED

THE Second Symphony, if not the finest of the four in conception and technique, usually makes the most immediate appeal. And since dark patches of true Brahmsian austerity in the music are the exception rather than the rule, it is hardly surprising that the Symphony's more patent qualities gained many friends long before the other three Symphonies had established themselves in complete favour. The pathway to its success was strewn with melodies of a kind more easily grasped than the rhetorical themes and motifs found in the greater part of the First Symphony. There were no problems to solve, nor could it be said of it at any time that the music contained subtleties of thought not appreciable at a first hearing. Such subtleties as existed were mainly confined to the slow movement, any recollection of them being soon forgotten in the naive charm of the third movement and the exhilarating *joie-de-vivre* of the finale.

The Second Symphony, coming almost directly after the First—it was completed in 1877 and labelled Op. 73— is a perfect contrast to its predecessor, despite the apparent fact that Brahms projected his mind from the one work into the other by the use of certain musical *minutiæ*, having in all likelihood more than a coincidental value. Whether the relationship between the great theme in the finale of the First Symphony, with its C, B, C three-note variants,[1] and the opening bar of the Second Symphony is other than accidental cannot, of course, be determined. But it should

---

[1] See Exs. 110, 111 and 117 in respect to the First Symphony and Ex. 76 in respect to the Second.

be remembered that Brahms devoted twenty years of his life to the First Symphony, an obsession of the mind not easily thrown off in the short space of time elapsing between the completion of that work and the composition of the next Symphony. And again, the great success attending the many performances of the First Symphony during the composition of the Second must often have stirred the composer's mind in happy or unhappy retrospection of the earlier work ; but rarely would he be able to forget the child of his own creation, his absorption in the Second Symphony notwithstanding. The cousinly relationship of the two is therefore quite possible.

" It could be shown, I think "—Ernest Newman writes in his essay in Musical Psychology *The Unconscious Beethoven* [1]—" that all composers' minds are more or less unconscious mechanisms. To some extent, indeed, this must be true of all artists : even prose writers will be found, on examination, to have each his own peculiar rhythm. But for some reason or other connected no doubt with the nature of the material in which the musician works, the composer is specially given to the unconscious repetition of the same formulæ. That these have so far not been noticed and isolated except in a few of the most obvious cases, such as Gounod's sequences or Grieg's falling thirds, is one of the mysteries of music ; for if any poet or prosaist were to employ the same verbal formulæ as many thousand times as the composer employs the same musical formula we should find him unreadable."

It may be argued that the three notes with which we are concerned both here and in the First Symphony belong merely to the matter-of-fact speech of music, and that they contain no more merit than can be found in any other platitudes of like kind. Taken without their context that may be true. Yet the same can be said of almost any

---

[1] *The Unconscious Beethoven* (Leonard Parsons, Devonshire Street, London). The latter half of this deeply interesting book is devoted to the analysis of certain formulæ in Beethoven's music, showing the evolution of themes through various stages towards their eventual form.

phrase in music once iconoclastic criticism gets to work with disruptive energy to shatter all on which the art is founded.   It has been demonstrated on page 58 how Wagner himself, with all his complicated machinery of leit-motifs, was compelled, willy-nilly, to build his thematic structures with materials as ingenuously simple as anything Brahms ever wrote.   And (to carry the thought still further and into another field) the same argument holds good with phrases such as " To be, or not to be," which, deprived of their context, merely suggest empty platitudes of a kind not a whit better than the D, C sharp, D of the Second Symphony.

And so the hard criticism levelled on occasions against the Second Symphony is often the result of a limited appreciation of those simple phrases which by enthusiasts are regarded as a meritorious feature.   As Mr. Newman points out in other words in *The Unconscious Beethoven*, insistent repetitions of word-formulæ by poet or prosaist would soon render him unreadable.   But with music—to return to my argument—it is different.   Such phrase-formulæ as the three notes D, C sharp, D, for instance, are the very life-blood of the art.   Their constant repetition and variation serve, in the hands of a master, to bind the music in intelligible fashion.   And I think it can be reasonably argued that the patterned evolution of a phrase, even in the most formal (but less desirable) academic manner, is of higher value to the art than the disintegration of thought by conscious and continual adoption of the asymmetrical. There we must leave this problem to itself, for we can spin thousands of words round it and yet never arrive at any definite conclusion.

The basis of the Second Symphony is nothing more than these three artless notes, D, C sharp, D.   Much like the First Symphony, which owes everything to a single *note*, so is the Second evolved from one *phrase*—a phrase that sets the whole machinery in motion.   But Brahms was far too good a craftsman to rely on this alone.   Left with no complementary thematic support, the phrase would have worked itself out in a very short time, for it is, as we have seen, nothing but the merest platitude. And just as Shakespeare took his simple opening " To be, or not to be " and clothed it with priceless gems of thought and wisdom—and almost every line of the Soliloquy has long since passed into current speech—so did Brahms, in this first movement, add two other themes to the three-note phrase and create from his tripartite combination a movement of the greatest interest and beauty. And, strangely enough, more is achieved therein with the insignificant three-note phrase than with the other two stronger themes. That is, of course, the Brahms way. In little things he discovers unsuspected greatness ; his sympathies extend to the humble things in music ; nothing is too small to escape his attention, nothing of so little value that it will not serve some definite purpose when the right time comes. And so the development of the music from the two stronger themes at or near the beginning serves to transform the three-note phrase into something of even greater strength than its companions.

As will be seen in Ex. 118 the three notes act as

Ex. 118

a bass to a lyrical theme on the 1st Horn and also to the responding phrase on the Wood-wind. [Later on, a third theme (Ex. 120) is used in conjunction with these.]

Enough of the music has been quoted here to show the main features of both theme and accompaniment. Since the three notes will eventually become the most important feature of the Symphony, it should be noticed how they recur at regular periods and at different pitches against the continuation of the theme, being given a quiet importance that foreshadows their incorporation in the movement, not only as a bass, but also as a very definite theme. Before the twenty-two bars of the theme have run their course, the 1st Violins and Violas creep in mysteriously with a subsidiary idea, mainly in crotchets.

Ex. 119

This keeps the music in a state of suspense round the dominant note A, and ushers in those sleepy Trombone-Tuba chords to which reference has already been made in Ex. 33 on page 90. After a few more bars of Brass chords have alternated with stray Wood-wind appearances of the three notes, we arrive (letter A) at the third member of the tripartite combination—a lovely flowing theme on the 1st Violins, of which much use is made from time to time, and which is definitely related in its first bar to the three-note phrase.

Ex. 120

Brahms's technical skill is now shown to great advantage, for the combinative qualities possessed by the three themes forming the opening D major section are apparent the moment Ex. 120 is heard. One can imagine what Brahmsian jugglery there will be with these themes later on, for each commences with a different note of the D major triad, and each has independent features in the actual shape of the phrase. And so, in such things, it is a case of the First Symphony all over again, even if the themes differ in character as much as the wooded Chilterns do from the snowclad Alps.

Here in the Second Symphony we live in pastoral surroundings, inasmuch as the opening phrases have all the graceful lines and quiet content of the countryside. Consequently, the early appearance of a placid theme having a major-third opening on a strong beat (Ex. 118, bar 2) does not cause any surprise : it is no more than we have learnt to expect. And Brahms, always on the alert for false quantities, takes steps to counteract the possibility of redundant major thirds by employing at the same time two other themes not accentually dependent on this note.

It must be admitted that this Horn theme has both beautiful and yet commonplace features. There is beauty in the simplicity of its opening and the exquisite response by the Wood-wind, and a somewhat commonplace effect in the supertonic repetition at the tenth and eleventh bars.[1] Happily, this supertonic repetition is heard only once again, namely, at the corresponding place in the recapitula-

---

[1] The *supertonic* repetition of a phrase, just after the phrase has been heard in the *tonic*, is generally regarded as an unsatisfactory effect. Brahms approaches this repetition through a chord on the *submediant* (Ex. 118, bar 9), as if conscious of his temporary weakness and anxious to disguise it if possible. But, for all his ingenuity, he fails in the effect, not only in his inability to disguise the supertonic repetition, but also in the clumsy drop from the pedal D in the bass of the eighth bar to the B (submediant) in the bar following. This desertion of the pedal D before the dominant harmony of the Wood-wind melody has been resolved produces an uncomfortable feeling of dislocation. Brahms was obviously reluctant to surrender either his three-note phrase in the bass or its four-bar periodicity, and so fell from the frying-pan of a poor supertonic repetition into the fire of equally poor harmonization.

tion (9th bar after J). There it is not so naked in the effect because the Violas clothe it with an E minor variant of Ex. 120, while the repetition itself is on the less noticeable timbre of the Oboes.

After this unpretentious opening, followed by the section already described (commencing with Ex. 119), the music soon bursts into flower with the entry of the 1st Violins (Ex. 120). The 2nd Violins make a very belated first appearance at the tenth bar after letter A and help to drive the music along in vigorous cross-phrasing to its first climax.[1] At the fifteenth bar after A the three crotchets are given weighty utterance in a fine piece of invertible counterpoint that demonstrates how successfully Brahms can endow his smallest phrases with more than ordinary vitality.

Ex. 121

And in this invertible counterpoint we also hear, in most unexpected fashion, with what a tenacious grip Brahms can hold the thematic substance of this Symphony, even apart from the three crotchets themselves. If the quavers in Ex. 121 be examined in detail, it will be seen that they are formed, in part, out of the lyrical Horn theme of the opening (Ex. 118). From a flowing melody they are now metamorphosed into a rhythmical figure that will pervade many bars of the music from this point onwards until it fades away into *p sempre dolce* during the course of the second subject (Ex. 123). There may be a scintilla of truth in the criticism of a French writer that Brahms " *travaille extré-*

---

[1] See Ex. 13*a*, p. 53.

mement bien avec idées qu'il n'a pas," [1] yet, I am tempted to
ask, is there any other composer of symphonies who could
take his ideas one by one in this highly original manner,
and, by alteration, variation, inspiration, conjuring, or
what you will, make them serve first primary and then
secondary purposes with such naturalness and such felicitous workmanship ?

The three crotchets are now turned into quavers, played
legato in vigorous cross-phrasing.[2]   Then, two bars later
(letter B), their whole character is changed by the introduction of light *staccato* effects against a *legato* version of the
quavers heard in Ex. 121.   These contrasts are shown in the
following example :—

Ex. 122

Later on Brahms develops these two features a great deal ;
(*a*) in the development section and (*b*) in the coda.   And
by this reversal of *legato* and *staccato* effects he softens, too,
the general mood of the music, preparing the way for the
second subject—a lovely *cantabile* melody for 'Cellos, supported by Violas in an underpart of equal beauty (letter C).

Ex. 123

[1] I am indebted to Mr. Ernest Newman and the *Sunday Times*, April 30th
1933, for this quotation.
[2] For a general analysis of this feature see p. 53 and Ex. 13*b*.

Round this the figure derived from the Horn theme weaves
delicate traceries. These disappear at the eighth bar after
C and return only in the concluding bars of the movement
—at the second bar of the *in tempo, sempre tranquillo* section.

The second subject itself has irregular features, determined,
maybe, by its accompanying figure. Commencing in the
key of F sharp minor, it soon gravitates rather surprisingly
towards D major, where it remains until three bars before its
second entry on the Wood-wind (letter D). From the F
sharp minor key it modulates once again, this time through
other keys and with contracted phrases.

At letter E a new section is reached, *quasi ritenente*, which,
as far as can be fathomed—though one can never be quite
sure with Brahms—contains no reference to anything
heard previously, except the transference of a modest
supporting rhythm from an A Drum to Wood-wind, Horns
and Trumpets.

Following this, ten bars later, is another sturdy, rhythmical section, obviously compounded of (*a*) the three-note
phrase, and (*b*) in the bass, a two-note fragment of the
Horn melody.

Of both these much is made.   After a fine *ff* climax (17th
bar after E), wherein the Trombones and Tuba make
one of their rare appearances,[1] the three notes become a
continuous syncopated figure accompanying a new theme,
both theme and accompaniment being developed from
what has just been heard (Ex. 125).

The music is now driven along in imitative, semi-canonic
style with spirit enough to produce a further *ff* climax
(4th bar before F).   And at letter F itself the second
subject (Ex. 123) reappears in A major on Violas against a
very beautiful embroidery of triple quavers on the 1st
Flute, these triple quavers obviously owing their presence
here to the oft-quoted three-note phrase.   The dominant
key of A is now firmly established, and the further partial
repetition of the second subject on Flutes and Oboes (9th
bar after F) serves to consolidate the closing bars of this
long and varied exposition.   Brahms concludes the section
with sequential and imitative passages, the origin of which
can be found in the third and fourth bars of the second
subject (Ex. 123).   The whole exposition is then repeated.[2]
   The development section commences very quietly with

---

[1] See Ex. 35*a*, p. 91.
[2] This repeat is disregarded nowadays by many conductors.   " Herr H——,
the high priest of Dresden critics, is of course at a loss to understand why the
first part of the first movement of the D major is repeated," writes E. von H.
in a letter to Brahms in 1878.   Undoubtedly the repetition of this idyllic
exposition takes away some of the freshness of what follows.

the Horn theme (Ex. 118), now given a beautiful solo entry in F major. To this is appended a response on the Oboe and 2nd Violins (a sixth below the Oboe) consisting of a further development of the same theme. The Flutes then imitate the Horn theme in the key of B flat, followed by the Wood-wind in crotchets against new quaver figuration on Violins and Violas. At this point the Wood-wind—with 'Cellos and Basses imitating them two bars later—play a development of the three-crotchet phrase from the Horn theme, but without any *slurring* of the notes. In this way new energy is released, which finds its outlet in a quadruple *fugato* of some dimensions commencing :—

Ex. 127

1st Vln.
2nd Vln.

Violas
Cellos
Basses

[While it is impossible to analyse each bar of this section, the four themes in this *fugato* are numbered in the above example so as to enable those interested to follow the course of the music to letter G, where a new section commences.]

Wood-wind, Horns and then Trombones help mainly with the harmony to build up this very contrapuntal music to another climax at letter G. And now the Trombones take charge of the situation in one of the strangest *stretto* effects ever written by any composer.

Ex.128

As will be seen from the above, the three crotchets of the first bar of the Symphony return in curious close combination, or, as it would be called by the theorists, in imitation *per arsin et thesin*.[1]   In the wake of this remarkable passage —whose dissonances are entirely logical to the contextual harmony—crotchet and quaver versions of the familiar three-note phrase both follow.   These lash the music along to three superb climaxes, in which the first two notes of the Horn theme (Ex. 118) are heard in greatly emphasized cross-rhythms on the full power of the orchestra.[2]   And between these moments of climax, Brahms gives us, in addition to all this remarkable concatenation of ideas, several versions of Ex. 120 that prophesy in unmistakable terms the imminence of the recapitulation (letter J).

The recapitulation—gently introduced by four bars of music developed from the second subject (Ex. 123, 3rd and 4th bars) against the significant D, C sharp, D on 1st Trombone—differs from the exposition.   Now the Horn theme is transferred to the Oboe and 2nd Violins, and is heard simultaneously with part of Ex. 120 on the Violas, the two themes appearing in real partnership for the first time.

[1] I cannot do better than refer the reader to *Grove's Dictionary*, which in its article on Metre, quotes from Baccheios's catechism (Meibom, p. 24) :—
Q. What shall we say *arsis* is ?
A. The time during which the foot is raised when we are going to take a step.
Q. And what is *thesis* ?
A. The time when it is on the ground.
[2] See Ex. 34, p. 90.

Ex. 129

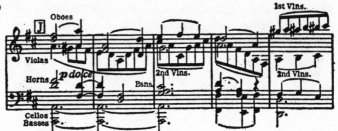

When Brahms was sketching this movement he must have calculated, with cunning deliberation, the eventual effect that could be obtained by this combination. The more the two themes are examined the more it is apparent how independent each is in character and yet how harmoniously both are made to blend.

But the simultaneous appearance of these themes alters the whole course of the movement. Instead of a vigorous restatement of Ex. 121, the Violins and Violas indulge in *dolce* quaver figurations of the " embroidery " kind. For many bars these twine round modulating Wood-wind versions of the crotchets shown in Ex. 119, while the music becomes partially obscured as if by some penumbra. Then, after three faint *pp* rumbles on the D Drum, during which the 1st Violins and 'Cellos cease their quaver movement, the Trombones, Tuba and two Horns prepare the way for the return of the second subject.

Did Brahms make further use of the pruning-knife at this point ? The three quiet Brass chords seem to be hesitating and spineless at this juncture, despite their harking back to the spirit of the opening, while the sudden modulation to the key of B minor through one abrupt dominant chord is by no means convincing in effect. And this causes the lovely 'Cello melody (Ex. 123) to steal on our ears prematurely ; we miss the seven modulatory chords that introduce it so soothingly at its first entry (5th bar before C).

On its reappearance in the recapitulation (letter K) this 'Cello theme is now decorated for eight bars with figuration of a different kind, derived from String *arpeggii* heard during the three *pp* rumbles on the Drum. At the ninth bar everything reverts to the plan of the exposition, the music being repeated for many bars together [1] with practically no variation, except in the orchestration. Indeed, the recapitulation is structurally somewhat unsatisfactory and inconsistent, as I will endeavour to show.

From the point where it begins (letter J) to the entry of the second subject (letter K) it is shorter than the exposition by no less than thirty-three bars.[2] Such abridgment in a recapitulation is, in a general way, all to the good (and is much practised by classical composers), provided the balance of structure in the *entire* movement is not disturbed thereby. But this is exactly what happens here, for the next section, *i.e.*, from K to the coda at M is a bar-for-bar thematic replica of the exposition from C onwards, but, of course, in another key. And as this section amounts in all to ninety-seven bars, it must inevitably sound, at this late stage in the movement, unequally proportioned to that part of the recapitulation altered so ruthlessly.

Yet Brahms always has great reserves of power on which to draw at the right moment. Whatever mistakes in structure there may have been made will be redeemed in the final peroration we can be sure. And such a moment comes with the coda at letter M, where the music, liberated from long-drawn-out argument round the second subject and its subsidiary themes, leaps into two-note fragments of the opening Horn theme with great freshness of effect. These fragments take up only four bars of music, giving way, after a rousing *crescendo molto*, to a further quotation from the same theme, namely, the third bar. Here the notes are given forceful *accented* utterance for the only time in the

[1] Eighty-nine bars, to be precise. Apart from the change of key and some fanciful new touches in the orchestration, the music from the ninth bar after C to the twenty-third after F is identical with that from the ninth bar after K to M.

[2] The exposition contains eighty-one bars as far as the second subject : the recapitulation but forty-eight.

movement, the Trombones following immediately with the *legato* version (Ex. 36) to which reference is made on page 91.

The mood of the music is now hushed for a passage on the Horn that is generally acknowledged to be one of the loveliest things in all music. From the three notes referred to above—which must not be confused with the other three notes, D, C sharp, D, used so extensively throughout the movement—there arises a new melodic line of magical beauty, a theme that carries us far away from the land of formal counterpoints, far away from everything that is concrete, technical or analysable. We are translated to a world of dreams and held there spellbound by Johannes Brahms in one of his finest moments of inspiration.

Ex. 130

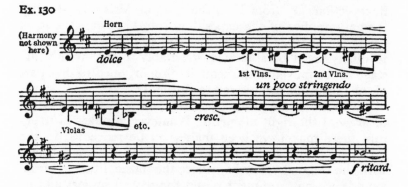

Here again is unsuspected greatness, lying hidden all this while in another small three-note phrase. Not only does Brahms transform these notes into a *cantabile* melody of the rarest beauty, but he accompanies the melody on the Strings with exquisite harmonies and deftly-woven counterpoints—the latter being recognizable as part of Ex. 120, etc. The passionate *stringendo* towards the climax of the Horn melody, with its eloquent B flat at the *ritard* bar, creates an atmosphere of romance ardent enough to melt the heart of any misanthrope, while the low-pitched Es on 'Cellos and Basses sustaining the chord at the climax, seem to reach

unfathomable depths of expression. This melody is the
longest, and, at the same time, the most emotional Brahms
ever wrote for the Horn. It extends to twenty-three bars
and covers, in addition, a wide range of expression. At its
wonderful close, we can only repeat with Langland—

"A marvel befel me—sure from Færy it came."

Brahms, transfigured, as it were, with his own inspiration,
continues in this mood of serene beauty with a new close
relationship of the two themes contained in Ex. 118, heard
on the Strings and marked *in tempo, ma più tranquillo*. Once
again the Horns add their touch of romance, to which the
1st Violins respond with an exquisite offshoot in quavers
that, it is seen, belong to Ex. 118. This is taken up by
the Wood-wind and Horns and brings the music to the final
section of the coda.

No words can adequately describe the loveliness of these
concluding bars, wherein the light *staccato* version of the
original three-note phrase (Ex. 122) alternates with allusions to the quavers shown in Ex. 121—quavers which, it
will be remembered, are developed from the original Horn
theme.

 Ex. 131

[For the sake of the analysis that follows, this quotation
begins at the 3rd bar of the *in tempo, ma più tranquillo*
section.]

Nor, it will be seen, does Brahms forget to give us a final
reference to the three notes in their original crotchet form.
Dovetailed with syncopated quaver *pizzicati* (in themselves
a new, important, and highly original variant of the same

phrase), this melodic strip is the most felicitous summing up imaginable.

Two other points of interest bring the movement to its tranquil close ; (*a*) the remarkable *stretto* between groups of the three familiar notes,

Ex. 132

and (*b*) a last reference, with Trumpets added, to the opening Horn theme. By this time we are no longer conscious of any structural defects, for the beauty of the coda has completely disarmed us.

· · · · · ·

We do not have to look in vain for a definite link binding the slow movement to the first, inasmuch as the opening melody on 'Cellos is the unmistakable child of the Horn theme shown in Ex. 130.

Ex. 133

Were we but superficially acquainted with Brahms's methods, to say nothing of his rare flights of imagination, this statement might be accounted a little fanciful. But

just as in the First Symphony Brahms came under the spell
of certain phrases that he conjured to life again in other
movements, so the reiterated F sharp, E of the wonderful
Horn passage (Ex. 130) must have affected him in like
manner here. "Nothing is lost" he once remarked to
Henschel. "If afterward I approach the subject again, it
is sure to have taken shape."[1] And that is the impression
created at the beginning of this movement. Those two
humble notes were not forgotten ; they must have persisted in the composer's mind, either consciously or otherwise, until they found a new outlet in this elaborate, deeply
romantic melody of twelve bars.

But, with Brahms, one melody by itself does not suffice.
And so, to ensure symphonic continuity of the music, he
adds another on Bassoons and a further phrase on Flutes
and 1st Trombone. Much is made of both. The Bassoon
theme is invariably used as a counterpoint against the first
two bars of the 'Cello melody or against variants thereof,
being often transferred to other instruments. It is easily
recognizable by the upward run of four demisemiquavers in
its second bar, an embellishment quite unlike anything
else in the Symphony.[2] On the other hand, the Flute and
Trombone phrase can claim no such distinction ; it relies
on plain crotchets and a stray minim or two. Yet, in spite
of this, its first two notes, B and E, soon play an important
part in the development of the movement. After the first
four bars of the 'Cello theme have been repeated on Flute
and Violins against a much more resonant accompaniment,
these two notes are used to initiate an entirely new idea,
given to the Horn (letter A) and reinforced by the Bassoon
two bars later.

Ex.134

etc.

[1] See p. 18.   [2] See, more especially, Ex. 38, p. 93.

This is then developed into curious imitative passages for Oboes and Flutes, the Strings remaining silent for some bars until 'Cellos and Basses break in with the same phrase. A rich warm-hued climax is now reached as the String sections enter one by one with phrases gathered from the opening 'Cello melody.

After a few bars of this kind, the music is again transferred to the Wood-wind. Here the 1st Flute and 1st Oboe (letter B) announce a new and graceful phrase of somewhat syncopated character that finds its immediate continuation on the Clarinets.[1]

This section is developed for twelve bars, the phrases being shared in contemplative exchange of thought between the Wood-wind and Strings.

Then an impressive silence of one beat is followed by yet another important theme that seems to contain allusions to the first movement, though this is probably just coincidence.[2]

A great deal is heard of this. From its suave opening it soon reaches a climax (letter C), out of which there emerges a restless, impatient mood quite contrary to the general

[1] See Ex. 37, p. 93.
[2] Compare the first five notes of Ex. 136 with the shape of (1) in Ex. 127, and certain three-note groups in Ex. 136 with the opening bar of the Symphony.

spirit of this " gay Vienna " Symphony. Dark forces find their expression here in strange and rambling semiquavers that seem to be in conflict with Ex. 136.

The music now swells to another and bigger climax and then suddenly subsides for a few bars, during which disjointed quaver fragments of the theme are heard on the Wood-wind against a dramatic *tremolando* accompaniment on Strings. Then, while Flutes and Oboes continue the quaver phrase, Brahms gives a two-bar hint (letter D) of the imminence of the recapitulation. But this effort—on Violins and Bassoon—is soon silenced by another dramatic outburst similar to that heard a few bars previously. Nothing daunted, the opening themes return again in still incomplete shapes, and, on this occasion, displace the restless music of the middle section (6th bar after D). For a further six bars they wander about rather aimlessly until the rough road to the recapitulation is at last traversed (letter E).

Although this strange section makes a considerable effect on the mind, probably by reason of the unexpected touches of drama contained therein, yet at times there are certain turgid sounds, more particularly in the first four bars (letter C onwards), which are not entirely convincing. Dr. Colles has put the case with fine acumen in his book on Brahms.[1] " The impression left is that here Brahms, more than in the slow movement of any other of the Symphonies, struggled for complete expression of his complex artistic nature. If he only partially succeeded, that part is of such beauty as to be of the highest value."

When the recapitulation is reached Brahms transfers

[1] *Brahms*, by H. C. Colles (John Lane, The Bodley Head, London).

the lengthy 'Cello theme to the 1st Violins. But it is now so much altered that its identity would be in doubt were it not for the context.

Ex. 138

If reference be made to the score it will be noticed how the three quavers that originated in Ex. 136 are taken up by the 1st Violins at the third bar before letter E. These run on until they merge, in an effortless way, into the variation of the 'Cello melody shown above. Thus, through these simple triple quavers—that have in themselves no more claim to distinction than their poor relations in the first movement—a new interest is created which carries Brahms along another path of inspiration. Who could have foreseen that through this group of quavers there would arise such a richly emotional climax as is found at the twelfth bar after letter E? Nor does Brahms release his hold on the music even after this climax. He is now deeply stirred by the course of events, and, after two beautiful and freshly-harmonized references to Ex. 134 (the A natural on 'Cellos and Basses at the 16th bar after E, supported by the harmony on Wood-wind, is a moment of rare inspiration), another fine climax is reached that seems to reflect the stern mood of the middle section, though reverting to the music developed from the 'Cello melody. At this point Trumpets, Trombones, Tuba and Timpani lend their weight to a *forte* minor-key version of the rich chords heard in the second and third bars of the movement, while the Violins add to the general agitation with strongly-bowed semi-quavers that are also very reminiscent of the middle section. Then, at the top of the climax, Brahms is inspired to the highest degree in an emotional development of Ex. 136 that carries one completely away with its intense feeling (letter F).

And finally, when the music fades away to its mournful close with the dual phrases of the opening, we cannot but think that Brahms, in this movement, must have been following the dim shadow of some elusive romance.[1]

> After listening to the sombre complexities and unequally sustained beauty of the slow movement, the third comes with all the freshness of a sunny day in spring—a day on which Brahms might well have sung with Herrick :—

> " See how Aurora throws her fair
> Fresh-quilted colours through the air :
> Get up, sweet slug-a-bed, and see
> The dew-bespangled herb and tree."

There is nothing in the Symphonies to equal this movement for easy grace and manners. It goes on its way unconcernedly, stopping here and there as if in happy contemplation of some country scene or wayside flower, running along at times in sportive fashion, or, maybe, doubling back on itself with almost childlike innocence. It comes to us with a fragrance of major key as sweet-smelling as the hawthorn or newly-mown hay. Even the major third B (in the opening melody on the Oboe) needs no defence of its four successive appearances on the strong beat of the bar ; its gentle reiterations are exactly right to the mood of the music, bringing a sense of peace requiring no apology.

Ex. 139

¹ See Ex. 38, p. 93.

And if these Bs be further examined with regard to their other reiterations on the *second* beat of each bar, I fancy their origin can be heard on the B Drum, three bars from

the end of the slow movement—

Though such a link may be but a coincidence, it is quite within the bounds of possibility that Brahms unconsciously altered the formula of those Bs and made up a fresh prescription with them.

Despite a certain kinship with chamber-music, the movement is undoubtedly an organic part of the Symphony as a whole. Compared with the other movements it is written in much lighter vein. Nevertheless, this very lightness is but another aspect of the vernal character of the Symphony, bringing the movement into a proper relationship with all that precedes and follows it. Had Brahms, for third movement, written a boisterous Scherzo in the Beethoven manner as a contrast to the seriousness of the second, there is no doubt that the finale would have hung fire for want of fuel more than is the case. Had he, on the other hand, given us a much more sedate third movement of the type found in the First and Third Symphonies, he could only have failed in effect (and probably in inspiration) through its juxtaposition with the very serious slow movement. Perhaps, all things considered, Brahms was right in discarding his alternatives, despite the opinion of Specht and others who do not admit the continuity of thought between this and the other movements.

The light, floating quality of the music is its great charm. The simple melodies and harmonies of the first section are confined entirely to Wood-wind and a single Horn, while against these instruments there runs a delicious *pizzicato* 'Cello accompaniment, mainly in quavers. Analysis seems almost unnecessary here, so transparently clear is the music. But the silent pause on the bar-line between the twenty-second and twenty-third bars—coming like an

" angel's whisper " before the repetition of the Oboe melody (Ex. 139)—must not be overlooked. Nor should the remarkably beautiful alternations between major and minor chords of G, heard seven bars before the close of this section.

The music now changes to a *Presto ma non assai* section wherein Brahms displays all his usual ingenuity. Taking his first melody (Ex. 139) as his model he proceeds to elaborate it in most unexpected fashion. In place of the comely grace that characterizes the opening section there now springs to life a dancing rhythm—in a fantastic duple measure—one that suggests the tireless play of sunbeams on a rippled lake. At this point Violins and Violas make their first appearance in the movement.

Ex. 140

The music follows the original theme quite closely for some bars until rapid exchanges of detail between Strings and Wood-wind, delicious in their " dew-bespangled " freshness, drive the music along with increasing impetus to a new rhythm of sturdy character that is obviously acquainted with the eleventh and twelfth bars of the first section (letter A).

Ex. 141

Here the Basses enter the movement with loudly-proclaimed
Cs that continue, two to a bar, for ten out of the twelve
bars forming this jocund section of the dance.[1]   This,
however, is only incidental.   The light *staccato* music soon
returns in new developments on the Strings, and now, as
previously, is shared with the Wood-wind in as pretty a
battle of wits as could be desired.   And then Brahms leaves
us in no doubt as to his immediate intentions when the
Oboes, Bassoons and 3rd and 4th Horns, six bars before the
Tempo primo (the 3–4 time), prepare the way for the return
of Ex. 139.

The half-hidden allusions to the returning first section, heard
here simultaneously with the outgoing *staccato* quavers of
this fantastic little dance, might well represent Prospero's
words to Ariel :—

> " This was well done, my bird ;
> Thy shape invisible retain thou still."

The original melody now returns with other harmonies.
But at its fourth bar the Horn has a new phrase, repeated a
bar later on the Oboe, and which, further on, is used with
beautiful effect on Violas and 'Cellos in the concluding
bars of the movement.

---

[1] One is reminded here of the story told of Johann Jakob Brahms (Johannes'
father) who, on being admonished by a Hamburg conductor for over-zealous
playing, retorted : " Herr Kapellmeister, I would like you to understand that
this is *my* Bass and I shall play on it just as loudly as I please."

Ex. 143

From the entry of these quavers the music breaks away from the original rather curiously. An *ostinato* figure for Strings, founded on the fourth bar of Ex. 139, forms the basis of the next twelve bars (from letter C), and on this figure various phrases of new shape and of slight value are grafted with a subtle touch, the whole ending somewhat piquantly with a sudden cadence into E major.

Once again another *Presto ma non assai* section arrives; much like the other in thematic content, but quite dissimilar in rhythm and length of phrase. Here one can again imagine some Ariel or puckish fairy weaving strange threads round these quaint metres.[1] And in this fanciful style the music follows the plan of the other *Presto*. There is the same heavy pounding of Cs by the Basses for ten bars, the same alternations of light *staccato* passages between Strings and Wood-wind, and the same dovetailing of the returning Bs with what is being concluded.

But in the few bars preceding the final return to the *Tempo primo* section (letter E) Brahms modulates unexpectedly into the key of F sharp. This subtle avoidance of the key of G at this point, together with the transference of the theme to the Strings, brings an added sweetness to the music for the next thirteen bars and inspires the composer to further exquisite variations of Ex. 139. After these thirteen bars the music falls back into the original key through a lovely modulation and then continues for eighteen bars in the manner of the opening section, though with different orchestration. In this way a short coda is reached (7th bar after F) that serves to epitomize the whole spirit of the movement, imparting to the concluding

[1] Tribrachic, and iambic of a distorted kind.

bars a fragrance unequalled anywhere else in the Four
Symphonies.

In any valuation of this movement in relation to its place
in the Symphony it should be borne in mind that Brahms,
of his own choice, preferred a delicate type of music in all
but one of his third movements, inasmuch as it afforded a
welcome relief to the more rhetorical moods of the preceding
movements, and, at the same time, anticipated nothing of
the massive strength of what was to follow. In fact, such a
third movement must have been a personal necessity to
Brahms. Through light music of the kind just analysed he
sought and found the interlude during which he could
conserve his strength for the final crowning of the Symphony.
Much can be allowed a composer in latitude of style within
a symphony when he is able to prove his case as conclusively as did Brahms in his four finales.

.   .   .   .   .   .

And after reaching the finale of a symphony having all
its movements in the major key, how was it possible to
maintain the musical interest? The task was not easy, as
Brahms knew full well, for " the gentle D major, breathing
beauty, dropping balsam into the soul," [1] had already
solved all its problems, once it was past the tension in the
slow movement. Thereafter everything must be " merry
and tender " (as Clara Schumann said of the Symphony),
and so the return to the *status quo ante*, after many minutes
of easy-paced, happy music, was made as hard a task as
any symphonist could give himself. With Haydn and Mozart
such difficulties hardly arose. Their Symphonies presented
no problems that more than scratched the surface of human
emotions, however expressive the music might be in itself.
For that reason these composers could plunge into their
merry *Presto* finales almost without a thought. Not so
Brahms. The lofty mood of the first two movements, followed by the light and fanciful third, demanded a return to

[1] E. von H. to Brahms, January 19th, 1878.

something more than a racy *Presto*. Brahms realized that
he must recapture the spirit of his first movement in the
finale or the whole Symphony would lack cohesion.

So this finale commences with a theme that has somehow
shaped itself from the D, C sharp, D of the first movement,
and, by this token, gives us a clear indication of what is to
follow.

It is all very delightful in its happy-go-lucky way. There
is a freshness about it that carries its own conviction, while
the quiet " pealing of bells " for eight bars (9th bar
onwards) reminds us once more of Clara Schumann—
" it might have been written for a newly-wedded couple."
And the theme has so much joy in its phrases that its dissection seems something of a cruelty here. Yet, for several
reasons, it must be accounted the weakest of Brahms's
symphonic themes, and, in view of this statement, requires
analysis.

The first four bars are admirable in their upward curve
and in the promise that out of them will grow something
really big. But at the fifth bar the theme weakens somewhat
to a figure in descending fourths that is repeated in the
following bar—an example of melodic stagnation happily
rare in Brahms. At the seventh and eighth bars the melody
recovers in splendid style, and then again loses its continuity by an unexpected fourfold statement of a new phrase,

also founded on descending fourths. And at this point the
weakness and general discontinuity of the theme is felt still
further because the fourths fall from the *weak* to the *strong*
pulse, as against the reverse in the instance of the fifth and
sixth bars. Such close proximity of descending fourths *in
rhythmic opposition* sounds a trifle artificial and unsatisfactory,
and, without doubt, creates the same uneasy feeling as was
experienced in the opening bars of the Symphony.

However, these weaknesses should not make us forget the
sterling worth of the Symphony as a whole ; its onward
sweep ; its lovely lyrical melodies ; its eventual cumulative
grandeur ; and its great efforts to sustain with interest the
happiness of mood achieved long before the concluding
bars have arrived. If it fails at times to win our more
critical appreciation, it is because Brahms, as stated already,
preferred to find the way to happiness rather than have it
disclosed to him at the outset. He needed more of a minor-
key impulse than was obtainable here.

After this quiet beginning Brahms (at letter A) soon
leaps into the saddle with a sudden access of energy that
sends the music along with great brilliance to a fiery climax.
This section is a *forte* development of the opening theme,
with many a reference to the familiar D, C sharp, D—soon
to become the quintessential feature in the final building up
of the coda :—

Ex. 145

f (Theme only shown here)

and also containing a new virile version of the ninth and
tenth bars (22nd bar after A onwards).

Ex. 146

(Thematic
structure
only)

This, it will be noticed, is accompanied by vigorous running quavers on the 2nd Violins that also have the three notes as their mainstay. On them Brahms builds up the fine fiery climax at letter B, gripping his ideas with a tenacity of purpose that is wholly admirable ; using the notes over and over again in degrees of expression varying from *ff* to *pp leggiero*, and in such a way that monotony of effect is avoided throughout. A little *legato* Clarinet phrase, founded on the descending fourths of the opening bars, serves, with repetitions on Flute, Horn, and then on Oboe, to introduce the second subject (letter C).

All this time the three-note idea has been as busy as ever. Nor do its activities cease with the entry of the second subject.

Ex. 147

This theme, with its great breadth of phrase and magnificent singing quality, comes with inspiring freshness of effect at this point, notwithstanding its faithful allegiance to the three notes (or first subject) as an accompanying figure. Following his usual plan, Brahms soon transfers the theme to the Wood-wind against a development of the quavers on Strings. At letter D there occurs a strong offshoot from the first two bars of Ex. 147—an unharmonized passage of a few bars that stirs the music to renewed vigour.

Ex. 148

Strings and Wood-Wind in 8ves

For sixteen bars from this point the three-note idea is
dropped while the music develops into curious syncopations all founded on Ex. 148. Here one can detect some
flagging of the composer's spirits, for the music has not the
ring of true inspiration nor the naturalness of orchestration
heard elsewhere. Moreover, Brahms—with something of
the thankfulness of a man who has extricated himself from a
difficult position—drops the idea the moment he reaches
the *ben marcato* in A major (17th bar after D). Here
the three-note (first subject) idea is resumed most convincingly. But, at letter E, even that has now lost some of
its freshness and Brahms is obliged to resort to expedients
that stamp the music as being rather more manufactured
than inspired. Reference to this has already been made on
page 95 and in Ex. 39. But, with the consummate skill of a
master, Brahms recovers his equanimity almost at once.
After what seems like an artificial, calculated piece of
cerebration (8th bar before F), wherein we find the fifth
bar of the second subject (Ex. 147) used as a basis for a
monotonous display of quavers in double thirds,[1]

Ex. 149 Clars. and Bsns.(8va lower)

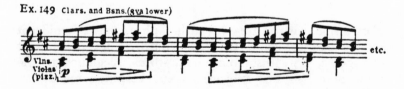

and wherein there is also, by contrast, a vigorous and convincing piece of rhythmic *stretto,*

[1] The inspired use of these quavers in the coda of the movement is a
reminder of the French critic's remark that " Brahms *travaille extrêmement bien
avec idées qu'il n'a pas.*" See Ex. 156.

we arrive at a new and vital point of interest (letter F).

Here, in the next four bars, Brahms makes use of a dramatic silence on each first beat, following these silences with minim and crotchet chords that give a new strength and impetus to the music. The end of the exposition is now quickly reached, terminating in the dominant key of A on an entirely new rhythmical device that sounds as if its origin were in the ninth and tenth bars of the movement.

[Compare the shape and length of this with the *legato* phrase in the 9th to 11th bars of Ex. 144.]

Then, at letter G, after a modulation back to D major on the rhythmical figure just quoted, the development section commences with a four-bar reference to the opening theme. At the fifth bar the music develops afresh in shortened phrases, all arising from the fourth bar of the theme and given out in the mysterious *pp* usually found at this stage in extended movements.[1]

At letter H the theme is altered still further with many a deft touch of inversion or diminution.

[1] It is a very observable fact that the development section in nearly every symphony commences with, or contains, early on, some such mysterious *pp*. From this the music gradually gains in volume until the recapitulation is reached.

Ex. 152

and flows along in quiet contrapuntal style until a forceful development is reached at the fifteenth bar. Here Brahms follows a new line of thought derived from the ninth and tenth bars of the opening theme. And against its continuation he incorporates a *marcato* phrase in quavers, closely related, it will be seen, to the quavers in Ex. 152, bar 3.

Ex. 153 (19th bar after H)

The music now forces its way, *crescendo*, through many rapid modulations (9th bar before I onwards) which culminate in a splendid climax, with the Trombones and Tuba entering the movement for the first time.

From letter H to this point there has been almost unbroken quaver movement of vital character. But, at letter I, Brahms changes the mood and also the shape of the phrases in a *Tranquillo* section that will be found illustrated in Ex. 40 on page 95. This is but another and smoother triplet-crotchet version of the opening theme, one that bears an even more striking resemblance to the parent thought heard in the first bar of the Symphony. Further allusions are then made to the opening theme (9th and 10th bars) seven bars before letter K, while at K itself the triplet-crotchet phrase returns, marked *Sempre più tranquillo*. From this point the music gradually fades into that twilight gloom without which no Brahms Symphony would be complete. Crotchets from the opening theme—see Ex. 41, page 96—become minims on Wood-wind, Trombones and Tuba at the fourteenth bar after K, creating a momentary bleakness of effect and chastening the spirit of the music during its mysterious *pp* approach to the recapitulation (8th bar before L).

As happened in the first movement at the same point, Brahms repeats very little of the opening music. His fertile imagination soon wanders off into some new contrapuntal device, which, in this instance, is an *inversion* of the music from the ninth bar of the theme.

Ex. 154

pp sempre

[Compare with Ex. 144, 9th bar onwards.]

This inversion alters the whole course of the music as far as the *forte* outburst that corresponds to Ex. 145. And then, if the thirteenth bar after letter L be compared with what occurs in the exposition from letter A onwards, it will be seen how much more virile the recapitulation is. The energetic quavers woven round the theme (16th bar after L onwards) keep the music in a continual state of excitement. Out of this finely-wrought passage there emerge two bars of descending triplet crotchets (on Strings) that usher in the second subject (Ex. 147) in triumphant irresistible fashion (letter M). The key of D now being definitely supreme for the remainder of the Symphony, Brahms follows the beaten track for more than sixty bars. What has been already written about Exs. 147 to 151 applies equally here ; apart from the pitch of the music, everything is identical with the exposition until a few bars before the coda at letter O. Here the figure quoted as Ex. 151 leaps about with great vigour.

Once more in his stride, Brahms begins the coda with

minor-key allusions to the second subject.[1] These mount higher and higher till they reach a powerful, ecstatic climax terminated by three dramatic chords.

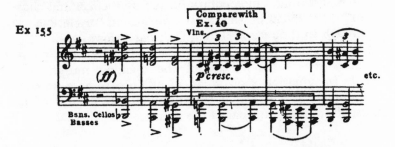

[Note the minim rest, for it plays an impressive part in the context.] Then, taking the third bar of Ex. 155 as a new starting-point, Brahms finally welds his material into a masterly peroration of great strength and compelling effect, wherein phrases from the first and second subjects are combined to produce a truly magnificent climax (letter P onwards). Even now Brahms has not shot his bolt, for, at the nineteenth bar after P, Ex. 149 makes a dramatic reappearance in three successive phrases that are made all the more eloquent by being punctuated by minim rests.

The end of the Symphony is then quickly reached with further references to the second subject, blared out with thrilling effect by the Wood-wind and Brass.

In this completely satisfying coda, Brahms makes ample amends for the lack of interest apparent here and there.

[1] See Ex. 43, p. 96.

Truly, he spurs everything along to superb climaxes before which the occasional weak moments seem to disappear as if by magic. Do such shortcomings matter ? Not very much. The general spirit of the finale is magnificent and the structure of the music all that can be desired. And what the first movement says with so much lyrical beauty the finale completes with vigour, nobility and real conviction. We are left in no doubt as to the return of the music to its own thematic kith and kin,[1] and when it does return we experience that sense of complete æsthetic satisfaction that only the greatest masterpieces of music can give us. The Second Symphony, if not the finest of the four, is at least the most human. In that fact, perhaps, lies its great and deserved popularity.

[1] Even the *ff* triad—D, F sharp, A—blazed out on the Trombones five bars from the end strongly recalls to the mind the three themes quoted in Exs. 118 and 120 and analysed in para. 1, p. 177.

CHAPTER XI

THE THIRD SYMPHONY ANALYSED

BRAHMS, now a man of fifty, settled in Wiesbaden during the summer of 1883 for the purpose of completing his Third Symphony. There, with the inspiration of the Rhine and the lovely Taunus mountains, he busied himself with the new venture and by October was able to return to his home in Vienna with the score ready for performance.

This Symphony is so unique in several important features and of such great beauty that its origin and general characteristics deserve more than passing mention. It is a work of apparent contradictions. Commencing optimistically, even heroically in the key of F major, with a passionate onrush of sound that sweeps everything before it, it relapses, at the third movement, into a minor-key mood far removed from the character of the opening and from the traditional expectation that a major-key symphony should have its third movement also in the major. Such an exceptional and rather sombre digression would in itself call for little comment but for the fact that the major key is thenceforth banished almost entirely from the remainder of the Symphony, being restored with permanent effect only in the concluding bars of the finale.[1] It is, indeed, no mere idle conjecture to wonder if Brahms, when writing the Symphony, had in mind a music-picture of the changing seasons. He was an observant student of nature ; a great walker in his young days, and an ardent lover of the countryside in its every aspect. " He is sparing of words, this remarkable

[1] Since the *bulk* of the music is in the minor keys of C (third movement) and F (finale), the argument is not invalidated by the occasional appearance of a theme or episode in the major.

man, and often gives an impression of dryness ; but every genuine experience of his turns into gold within " [1] wrote Elizabet von Herzogenberg to Ethel Smyth in a letter dated August 14th, 1878. And again, those who have read Henschel's *Musings and Memories* will recall Brahms's absorbed interest in such wayside diversions as, for instance, the quaint call of the bullfrogs—" the undefinable sounds of which for ever and ever move within the pitiable compass of a diminished third " (C flat to A natural), to which the author adds his own comment that this interval is found frequently in Brahms's songs dating from this period. Equally, might not the environment in which the composer found himself at Wiesbaden in 1883 have affected him in a similar way, directing his mind into channels of autumnal sound, which, in the initial stages of the Symphony, were as remote as could be from his consciousness ?

In an enthusiastic letter to her old friend, dated February 11th 1884, Clara Schumann draws a fanciful picture of the Symphony.[2] Even after making due allowance for a romantic pen that sometimes ran away with her, we cannot but admire the keen perception shown in her analysis.

" I have spent such happy hours with your wonderful creation, . . . that I should like at least to tell you so. What a work ! What a poem ! What a harmonious mood pervades the whole ! All the movements seem to be of one piece, one beat of the heart, each one a jewel ! [3] From start to finish one is wrapped about with the mysterious charm of the woods and forests. I could not tell you which movement I loved most. In the first I was charmed straight away by the gleams of dawning day, as if the rays of the sun were shining through the trees. Everything springs to life, everything breathes good cheer, it is really exquisite ! The second is a pure idyll ; I can see the worshippers kneeling before the little forest shrine, I hear the babbling brook

[1] *Impressions that remained* (Vol. 2), by Ethel Smyth, D.B.E. ; Mus. Doc.
[2] Brahms had lent her his own two-piano arrangement of the score. He frequently forwarded his compositions either to her or the Herzogenbergs prior to their publication.
[3] But so far she does not seem to have discovered the motto F.A.F., though she obviously sensed its unifying presence.—J. H.

and the buzz of the insects. There is such a fluttering and a humming all round that one feels oneself snatched up into the joyous web of Nature. The third movement is a pearl, but it is a grey one dipped in a tear of woe, and at the end the modulation is quite wonderful. How gloriously the last movement follows with its passionate upward surge ! But one's beating heart is soon calmed down again for the final transfiguration which begins with such beauty in the development motif that words fail me ! " [1]

In setting such a large part of the Third Symphony in the minor key Brahms might conceivably have had its very different predecessor the Second in mind, where, as we have seen, the major key did yeoman service throughout. He was wont to write his works in pairs—e.g., the First and Second Symphonies (1876–1877) ; the Third and Fourth (1883–1885) ; those first publications, the C major and F sharp minor Piano Sonatas (Opp. 1 and 2) ; the Serenades ; the two Piano Quartets (Opp. 25 and 26) ; the two Clarinet and Piano Sonatas (Op. 120) ; the *Academic Festival* and *Tragic* Overtures (Opp. 80 and 81),[2] etc.—but yet he was never known consciously to transfer the formulæ of the work first written into the second : each had its separate life. And so we can safely assume that when the Third Symphony was being composed Brahms set out deliberately with the intention of avoiding everything that savoured of repetition. The door had been closed on the first pair ; there could be no going back, no retrospective survey of music already composed. There could be but one symphony of spring-time, to be followed, in turn, by another representative of summer or autumn. And the summer of Brahms's music is perhaps most to be found in the first large-scale composition that followed the Second Symphony, namely, the Violin Concerto in D (Op. 77), written in 1878. Thereafter, the high lights begin to disappear ; his compositions take on the tints of autumn with all the mellowed abundance of the

---

[1] *Letters of Clara Schumann and Johannes Brahms.* Ed. by Dr. Berthold Litzmann. (Edward Arnold & Co., London.)

[2] Contrast was the very essence of Brahms's musical nature, though, it must be added, this quality goes unrecognized in some critical quarters. Of the two Overtures Brahms said—" The one weeps and the other laughs."

harvest ; a chill wind blows when not altogether expected, and lengthened shadows mottle the music with many a dark patch.

Brahms's music tells his age with unfailing certainty, and most of all in his four symphonies.   His youthful exuberance with all its forthrightness, his romantic disposition with its shy inhibitions, his high seriousness of purpose, all are heard in the early compositions written before the Piano Concerto in D minor.   Then about this time came the Schumann tragedy, and either through it or simultaneously with it came also a still more manly seriousness and a rational romantic outlook that refashioned the expression of his great genius on more classical lines.   And by the time he had arrived at the autumn of his life the Autumn Symphony (for so it is) was waiting to be born.   Small wonder then that this Symphony could not emulate the carefree spirit of the earlier work and remain in the florescent state of the major key throughout its length.   Clara Schumann, in the letter quoted above, sensed the general mood of the work with acumen.   In the " passionate upward surge " of the finale, with its headlong drive in the minor key, we hear Brahms rebelling with all his might against the march of the years.   The autumn of his life has been reached, and that to Brahms, the would-be-young-at-heart, is a devastating thought.   Calm philosophy comes to his aid again only in the last bars of the Symphony, where, in splendid self-forgetfulness, he once more views the glories of nature, the golden harvest, or the sun disappearing behind the western spurs of the Taunus range and beyond the legend-haunted Lorelei rock.   Human life may be transitory, and the spring and summer equally impermanent, yet, says this wonderful, placid music, there is a splendour about the world that extends far beyond personal discontent and rebellion.

And in this way Brahms makes his Symphony a very vital piece of music, for it combines the emotional and the philosophical in satisfying proportions.   This most reticent man, whose heart probably no man or woman ever wholly unlocked, here, and quite unconsciously, reveals himself as he would never have done in speech. Autumn makes him retrospective. The Symphony is the story of lost youth. Its very motto F.A.F.—" Frei aber froh "—harks back to those early years, thirty years before the Symphony, when *freedom* and *gladness* were the nectar of inspiration to the young Johannes. Now a graver import seems to lie in those words. Free he might be . . . but glad ? That was another matter. The many bold appearances of the motto-phrase betoken a man of fine courage, but behind them there is a passionate intensity that tells the tale of a fight that cannot be won. It is Brahms's most enigmatic symphony ; a work to puzzle us continually because of its obvious highmindedness set so curiously in a romantic, autumnal garden. But whatever it may have meant to Brahms, we can appreciate the loveliness of the music without any ado.

We shall never know the real autobiographical reason (if any) for this sudden and finest revival of a youthful motto ; it might refer—and yet it might not—to so much that Brahms could not bring himself to formulate in words. Clara, Agathe von Siebold, Clara's daughter Julie,[1] Elizabet von Herzogenberg, Hermine Spies the contralto—whom Brahms first met in the year of the Third Symphony, and who, subsequently, stirred his feelings even into the contemplation of matrimony—all pass by in a cavalcade of the years like some shy Brahmsian parallel to Villon's *Dames du temps jadis.* On the other hand Brahms may but have delighted in weaving this motto into the fabric of his Symphony just for its own sake, and for the amazement of those friends who always expected great technical feats from him. The *cri du cœur* that is heard so unmistakably in the later stages of the work seems to be the logical but totally unexpected development of the music, as unforeseen by Brahms as it would have been by us on our first acquaintance with the Symphony.

[1] She made a deep impression on Brahms when he met her again at Clara's house in 1869. When Julie became engaged to Count Victor di Marmorito, Brahms could only stammer out his confused congratulations. The next day he left the house, fearful of betraying his feelings still further.

The heroic uplift of the motto in the first movement is truly magnificent—Brahms would have us and himself believe that he is young again—and the big theme (Ex. 157) that this phrase accompanies has a vigour the equal to which is scarcely to be found anywhere else in the master's works. With many felicities of this kind—the brave character of the first movement ; the lyrical beauty of the second ; the sad, retrospective third, with its chill touch of autumn and old age ; and the rebellious finale, with its supremely tranquil close—Brahms consolidates the whole Symphony into something of the rarest beauty.   And then he would have us judge it ultimately (as we should do), not on any autobiographical grounds, but because of its intrinsic worth as music.   The experiences that have gone to its making have been turned into the pure gold of absolute music ; we listen to it unhindered by any programme, unconscious of any external circumstances, drinking in its beauties, amazed at the perfection of its design.   " Brahms," wrote Hadow in his study of the master, " who has at his command every shade in the whole gamut of colour, can make an abiding masterpiece with a few strokes in black and white."   The Third Symphony, with its mellowed style, affirms the truth of that discerning criticism.

The extravagant praise showered on the Symphony by the Viennese Press after its first performance annoyed Brahms.   He felt he could not live up to it.   But there was more than good reason for this praise.   The Wagner and Bruckner elements in the audience had transgressed the etiquette of the concert-room by deliberately hissing the work and its composer, an unmannerly outburst that was soon drowned in the enthusiasm of the faithful.   And so, in face of this demonstration, the critics—adherents of Brahms in ever-increasing numbers—could scarcely have refrained from showing a certain amount of bias.   " The too, too famous F major "—as Brahms called it so humorously in a letter to Elizabet—was hailed on all sides as a great advance on the other two symphonies. And what listener, hearing these opening bars for the first time, could resist prejudging the work wholly in its favour ?

Ex. 157 Allegro con brio

Those who know the Symphony well will recall the immediate effect produced by the opening chords of the motto-phrase.[1] In an instant the atmosphere seems charged with electricity. F.A.F. has fired Brahms's blood as never before ; he hears it again after all these years, not as a trivial incident, but now as a foundation for something of the greatest moment. And since this highly-charged opening is followed immediately by that passionate, masterful theme

[1] In the Symphony the musical strength of the motto lies in the fact that F is the *key-note*, whereas in the D major Ballade, Op. 10 (see Ex. 1, p. 21), the F (sharp) is the *major third* of the key—a comparison between strength and weakness that has been argued on pp. 48–50.

on the Violins—a theme that instantly belies Nietzsche's
phrase " the melancholy of impotence "—it is no wonder
that the critics of 1883 were caught up in its surge, loudly
proclaiming that Brahms's greatest masterpiece had arrived.

There is a double strength in the music ; the giant strides
of the motto, and the far-flung range of the virile theme
itself, spread across a compass of no less than three octaves.[1]
The very shape and length of the latter must command our
admiration. Dotted minims, minims, dotted crotchets,
crotchets and quavers are used here in a profusion of
rhythmic effects unequalled anywhere else in the Four
Symphonies. The vital material contained in the twelve-
and-a-half bars comprising the first theme could have
stocked another movement, had Brahms chosen ; and his
subsequent use of its main characteristics in a wealth of
incident in the coda (four bars before letter L onwards)
reaches a level of the highest inspiration and workmanship.

And, apart from the theme itself, there is another feature
of remarkable interest contained in the motto-phrase
F.A (flat). F.—one of those apparent contradictions to which
reference has been made at the beginning of this chapter.
No one would deny the heroic character of the music, its
optimism or its general loyalty to the F major key.   Yet in
the second bar of the Symphony we are confronted with an
A *flat* much more akin to a *minor* than a *major* key.   And this
contradiction becomes all the more emphatic and striking
when we also hear, as prematurely as the fourth bar, the
A flat figuring in an F *minor* chord (*).

Ex.158

(Short
sketch)

[motto two 8ves lower
than shown here]   etc.

---

[1] In this respect it compares advantageously with the opening theme of
Mozart's " Haffner " Symphony in D (No. 35), and with the main theme of
the finale in Beethoven's Symphony in D (No. 2).

This A flat has given rise to much academic speculation
on account of its apparent false relation to the A natural of
the theme in the third bar—a breach of the law more objec-
tionable to the eye of the pundit than it could have been to
the quick ear of Brahms. But in it there is a far deeper
significance, for from its precocious appearance must have
arisen that eventual strong urge towards the minor key.
" As with the seed corn " : said Brahms to Henschel, " it
germinates unconsciously and in spite of ourselves." And
just as the note C influenced the whole of the First Symphony, so does this A flat take gradual possession of the
music here. But for the present cheerfulness is the prevailing
mood ; the A flat is purely incidental, a tiny cloud barely
visible.

The vigorous first theme is immediately followed by
another of entirely different character, one that strikes a
feminine note (letter A).

Ex.159

This makes a very beautiful episode of four bars, broken at
the fifth by modulatory references to the motto F.A.F.
Then, at letter B, we hear it afresh, transferred to Wood-wind

Ex.160

in the key of D flat, and again abandoned in favour of the motto a few bars later (Ex. 160).

Here the eager spirit of F.A.F. begins to subside ; no longer do we find *sf, fp,* or even ordinary accents attached to the notes ; the way is being prepared for the second subject—a melody of rare charm, and, as will be seen later, of exceptional interest.

But before this is reached, there is a further episode of five bars, harmonically reminiscent (and no more so) of the Sirens' chorus in *Tannhäuser*—" Naht euch dem Strande." [1] But I myself hear in the Brahms episode not this so much as some kind of dream-relationship to a vigorous passage of four bars, found twenty bars from the end of Beethoven's Violin Concerto. [2]

Ex.161

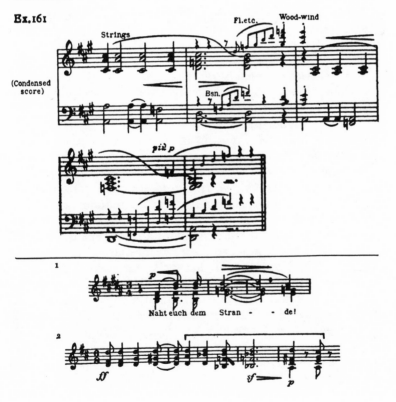

Naht euch dem Stran - de!

This episode in A major astonishes us by its anticipation of the key of the second subject.[1] Were it not for the prolonged cadence in its fourth and fifth bars—a most beautiful minor chord effect, made still more eloquent by the suspended C sharp in the 1st Violins—Brahms might have found it difficult to convince us that he was not casting about rather aimlessly for the exact moment of entry for the second subject.

Ex. 162

With this lovely melody, which seems to get into a delicious tangle with itself, Brahms extends his rhythmic scheme to a 9-4 time. On a drone bass of A and E—with the Flute pulsing a higher-pitched E over everything else—he is inspired to a theme of most intimate charm, one remarkable for its idyllic quality, and, technically, for the uncommon shape of its phrases. The opening is a graceful duet between Clarinet and Bassoon, with the Clarinet on the melody itself. And of especial interest is the manner in which Brahms has varied the theme by the subtle transference of accentual notes from one beat to another. [For the sake of reference, these points are respectively marked (a) and (b) in Ex. 162.] Nor is that all, for at the third and seventh bars there are echo effects of the rarest beauty that serve to enhance the wayward nature of the minim, here transferred from the second to the first beat of the bar. The theme is now repeated on Oboe and Violas, the Flute joining them

[1] Is it more than a coincidence that the key of the first subject is *F*, that of the second subject *A*, and the recapitulated first subject *F*?—J. H.

two bars later, while the drone bass continues on various
instruments for eight bars altogether—a static condition rare
in Brahms, yet most effective in this instance.

It is interesting to note the almost brusque manner in
which Brahms creates a new mood, one bar before letter C.
In his music he rarely seems at a loss for means to continue ;
there is always some intriguing contrast between *legato* and
staccato effects.   At this point the sudden guillotining of
the *legato* cadence (*)—compare the first bar of the following
with the fourth bar of Ex. 162—at once produces a fresh
development of the music on the Wood-wind that is a sheer
joy for its rhythmic variety.

Then the music returns to *legato* Strings for the final and
exquisite phrases of this second subject, and the 6-4 time is
resumed with the tranquil version of F.A.F. shown in Ex. 45
on page 100.

A new descending *arpeggio* figure begins directly after this
resumption.   This is developed very extensively against the
phrase originating on the 'Cellos in Ex. 45, the combination
of the two producing an entirely new and impatient mood
at letter D.

The *arpeggio* figure (*a*) bears a cousinly resemblance to the main theme (Ex. 157, bars 3 and 4), and, in all likelihood, was prompted to Brahms by the proximity of the motto referred to above.   At the second bar after D this figure is metamorphosed into an important new figure (Ex. 164*b*) that carries the music onward to the impetuous climax of the exposition, and is also combined with various thematic fragments easily recognizable.   From the point just mentioned the music keeps in or around the key of A minor, its mood being far more exigent than one might have expected. After the exposition has been repeated Brahms develops this forcefulness still further, and, through a series of modulatory chords that are coupled to a stirring rhythm in syncopated crotchets, arrives at the key of C sharp minor (letter E).

Two matters of interest stand out at this point : (*a*) the strong and unexpected minor-key trend of the music, and (*b*) the unusual appearance of the second subject (Ex. 162) in very agitated form.[1]

Ex.165

Here Brahms shows himself at his best.   The music between letters E and F is on a very high level of inspiration ; its passionate intensity holds the mind enthralled, possibly because this C sharp minor development is so unique and so far removed from the key of the Symphony, possibly because we rarely hear a lyrical second subject of this kind treated in such rhetorical fashion.   Nor is it surprising to find

---

[1] It is comparatively rare for a second subject to appear in the development section of an *allegro* movement of a symphony.   Instances of these exceptions can be found in the first movement of Beethoven's Symphonies Nos. 2 and 5. There is no other instance in Brahms's Symphonies.

Brahms once again interested in the *minutiæ* of his subject.
If the passage marked (*c*) in Ex. 165 be compared with the
similar passage in Ex. 162, the development of the music is
apparent immediately. Brahms's music may exult but
seldom—this was Hugo Wolf's lifelong and bitter diatribe
against the composer—but at least it has vitality of movement, and that vitality is mainly due to the fact that Brahms
had an uncanny genius for turning to great account such
small phrases as the above. Give him a group of quavers
set in some compound time and he will develop it almost
to the *n*th degree, maintaining interest to the end. If he
is not given to exuberance the fact should not be urged
against him. Had it been otherwise, we might never have
seen the finest flowers of his genius, those masterpieces of
abstract thought that depend, not on the spirit of exultation,
but on something more remote in character and feeling.

Between letters F and G we find the second subject being
further developed in a style similar to that at letter C
(Ex. 163), yet more ornately, for the Violas and 'Cellos are
employed imitatively with an inverted form of the Oboe
phrase shown in the second bar of Ex. 163—a succession of
quavers that seems to have strayed from the first movement
of the same composer's Violin Concerto in D.[1] In these few
bars the agitation in the music subsides rather suddenly,
broken fragments of the inverted quaver passage displacing
the original from which they sprang. The three bars before
letter G are so interesting as an example of Brahmsian cross-
rhythm and development that they must needs be quoted
below (Ex. 166). Nor, in these moments, must we overlook
the harmony that moves with such firm steps and beauty
towards the entry of the motto-phrase in E flat, where the
Horn plays with such magical effect.[2]

The Horn melody has come under review elsewhere
(pp. 100–101). There only remains to add that it elaborates
the motto F.A.F. into something of deeply romantic

---

[1] See the 27th and 28th bars after letter A.
[2] See Ex. 46, p. 101, for the complete passage.

Ex. 166

character, especially if we take its accompaniment into consideration. Here the Strings pulse along in breathless syncopation, as if too timorous to express themselves fully lest the magic spell be broken.

At letter H the time slackens to *Un poco sostenuto*, at which point Brahms gives us a shadowed hint or two of the imminence of the recapitulation section (*Tempo I,* 9th bar after H), though the key of the music is still E flat—a far enough remove to make us wonder how Brahms will be able to get back convincingly to the key of F in the short space of time at his command. That, however, he does by the simplest means, and with not a little ingenuity. His object is to get rid of the E flat that makes its presence felt so strongly in the

Ex. 167

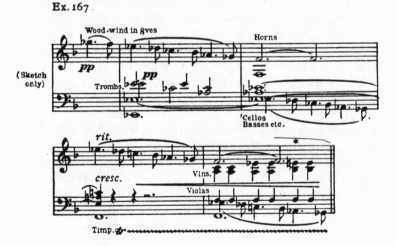

eight bars comprising the *Un poco sostenuto* section ; it is foreign to the key of F major and must eventually be contradicted either by an E *natural,* or by modulatory harmonies that will banish all recollection of it.

The quotation above (Ex. 167) shows how Brahms takes the figure ♩. ♪ that belongs to the main theme (Ex. 157), and, by means of it, arrives at the *note* F. This note is then retained throughout the next three bars, thereby claiming a good share of our aural attention. But this is not enough definitely to re-establish the *key* of F, for the required E natural (*) receives but scant attention, and cannot over-come in such a brief appearance the strong influence of the E flat.[1] So Brahms, with a rare intelligence, modulates still further the moment he strikes the motto-phrase at the recapitulation (*Tempo I*), passing through the key of D flat and thence to F major.

Ex. 168

(Sketch only)

Now the tonality is made secure, the double presentation of F.A.F. contributing not a little to this.

Reviewing the development section as a whole, we see Brahms in a somewhat different light. He attempts nothing in the way of an extended working-out of the music, but prefers compression and concision of thought. And so there are no flights of fancy of the *fugato* kind, such as are heard in

[1] " The dominant's persistence, till it must be answered to " is here con-spicuous by its absence. It is somewhat outside the scope of the present book to explain the chromatic chord that contains the E natural referred to above.

the Second Symphony's first movement ; no dramatic *dénouement* which clenches the subject-matter in masterful style ; nor yet any conscious endeavour to put the music through the more academic paces of strict counterpoint. Brahms follows his fancy more harmonically than contrapuntally here, though it would not be quite accurate to deny the lurking presence of the latter quality. His finest moments of counterpoint are reserved for the climax of the recapitulation, as will be seen later ; in the development, mood has interested him more than matter, and tonalities far removed from the key of the Symphony have added their spice to this remarkably original movement, stirring his imagination to some lovely utterances.

The combined recapitulation and coda sections (105 bars) are, in length, little short of the remainder of the movement ; the exposition and development totalling 72 and 47 bars respectively. In other words, Brahms seems more intent on driving home his argument than on developing a middle section in some elaborate, wayward manner. He seems to be almost impatient to get to the coda. There is but one reference to Ex. 159, as against its two appearances in the exposition, and, after the music has modulated to D for the reminiscential episode (Ex. 161), only a shortened version of the second subject (Ex. 162), also in D.

Back at the 6–4 time, the music, now established once more in the key of F, follows generally the track taken in the exposition, but yet with marked differences, such as the fine development of the quavers in cross-rhythm three bars before letter K. By now the key of D minor has been reached and is retained until the coda (six bars before L).

Here Brahms musters all the resources at his command, and makes the coda by far the most thrilling section of the movement (see Ex. 169).

The first two notes of the motto are played in octaves by Horns and Bassoons in a dramatic *crescendo* that stretches upward to the entry of the main theme on the Violins, the motto itself being completed on Flute, Oboe, 4th Horn and

Ex. 169

(Condensed score)

Bsns.
Hrns.

Timp. on C throughout....

etc.

Trumpet.   But the harmonies differ from those at the opening of the Symphony.   Now they revolve round a pedal C
in the bass, heard most effectively on the Timpani, while the
Bassoons, Contra-Bassoon, 3rd Trombone and Basses are
engaged on another instance of the motto, set to the notes
C, E flat, C.   And our interest is still further aroused by the
dissonant chromatic version of the now familiar phrase of
the main theme (Ex. 169, at the asterisk).   This tightening-
up of the thematic material produces the desired drive to the
climax.   At letter L Brahms is carried along by his own
momentum, and gives us a magnificent development of the
four notes that make their first appearance in the seventh
bar of the movement (Ex. 157, 7th bar).

Ex. 170

Wood-wind in 8ves

Strings *f marc.*

etc.

Against this the Wood-wind and Horns have independent
counterpoints that assist the Strings through a perfect maze
of modulations, the way out of which Brahms finds with
wonderfully sure steps.   A great climax is reached amid a
wealth of contrapuntal devices, all being traceable to some

fragment of the main theme, or to some development
therefrom. And now the apex of this climax is reached two
bars before letter M, and, from this point, the music begins
to fade away on an emotional and inverted phrase (Ex. 171*a*),
that owes its origin to part of the main theme (Ex. 171*b*).[1]

But Brahms's passion for development by inversion is not
yet appeased. He must needs *re-invert* the three notes that
are bracketed in Ex. 171*a*, thereby " double-crossing "
himself until the music once again shapes itself something
like its original in Ex. 171*b*.

All these contrapuntal devices are used in such a natural
effortless manner that we barely notice their presence.
During this time the music sinks to rest in a *pianissimo* of
rare loveliness, the phrases being divided by silences that
make them all the more impressive. No composer understood or felt the value of such silences better than Brahms.
The Symphonies abound in instances which go to prove how
meticulously he weighed everything in the balance, measur-
ing out his effects with fine precision. Hence, in this
movement under consideration, he maintains a perfect
equilibrium between the restful and the restless elements in

[1] As a matter of fact, this passage also grows logically out of the preceding
matter, as will be seen by an examination of the 2nd Violin and Viola parts
from letter M onwards.

the music ; between the major and the minor keys ; even
between sound and silence.   Those who can appreciate such
manifestations of genius recognize Brahms as one of the
greatest composers of shapely, symmetrical music.   Those
to whom only the asymmetrical appeals find in him a
wearisome collection of alleged platitudes that provoke much
general, but little detailed criticism.   Criticism of today
demands more than sweeping generalities ; it requires
evidence : chapter and verse.   And that, in the case of
Brahms, is not always forthcoming from those who are
loudest in condemnation of his music.

At the sixteenth bar after M, Brahms resolves the end of
the movement in F major with a combination of the 'Cello
phrase quoted in Ex. 45, the F.A.F. motto (shared between
Clarinet and Flute, and buttressed by other instruments),
and, five bars from the end, a last allusion to the main theme
(Ex. 157).   Altogether it is a remarkable movement, with
a lovely and tranquil ending that seems as if it must return
(as it does) in the closing bars of the Symphony.

To appreciate fully the beauty of the *Andante* movement in
its opening phrases, the Brahms student is recommended to
a close investigation of the detail in the score.   He will notice
that from the beginning to letter B the melodic strains are
given to the 1st Clarinet, with the other Clarinet and
Bassoons completing the underlying harmonies.   In addition, he will discover that the Flutes and Horns assist the
harmony every few bars with supplementary touches

(◄►) as eloquent as they are effective ;   while the

Violas and 'Cellos hold us enraptured with brief phrases
echoing the Clarinets and Bassoons.   Neither, incidentally,
must we forget the Oboe strip of melody one bar before A,
nor yet the modest touches on the Basses that help to define
the answer to the " dominant's persistence."

As the following and all too brief quotation will show,
there is a guileless simplicity about the music.

Ex. 173

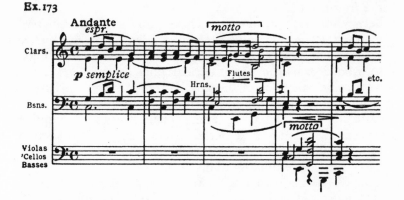

This very simplicity of theme and harmony has often made many a musician deride the opening of the movement for its momentary likeness to the Prayer in Hérold's *Zampa*, merely because the first four notes happen to traverse the same path.[1] Coincidences of this kind must occur with all composers, and more particularly in music constructed on short phrases such as the above. Brahms played the *rôle* of unconscious plagiarist to perfection.

Clara Schumann and Elizabet von Herzogenberg seem to have rivalled one another in their fanciful pictures of this movement. There is real insight and also imagination in a description by the latter, written to Ethel Smyth in 1884.[2]

" The Andante moves me as do few things in music, so restrained, and in spite of its tenderness, so virile—an exquisite product of matured power. When first I heard it I thought involuntarily of a giant holding his breath for fear of waking a child. How adorable and beautifully articulated the first theme is—and the divine G major bit ![3]

[1] Comparison with Brahms's own *Death of Trenar* (the first four notes) would, perhaps, be more profitable.
[2] *Impressions that remained,* by Ethel Smyth, D.B.E. ; Mus. Doc. (Longmans, Green & Co., London.)
[3] See Ex. 176 for a more complete version. E. von H.'s quotation (p. 229) is not quite accurate in detail.

The man who can write that is not on the down-grade as Levi declared him to be ; but Levi has become blind in that direction." [1]

This *Andante* is the most transparently clear of all the slow movements in the Brahms Symphonies. It remains in the key of C, or its dominant G, for the greater part of its length, excursions to more remote keys being very few. Consequently, there is about it a placid atmosphere that comes as a very satisfying contrast after the many tonalities exploited in the first movement ; the time for adventure is past and Brahms lapses into dreamy contemplation. But of what, who shall say ? At the third bar the 1st Clarinet drowsily suggests the motto-phrase and, one bar later, is echoed by Violas and 'Cellos. But, it will be seen, this echo is deprived

of the rhythmic feature— ♩.♪♩.♩ —that is associated with the Clarinet melody, the Violas merely sketching in the phrase with plain crotchets. This happens five times before the general style of the music is varied at letter B, and produces a mood of serene contentment, like an autumn landscape lost in the haze of a westerning sun. The twenty-three bars forming this section (to letter B) have so many interesting features that to analyse each one would prolong this chapter out of all reason. But one feature stands out more, perhaps, than any other ; namely, the number of harmonies used in the *root* position. This gives the music an almost modal flavour, calling to mind Grieg's opinion that Brahms's music was often like a " landscape, torn by mists and clouds, in which I can see ruins of old churches, as well as of Greek temples."

And that flavour is brought out even more fully when at

[1] Hermann Levi (1839–1900), a famous German conductor and wholehearted Wagnerite, who directed the first performance of *Parsifal* at Bayreuth on July 28th, 1882.

letter A the melody itself is varied by the substitution of an
A for the B heard in the first bar—one of those subtle turns
of phrase to which Brahms was often given.

Ex. 174

Analysis of this section has gone far enough. Those who
can appreciate the æsthetic points already reviewed will not
be slow to discover other things of equal beauty ; those to
whom the music conveys no message will still hear in it the
prattle of small talk.[1]

The simplicity of the music is now matched by the
simplicity of the semiquaver decoration that elaborates the
opening theme at letter B. Here the Violins enter the
movement and soon take the music along to momentary
outbursts in G major that are swung into A minor almost
at once, the F *sharps* of the G major key being sharply
contradicted by F *naturals*. These will be found in the sixth
and eighth bars after letter B, marked *sf*. And now (10th
bar after B) the semiquavers are abandoned, for a gloom
settles over the music in a remarkable passage in crotchets,
founded on the second bar of Ex. 173. As we approach
letter C during this passage there is a gradual attenuation
of the musical substance—the simplicity of Brahms's music
is really extraordinary here—until we instinctively find
ourselves expecting a new and important theme.

[1] There is probably no composer living (and I write as one) who, in his
inmost heart, does not desire a drastic simplification of style. But in this
restless age, minims, crotchets and quavers (flowing along calmly in an *Andante*
movement) seem utterly beyond the reach of most composers. And since
many such composers are warped by an inferiority complex that apes the
superior, barriers of self-defence are erected which cause them to condemn
what most they covet, and to turn to nerve-racked rhythms in superabundant
notes as their chief means of expression.—J. H.

This makes its appearance at letter C as a five-bar phrase of very intimate character : one that greatly influences the movement both harmonically and rhythmically, and which makes a disguised reappearance in the finale—whether by design or accident, who shall say ? [1]

Ex.175

Again the Clarinet and Bassoon are chosen for this theme, the Strings punctuating the harmonies with a two-note reference to the theme itself.   In the fourth bar after letter C there is an interesting clash of an F sharp in the theme against an F natural in the accompaniment, the combination of the two sounding so logical as to pass unnoticed in performance. The theme is now repeated in similar manner on Oboe and Horn a fourth higher, and then melts into the strip of melody reproduced somewhat inaccurately by Elizabet von Herzogenberg.

In reality, this reticent and lovely phrase (Ex. 176a) seeming so new, is a further development of the opening melody, for the 'Cellos have four notes (D) that correspond to the Gs on the Clarinet in the second and third bars of Ex. 174.   The phrase is repeated on the Wood-wind and

[1] Compare Ex. 175 with the general shape of Ex. 187, p. 243.

Ex 176a

Ex.176b

then developed by inversion on the Strings (Ex. 176*b*)—a typically Brahmsian touch. Once more the Wood-wind add their symmetrical rejoinder, after which the music relapses into a remarkable development of the first two notes of Ex. 175.

Ex.177

"It must be remembered," wrote Mr. Fuller Maitland, "that in 1884 such a passage as this was considered almost too advanced for most hearers, although nowadays if anything as logical as this appeared in the work of some modern composer, how thankful we should be."

The music now develops in much more ornate style
(letter D). Round a rich variant of the first theme—shown
as Ex. 47 on page 103, and given to Bassoons, Violas and
'Cellos—Violins weave a new counterpoint in hesitant triple
quavers. Many dark harmonies gather louringly about the
theme as it is taken through various tonalities ; strong
accents and *sforzandi* tell us that a climax is approaching ;
and high-pitched notes on the Strings impart to the music
a sense of momentary passion that seems to have strayed
from the first movement. The semiquavers reappear three
bars before letter E, while at E itself the climax is reached
with the Violins hammering out a rhythmic variant—

♫♫ ♪ —of the first three melodic notes of Ex. 173. And
C C D B C

here the Trombones enter with harmonies that darken the
mood still further, while Clarinet, Flute and Bassoon, in
successive phrases, hint at the return of the earlier music.
Note also at this point the long-held pedal C in the Bass.

The actual return is made at the end of the fifth bar after
letter E, where, in a strange and indefinite way, the theme
creeps back in crotchets that are seemingly pulled awry.

Ex.178

Note the exquisite pendant on the Clarinet in the last bar
of the quotation.

From this point the movement follows the plan of the
opening, yet in much more ornate style. The theme and its
echoes are given to Wood-wind and Horns, during which
time the Strings are engaged on embellishments in simply-
written semiquavers and triple- quavers which enhance
considerably the clear-cut beauty of the music. The motto
shines out clearly on the 1st Horn on the notes E, G, E(8va),

just before the end of the section. Then, at letter F, the Violins take charge of the melodic outline in a lovely theme indirectly derived from the opening.

Ex. 179

They soar to an ecstatic height in a rapturous moment or two, where, once again, we hear the old strife between A naturals and A flats—a point worth recording, because such incidents tell us in no uncertain manner what depths of feeling lie buried beneath the lyrical surface of this music.[1]

At letter G a return is made, but in another pitch, to the remarkable passage quoted in Ex. 177, at the end of which there is a lovely cadence on the Trombones into the key of the movement, and—what is so often overlooked—a further continuation on Basses and 'Cellos of the two-note figure heard so frequently, now reiterated in a hushed *pizzicato*.

Above it the Clarinet gives us a last commentary on the opening phrase over the chromatic passage on the Bassoons found in Ex. 48, page 103. This sinks through a beautiful *diminuendo* effect into quiet cadential chords, mainly on the Brass instruments—chords which (I have often thought) must have been lurking somewhere in Humperdinck's imagination when he was writing the final bars of the Overture to *Hänsel and Gretel*. And in this tranquil style the movement ends.

The third movement—*Poco allegretto*—is of much lighter texture orchestrally, while its general character, as music, is aptly described in Clara Schumann's " grey pearl, dipped in a tear of woe." " This wholly romantic woodland

---

[1] Here the A flat overcomes the A natural, as befits the character of the movement. At the great climax near the end of Beethoven's Third *Leonora* Overture, the reverse is the case. Those with a natural instinct for such æsthetic points will appreciate the distinction.

melody, spun over with triplets," says another writer, Richard Specht, . . . " is one of the twilight tunes sung longingly out of an apprehensive and overflowing heart which more than anything else endear Brahms to us. They remind us that his name is derived from the *Brams*, the gorse of the Low-German heathlands : we seem to see him with his arms full of twigs with golden blossoms and bronze-green leaves." [1]

Fuller Maitland, on the other hand, illumines the music further with a different, equally fanciful, yet wholly acceptable phrase. "No human emotion is here," he writes, " but rather the imagined sorrows of some fairy creature, some plaintive Ariel "—a criticism to which no one will take exception, so elusive, so intangible is the mood of this quasi-romantic *Allegretto*.

Brahms does not beat about the bush ; he starts the movement as unfalteringly as he did the others, striding into the 'Cello melody—a melody that is caressed so tenderly later on by other instruments, and more particularly by the Horn— with the sureness of a man who knows the way he is going.

Ex. 180

When this melody has run its course on the 'Cello, " spun over with triplets " by the Violins—triplets in which one

[1] *Johannes Brahms*, by Richard Specht, translated by Eric Blom. (J. M. Dent & Sons, Ltd., London.)

senses here and there the hidden play of the motto-phrase—
it is taken up afresh, and then brought to a full cadence
by the 1st Violins at letter A. At this point the 'Cellos and
1st Violins join melodic forces in a brief episode of much
charm, wherein points of imitation are a striking feature.

Ex.181

But of this Brahms soon tires, the music seeming to get caught
unexpectedly in an E major rut just when one is hoping for
something more extended (9th—13th bars after A).
Then, after forewarning us several times in thoroughly typical
fashion [music] that the melody
is shortly due again, he gives us a richer version of the original
theme, this time on Flute, Oboe and Horn (letter B), with
the Strings lending more ornate support.

Another full close (letter C) prepares the way for the
middle section of the movement. Without any delay
Brahms enters into his new subject-matter with a transitional chord (*) as effective as it is sudden (Ex. 182, p. 237).

In the First Symphony we saw how Brahms sensed
extremely subtle distinctions between the synonymous notes
E flat and D sharp.[1] Here there is something similar.
Carrying in his mind the sound of the B natural heard in the
bar before letter C, he uses this note as a link between the

[1] See pp. 41 and 42.

Ex.182

(Sketch only)

C minor key of the section just completed and the A flat major key of the section to come. If we can imagine the *B natural* in the chord as a (synonymous) *C flat* we hear a chord of A flat minor, from which, through the next chord, marked **, the transition to A flat major is straightforward and perfectly logical.

From the thematic point of view, the smallest thing seems to have set Brahms going in this middle section. He takes his C, B natural, and merely reverses their order (see (*a*) and (*b*) in Ex. 182). And he is so intrigued with this simple jugglery that he has quite overlooked the fact that his theme, *quâ* theme, is possibly the poorest found in the Four Symphonies. Yet, as stated in similar words elsewhere, Brahms always seems capable of redeeming or modifying his own weaknesses by the addition of interesting touches that hold the listener's attention. Here is a case in point. In most of this section the Strings are concerned with syncopated figuration in semiquavers that seems to counterbalance the poverty-stricken nature of the theme itself (see Ex. 182). I fancy that most listeners must switch their auditory sense mainly onto this rather fascinating decoration, for the rigid cross-phrasing of the theme itself does not hold the interest for long, since the three-note group ♪♪♩ has little to recommend it.[1]

Yet out of it grows a melody for Strings that is a very reproof to our impatience.

Ex.183

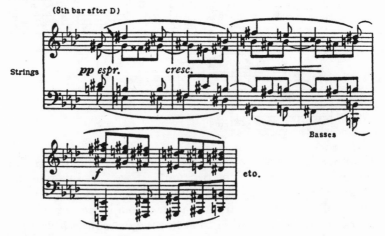

(8th bar after D)

Strings   *pp espr.*   *cresc.*   Basses

f   eto.

This theme does not last long, though it soars to a moment of great beauty. At letter E we are back on an A flat minor chord—the progression to it is quite Schubertian—and are then given a further but shortened version of the three-note phrase, with the syncopated Strings again in attendance. Thence to the resumption of the first section of the movement is but a short journey. Ex. 183 reappears in another key, hushed to the merest whisper—a lovely effect. Then, over harmonies that grow naturally out of this melody, the Wood-wind, in three successive phrases, intimate to us the return of Ex. 180.

This time a solo Horn replaces the 'Cellos, and then the Oboe has the responding section of the melody. Everything is much as before, save the orchestration. For instance, the duet between 'Cellos and 1st Violins is now heard (at

---

[1] Altogether there are twenty-four instances of it : sixteen " right off the reel " and eight after letter E.

letter G) on Bassoon and Clarinet. And when the 2nd
Bassoon and 2nd Clarinet join in for the E major bit (8th
bar after G), there is created a somewhat richer texture than
before which leads convincingly to a fine version of the
original theme at letter H.

The coda is reached at letter J. And here Brahms—fine
old craftsman that he is—gives us one of those delightful
surprises which make us realize what a genius he is for turning
a corner. At this point we half expect the return of the

three-note phrase ♫♩ , but are mistaken. Brahms is too

astute to trouble us again with this rather tiresome little
phrase, for, as we have seen, it had become one of those vain
repetitions such as the heathen use ; it had outstayed its
welcome. Instead, he treats his B natural (*) in as novel
and interesting a way as he did at letter C ; this time
as a note that helps to determine an entirely new, chromatic
harmony.

Ex.184

On this he founds his coda, making it the basis for two
phrases that conclude the movement in very pensive style,
while the harmonies merge into one another with great

beauty of effect. Here we seem to see Brahms in a woodland scene such as Specht imagines, with autumn leaves falling thick about him.

Tragedy lurks in the mysterious *sotto voce* opening of the final *Allegro* ; ghosts seem to steal past us along some shadowed wall, furtive and invisible. This " gnarled, ominously opening finale in Brahms's tragic key of F minor " (Specht) is indeed a contrast to what might reasonably have been expected when the Symphony started on its brave career. Yet, in truth, having heard so many excursions into the minor key—beginning with the F minor chord in the fourth bar of the Symphony—we recognize how inevitable has been the growth of the music toward the point now reached. Here Brahms's supreme mastery is again in evidence. He views his Symphony as a whole. It is not enough for him to forge links between the movements by the conscious employment of phrases of *leit-motif* type. Important as these are for obtaining thematic unity, there are much more fundamental matters yet. The root-matter lies in the conflict between the major and the minor keys. What is stated thematically is really governed by these forces. It is that tug-of-war between these opposites which gives this Symphony its unique character. What other symphony has indeed the strange sequence of tonalities found in this one ? Brahms seems compelled, as if by some invisible agency, to follow a certain course ; once under compulsion he is given all latitude to mould his ideas according to his personal idiom. In few symphonic movements do we feel the influence of some such dæmonic force as strongly as we do here. We sense it in the First Symphony, yet with the certain knowledge that the blackness of night will be followed by the glory of the morning sun. In the movement under consideration no such hope is there ; the forces let loose seem to exhaust themselves : they are certainly not overcome.

And then, regarded in the light of absolute music, the movement is one worthy of the highest praise. Its close affinity with the slow movement, in a most unsuspected way ; the malleable quality of its themes—at which themes Brahms hammers with all his might and with no hurt to them ; the fundamental power that holds the music in a vice-like grip ; all these things give it a character that binds it unmistakably to the spirit of the First Symphony.

Once more the note C is the link that carries the music forward logically from the preceding movement. Indeed the insistence of this note in nearly all the themes of the *Allegretto* must have possessed Brahms's soul in no small measure, directing his mind into that channel of thought which created the following theme.

Ex.185

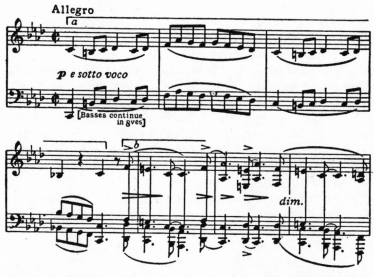

This mysterious theme, gaunt and hollow-eyed, bears a cousinly relationship to the opening phrases in the finales of the First and Second Symphonies respectively. The following quotations make this clear.

Ex.186

But the mood of the Third Symphony in entirely different. For four bars the theme creeps along without any harmony, curious accents and *diminuendi* giving it a sinister touch that presages a gathering storm. At the eighth bar *arpeggii* on 'Cellos and Violas appear, ornamented with notes dissonant to the harmonies. These continue for some bars as a florid accompaniment to a repetition of Ex. 185 section *a*, now given to Flutes, Clarinets and Bassoons in a harmonized version. Two points deserve recording here : (1) the early and desultory appearance of seemingly unimportant *arpeggii*, which, in the coda of the movement, are developed on muted Strings in passages of rarest beauty ; (2) the very interesting variation given to Ex. 185, section *a*, which now becomes a five-bar phrase through the prolongation of certain notes.[2]

Seventeen bars of this music bring us to letter A, where the Trombones enter with the solemn E flats described on page 104 (Ex. 49). At once Wood-wind, Horns and Strings answer this distant call with what must be a new version of the theme heard in the slow movement (Ex. 175), though Brahms might indeed have been entirely unconscious of this similarity when composing the finale.

---

[1] At the *Allegro non troppo ma con brio*.

[2] Comparison of the theme in the first four bars of the movement with the version obtaining in bars 9-13 inclusive will show at a glance where Brahms has varied the note-values. In a book of this kind where so many musical quotations are necessary it becomes impossible to illustrate points of this nature in every instance.

Ex.187

Whether this was a coincidence or done of set purpose does not really matter. We have only to remember that from this hushed theme, creeping along with muffled tread and seeming to be born of blackest midnight, there arises in time a mighty climax that tears its way through the music with tornado-like fury.

And then, eleven bars after Ex. 187 is heard, we might cry out with Dante in the *Inferno* :—

> "Broke the deep slumber in my brain a crash
>   Of heavy thunder,"

Ex.188

for the Trombones swell to a sudden *forte*, bringing in the whole orchestra on what, at first sight, appears to be an entirely new phrase, one which (on this occasion only) is abandoned as soon as uttered.[1]

Now this phrase is actually the rhythmical shell of the first two bars of the movement, as is shown by the small-type notes appended to the quotation. It gives the music a new character ; in it we hear once again that rebellious spirit that has so often driven Brahms along to his finest moments. Indeed, out of this agitated four-note group (C, D flat, A flat, G) there is created a new and rhythmical line of thought second in importance only to the great climax founded on Ex. 187.[2]

For a moment or two (see the third bar after letter B in Ex. 188) Brahms retreats to the music of the opening in yet another eerie *pianissimo*. But once again the challenge sounds forth in resolute tones of similar pattern to those at letter B, from which there develops a climax of real power, the approach to which is made quite thrilling with fine syncopations in the bass and middle harmonies. Here the ingenuity and neatness of Brahms's dovetailing of detail are once again disclosed to the score-reader's eye, though, in this instance, as is explained later, much of it is more visible than audible. At this point of climax (17th bar after B) Brahms gives us a version in crotchets of the quavers heard in the second bar of the movement, and this is immediately treated to a strenuous display on Wood-wind, Horns and Strings.

Ex.189

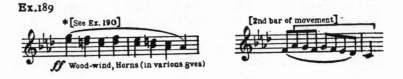

[See Ex. 190]   [2nd bar of movement]

ff Wood-wind, Horns (in various 8ves)

[1] The Timpanist has been silent since the close of the first movement, re-entering here with fine effect on the two Cs at letter B.

[2] See letter J onwards.

From it we are plunged without any ado into the second
subject of the movement—a large-hearted, major-key tune
that swings along in full strides, and which, in its opening
phrases, reminds us vaguely of the three-crotchet group
heard in the first movement.[1]

Ex. 190

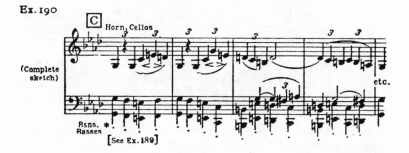

(Complete
sketch)

The 1st Horn and 'Cellos give out this melody with such
conviction and resonance that I very much doubt whether
anyone has ever listened intently to the bass of the
accompanying harmonies, which for two bars (and again
later on) copy the crotchets shown in Ex. 189. The effect
is clearer to the eye than to the ear; yet there it is on paper.
These crotchets, although of primary importance but a
moment or two back, are soon past their heyday; relegated
to serve the new melody in a secondary capacity. Such
is the never-ending fecundity of Brahms's imagination;
such the flow of his music in one continuous stream.

The brief second subject is now given richer treatment on
1st Violins and Wood-wind, and then, at letter D, reverts
to the minor key. In this passage of four bars will be found
the disguised version of F.A.F., referred to in Ex. 50 on

page 105, and also a figure

that breaks out in a fine frenzy six bars later.

[1] See the ' Cello part in Ex. 45, p. 100.

Ex.191

In particular, the theme shown at letter E in the above quotation is used in most compelling style, acting as a *point d'appui* for the further development of many fresh details harvested from themes already heard. The music now runs a fevered course past letter F—where there are many remarkable effects of distorted rhythm—to letter G, from which point everything quickly subsides to a less agitated mood on miniature phrases borrowed from Ex. 185.[1]

The development section proper is reached at the fifth bar after G. Here there is a momentary reacquaintance with the unharmonized version of the initial theme, but scored

Ex.192

[1] If the full score be consulted it will be seen how every instrument engaged in the music at this point is concerned in the three-note phrase : Wood-wind and

Horns in ♩ ♫ rhythm, and *pizzicato* Strings playing ♩ 𝄽 | ♩ ♩ ♩ | etc.

Brahms must have known the proverb : " Waste not, want not ! "

in another manner.[1] Within a few bars this passage runs
away in descending quavers, and is then displaced by minims
in a new development of the utmost importance (Ex. 192,
p. 246). Comparison of this passage with the section of Ex.
185 marked *b* tells us its origin ; comparison of its first two
minims with the two Trombone E flats in Ex. 187 tells us
what a rhythmic alliance exists here—an alliance that will
eventually set in motion the tempestuous and overwhelming
climax that lifts the Symphony right out of itself.

But for a few bars these minims are temporarily suspended,
for another and still more reticent version of Ex. 185 follows
(17th bar after G) that now turns the descending Wood-
wind quavers into veritable scale passages, while the
Strings accompany with the hollow whispers already
described elsewhere.[2] Then for a second time (5th bar
before H) the minims of Ex. 192 steal upon the end of this
with remote minor harmonies that become hidden more
and more in the general gloom, during which time the
Strings, in still hoarser undertones, play with the broken
fabric of the opening bars.[3] The minims are now definitely
established as an integral part of the music for many bars to
come, breaking out suddenly (in the 8th bar after letter H)
into a self-assertive mood that carries even more weight than
the thematic quavers associated with them, important as the
latter are.

Ex.193

[1] See Ex. 51, p. 106.
[2] See Ex. 52, p. 106. These owe their origin, it should be noted, to the
sf quaver groups heard on Horns, Trumpets, Violins and Violas at the eighth
bar after letter F.
[3] See Ex. 53, p. 106.

And then the most dramatic section of the Symphony begins at letter J with one of those silences the praises of which have been sung elsewhere. We feel as if Brahms were taking a breath long enough to cover this magnificent stretch of music extending over twenty-three bars, and which culminates in the exciting return to the recapitulation at letter K. The *forte* minims of Ex. 193 have already grown in strength to a *più forte*. Their transition to the minims of Ex. 187 at letter J is therefore an easy one ; in fact, the union of ideas is so perfect here that we are not aware that another theme has been broached until we hear the crotchet triplets in the third bar after J.

Ex.194

Against the tremendous weight of the theme on full Woodwind, Brass and Basses, the Strings indulge in a phrenetic display of quavers. They dart about in all directions like tongues of flame shooting hither and thither, untamed and devastating, all-consuming. And when the climax is reached Brahms unchains the thunder of his Drums like some Jupiter Tonans. The effect is overwhelming. With the force of an avalanche we are swept into the recapitulation before we are even aware that anything so formal has happened. But the *sotto voce* music of the opening does not return here ; it hardly could. We are long past any such restraint of mood. And so Brahms, with a sure instinct, leaps into the *ff* rhythmical section first heard in the exposition at letter B. There are, however, many differences in the treatment of the detail for the next ten bars, the quaver passages in the following quotation showing to what a tension the original theme is now subjected.

Ex.195

Then, at the eleventh bar after K, the music reverts to the plan of the exposition, but, of course, in an altered pitch.[1] We hear again the second subject (Ex. 190) now in F major. Once more it momentarily breaks the long succession of minor keys that has persisted with scarcely an interruption since the original appearance of this theme and once more it is swept into the vortex. Finally, in the last few bars of this powerful recapitulation (letter N onwards), while the forcefulness of the music is rapidly disappearing, there is a totally unexpected modulation into B minor. Through this the coda is reached. Here the Violas, now muted, enter with a new version of Ex. 185.

Ex.196

[1] In the recapitulation, the section from the eleventh bar after K to N corresponds to the exposition from the eleventh bar after B to G.

The effect is a complete surprise. The softened rhythmical flow of this theme, coupled to fragments of the original rhythm on 'Cellos and Basses, conveys to the mind the immediate impression that at last all those strange dæmonic forces have scattered, never to return. In fact, during the next twenty-one bars, such references to the original theme as do occur seem to have lost all power further to retard the progress of the Symphony to its major-key conclusion. As Fuller Maitland remarks, in his article on Brahms in Grove's *Dictionary of Music and Musicians*, there is " a touch of wonderful beauty at the end, in a tranquil coda to the finale, which has been well compared to a calm sunset after a stormy day." And to me that sunset seems pictured, not as one in a clear sky, but rather of the kind that streaks with a fiery red the clouds that still hang about loth to dissolve.

Half a bar before letter O we resume acquaintance with the semiquaver *arpeggio* passages that appeared in desultory fashion almost at the beginning of the movement. Now, as they spread to the muted Violins from the Violas and 'Cellos, they assume great importance. At *Un poco sostenuto*, where the music returns to F major, they seem to open up a vista of rare loveliness, while the Oboes and Flutes in an amalgam of familiar phrases (that are continued on 'Cellos and Basses, 1st Clarinet, etc.) tell us that the end is not far off. And during all that follows the muted Violins and Violas still continue to speed along in their quiet flickering colours—colours that vanish only in the last bars of the Symphony.

But the wheel has not yet come full circle. F.A.F. reappears—as was preordained—on the 1st Oboe at the seventh bar of the *Un poco sostenuto* section, entering shyly and in informal style in a cadential passage that also contains snatches of Ex. 185. The Oboe is then followed by the Horn in a still more beautiful allusion to the motto-phrase, accompanied by *pp* harmonies on the three Trombones. And then the long-delayed cadence melts, in shimmering half-light, into what must surely be one of the most inspired

conclusions ever penned by any composer, for, at letter P,
Ex. 187 returns in greatly altered form.[1]

Ex. 197

Being now firmly established in F major, it breathes an
atmosphere of ineffable peace.   We are in the sunset glory
of the music, spellbound by the shifting colours—those simple
but indestructibly beautiful harmonies.   And as the coda
progresses the theme rises to a moment of the noblest
expression (13th bar after P), from which point it sinks
to its final cadence.   There, the music being now anchored
to the pedal F in the bass, we hear F.A.F. in combination
with further allusions to Ex. 185.   But even now the motto

[1] See Ex. 55, p. 108, which shows the orchestration in more detail.

does not win its way easily to its final note. " Frei aber . . .
frei aber " it seems to say hesitatingly before the last " froh "
is reached, in this way delaying by two wonderful bars the
entrance of the F major chords that conclude the Symphony.

Ex.198

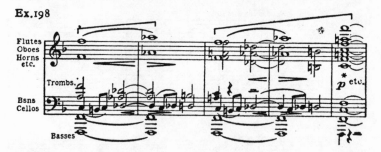

And when the first of these chords is heard (*), Brahms
gives us, on the Strings, a faint reminder of the heroic
theme from the first movement (Ex. 157).[1] As the theme,
in undulating semiquavers that are spread over seven bars,
descends into the bass, we seem to live the whole work again.
It floats before our eyes in all its moods ; heroic, lyrical,
stormy, gracious, wistful, then rebellious, and, finally,
enwrapped in a lovely peace. We re-enact the long strife
between the major and the minor keys and learn therefrom
that in this Third Symphony Brahms achieved a degree of
æsthetic and musical perfection possible only to those able
to turn the cup of tragic experience into a chalice of the
purest gold. A motto-phrase, quite an everyday one,
carries the burden of this Symphony, uplifting the mind of
a great composer into the realms of the most imaginative
and beautiful music. How many symphonies end in such
blissful repose ? They could be counted on one hand.

[1] See Ex. 56, p. 108.

CHAPTER XII

THE FOURTH SYMPHONY ANALYSED

RUMOUR stated that he was writing a 'Cello Concerto. Nobody seemed to know exactly what was happening. And when an eager public is left in the dark concerning the doings of a famous man, that lying jade will soon try to illumine things with a false light of her own.

Brahms was certainly in no communicative mood in the summer of 1884, when at least two movements of the Fourth Symphony were sketched at Mürzzuschlag in Styria. Between May and October there is a gap in the Herzogenberg letters and a still wider one in the Schumann ; and it is not till near the time of his return to Vienna that Brahms writes to Elizabet or Clara. To Elizabet he signs himself " with kindest regards," after writing that he will subscribe £25 to a fund for a musician who has fallen on evil days ; to Clara he rhapsodizes about the country—" It is wonderfully beautiful here and I only wish you could be with me on one of those magical moonlight evenings on the Semmering." Obviously great things were on hand, but as yet there is no mention of the Symphony.

Elizabet makes a tentative inquiry at the end of October and again in January and May 1885, but even her persuasive pen can get nothing from the great man. Then, like a bolt from the blue, he writes to her on August 29th from Mürzzuschlag, where he has returned to his quarters of the previous summer :—

" Might I venture to send you a piece of a piece of mine, and should you have time to look at it, and tell me what you think of it ? The trouble is that, on the whole, my pieces are nicer than myself, and need less setting to rights ! But cherries never get ripe for eating in these parts, so do not be afraid to say if you don't like the taste. I am not at all eager to write a bad No. 4."

To which she replied three days later :—

" DEAR FRIEND,—Yes, you may venture to send that piece of your piece, which—Heaven be praised !—appears to be a Symphony. It will make two people very happy. . . . It was a real disappointment to us that you could not come . . . well you were evidently better employed. No. 4 in process of construction was better company for you than all of us put together. Send as much as you have, only *at once*."

Within four days the " piece of a piece " arrived, accompanied by a brief note from Brahms. " If the piece should smile at you at all, I should like to ask you to pass it on to Frau Schumann—that is, play it to her. I hope to hear very soon. You will be sure to send the thing back before you leave ?—Meantime, in haste, yours,

J. BR."

And so in this way the first movement and a few bars of the *Andante moderato* were made known to Brahms's friends in 1885.

But Brahms was soon put out of countenance, for beyond a brief letter from Elizabet, dated September 6th (the spirit of which seems to have been misunderstood) and, eleven days later, one from Clara referring only in general terms to the Symphony, he received no further communication from either until the following month. He took these silences to imply adverse criticism that neither woman dare express. In a letter to Heinrich von Herzogenberg (September 30th) we find him referring in sarcastic and irritable terms to Elizabet's failure to write. " My latest attack was evidently a complete failure—a Symphony, too ! But I beg your dear lady will not abuse her pretty talent for writing pretty letters by inventing any belated fibs for my benefit." By October 10th all is well again ; he has by then received the very lengthy letter from Elizabet (containing also the enclosure written on September 8th, and unposted at the time), and so he sends the other two movements.

Yet, as is shown by a perusal of his various letters about this time, he is full of misgivings about the work. To Bülow he makes another reference to the unripe Styrian cherries and adds that in this Symphony he fears that he has been influenced by the climate ; in a letter to Elizabet dated October 10th, he questions whether she will have the patience to sit through the finale. He himself doubts whether he will ever inflict the piece on anyone else, and, if Richter performs it with the Vienna Philharmonic, " they announce it at their own risk." He thanks Elizabet for her kind letter of criticism " which was really essential to me " ; and, again, is " far from being so vain as to expect praise." Then, before the month is out he writes once more to Herzogenberg, impatiently demanding the return of the manuscript of the third and fourth movements, obviously irritated afresh because Elizabet had failed to acknowledge receipt of the music. The rehearsals with the Ducal Orchestra at Meiningen under his direction, prior to the first performance of the Symphony on October 25th, had failed altogether to please him. From the Duke's palace he writes yet again in mixed strain to Clara, telling her that he has worked long and hard at the Symphony, "thinking of you all the time, and wondering whether it would not perhaps prove a doubtful pleasure to you . . . but as the piece pleases musicians (and does not altogether displease me) I cannot refuse to allow Bülow to travel about with it for a bit." In such phrases and many like them he does not disguise his anxiety.

The advance opinions of the critics, moreover, were not always complimentary. Kalbeck begged Brahms not to have the Symphony performed. Hanslick, too, that staunch adherent of the master, found in the first movement nothing more than the sounds of " two witty people quarrelling "— a criticism made after Brahms had played the Symphony with Ignaz Brüll in a four-hand arrangement. Perhaps on this occasion the gentle sonority of Brahms's " tenor thumb " went unnoticed !

Undoubtedly the austere mood of the new Symphony found many would-be enthusiasts unprepared for the change of style. The lyric element so prominent in the other three Symphonies was not there to the same extent : the Symphony could not be " sung " like its predecessors. Nor could criticism be based on anything definitely pictorial, particularly in regard to the first and last movements.

Musical criticism is not self-dependent. Like the sister arts it must indulge in metaphor, simile or analogue. We of today react to Brahms's Symphonies much as people did in the 'eighties. In the First we hear (as it suits our fancy) the triumph of man over self ; or, maybe, the sinister forces of darkness dissolving in resplendent sunlight ; even, according to Kalbeck, the tragic drama of Robert and Clara Schumann, with Brahms as equally tragic onlooker.[1] In the Second, Vienna in springtime passes before our eyes, with all its warm and resinous smell of pine trees, its apple-blossom and its lilacs. In the Third we sense the breath of autumn's being and view a sunset of awe-inspiring grandeur. But those musicians in the 'eighties who had discerned in the Brahms of the earlier Symphonies an acceptable blending of the classical and romantic styles now found it difficult to invent a programme suitable to this uncompromising Fourth Symphony—a Symphony that avoided contact with every-

---

[1] After they had returned one another's more intimate letters Clara wrote to Brahms on July 23rd 1887 as follows : " At the present moment I am living immersed in your letters—a melancholy pleasure ! Words cannot describe what stirs the soul when one dips deeply once more into times long since gone by. In giving you back these letters I feel as if I were already taking leave of you. In reading them I become abundantly convinced that it would be a crying shame to destroy them. You ought to compile a kind of diary out of them for they contain almost the whole of your career as well as innumerable interesting remarks and opinions which are invaluable for a biographer. Please do that first and then destroy them afterwards. For what seemed good and at times sad to ourselves belongs to us alone. Nobody need know anything about it."

The letters to which she refers were all written during the years covering the composition of the First Symphony.

thing pictorial. And when music does not lend itself readily to colourful criticism steeped in metaphors its quality is perhaps all the harder to appreciate : we are thrown back on its absolute worth and find ourselves with insufficient words to describe it.

Specht (driven to metaphor) likens the first movement to an elegy that " draws a veil of dull silver across its most unruly themes and flows like a gentle brook among banks overgrown with meadow saffron," while Clara Schumann again indulges her pet emotions : " it is as though one lay in springtime among the blossoming flowers and joy and sorrow filled one's soul in turn." Sorrow certainly is not there, nor can we find anything to correspond to the earthly joy found in the other Symphonies, unless it be in parts of the third movement. We must suppose that to Clara, in her sixty-seventh year, almost any music by her old friend would sound like the blossoming flowers of springtime. How could it be otherwise ?

Brahms in this Symphony drives clean through the more worldly and physical emotions. Beauty is there in complete fulness, for loveliness of utterance possessed his soul to a degree hitherto unapproached. As Specht says in his description of another Symphony : " Brahms doubtless did create out of his inward experience, but never in the sense of a definite programme." Here, in the Fourth Symphony, the absence of any suggestion of a programme has without doubt tempered the enthusiasm of those who can approach Brahms's music only from the romantic angle.[1]

The music stretches far beyond any imagery : far into the realm of the abstract. Brahms here seems at one with Bach in his greatest moments. There is indeed a kinship of spirit that does in very truth link this Symphony with all that is best and noblest in music—with the opening chorus in the *St. Matthew Passion*, with the " Sanctus " and " Et

[1] In recent years Colonel de Basil's Russian Ballet have given frequent stage representations of the Symphony under the title of " Choreartium." Opinions are sharply divided as to the wisdom or folly of adapting such a masterpiece of abstract sound to the *milieu* of the theatre.

resurrexit " of the *B minor Mass*, with Beethoven's *Eroica* Symphony, or with Handel's " Surely He hath borne our griefs." Of sensuousness there is none. Brahms, the " thwarted romantic " now thwarts every romantic tendency. In particular the orchestration of the slow movement conclusively disproves the frequent criticism that here once again we have the same Brahms, grown older in the meanwhile, but still breathing the melancholy longings heard in the *Andante* of the First Symphony. But there is something in the music that goes much further than this ; something that allows little or no analysis by simile, metaphor and analogue. We are thrown back on its absolute quality, where beauty is found for beauty's sake and where we catch one of those " glimpses of the divine " to which in everyday life reference is so often made. The illusory world of sound becomes a vivid reality ; we feel it in and around us. That is why this Symphony sails among the stars and out into the spaces beyond.

Daniel Gregory Mason in his *From Grieg to Brahms* [1] writes : " It is Brahms's unique greatness among modern composers that he was able to infuse his music, in which all personal passion is made accessory to beauty, with the ' pure morning joy ' " (a quotation from Thoreau). " His aim in writing is something more than to chronicle subjective feelings, however various or intense. . . . Steadily avoiding all fragmentary, wayward and distortive expression, using always his consummate mastery of his medium and his synthetic power of thought to subserve a large and universal utterance, he points the way for a healthy and fruitful development of music in the future."

We can therefore understand some of Brahms's misgivings prior to that first performance. They can hardly have been on account of the music, for here, he must have known, was his supreme masterpiece. But very humanly, he feared for the reception of the work by the public, especially after the preliminary discouragement meted out by Kalbeck, Hanslick

[1] Published by the Outlook Co., New York.

and others. To many of Brahms's friends the work was frigid and inaccessible. Nevertheless, the composer had at last achieved his heart's desire : he had written his most classical symphony, a symphony that yielded little, if anything, to the weaker sentiments. He must indeed have cherished the thought as the work was created bar by bar in the seclusion of his Styrian retreat. Too much contact with the outside world might have shaped the Symphony very differently. As it happened, the absence of such contact retarded for many years a full understanding of the grave beauty of the music. Although Bülow scored a great success with it when he toured the Rhenish and Dutch towns soon after its first performance under Brahms at Meiningen, even that was insufficient to convert the general musical public. For twenty or more years the Fourth Symphony remained a disappointment to all but the few who kept the lamp burning. Today it ranks with the finest symphonies ever written, acclaimed and revered by all who have studied it in detail and grasped its meaning.

It has already been shown how the movements of this Symphony are held together in close relationship by the note E, and how (to quote from Dr. Hermann Deiters' reminiscences of the composer) Brahms continually strove to " arrive at perspicuity and precision of invention, clear design and form, careful elaboration and accurate balancing of effect." Still, if we are fully to grasp the extraordinary nature of the Fourth Symphony we must appreciate in some measure certain underlying characteristics in the sounds themselves, characteristics which appear and reappear throughout the work like outcroppings of rock on a green hillside. Masterful as Brahms was in all matters affecting the shaping and varying of the thematic or harmonic substance of his symphonies ; adamant, too, in the strict application of all the æsthetic principles which a lifetime of experience had taught him, yet, as he himself confessed, inspiration could only come from outside, germinating unconsciously like the seed corn.

We have seen these influences at work in the other Symphonies and they are none the less in evidence here. Brahms seems to have been caught in the toils of certain sounds which had to be re-expressed from time to time, sounds independent of anything the composer might do by sheer craftsmanship.

And of these sounds nothing strikes the imagination more than the recurrent F natural, which, so unusual, and even foreign to the key of the Symphony, makes its mark on the music with such strange and mysterious power. We hear it as early as the seventh bar of the first movement, gently and transiently, threading its way through a D minor chord and colouring both theme and harmony with a rare touch of beauty. But, as will be seen by reference to Ex. 59 on page 111, this F natural develops into something more austere, even slightly sinister. In the second movement it acts (incidentally) as some kind of powerful prefix and suffix to everything else.[1] It also permeates the greater part of the third movement. Here, uncontrolled in its gaiety, sounding as a strongly rhythmical and pivotal note in many of the themes—noisy on the Drums and lyrical on the Horn— it dominates everything with an insistence that at times shakes the very foundations of the C major key in which the movement is written. Finally, in the passacaglia movement, it reappears in that remarkably arresting chromatic chord in the seventh bar ; then again, eight bars later ; and, after the prolonged quiet sections, once more, and with overwhelming effect, in the twenty-fourth variation (15th bar after letter H) and, as a last instance, in the coda of the Symphony (letter M, Ex. 75, p. 121).

Nor is that all. Were more space available it would be of great interest to examine in detail the melodic use to which Brahms puts the interval of the fourth. This interval —in its perfect, diminished or augmented forms, used either

---

[1] See Ex. 210, p. 275, and p. 281, para. 3.

by direct leap or by implication—colours a large part of the music, more especially the first movement. The themes quoted in Ex. 199 (c) and Ex. 200 indicate the importance of this feature. On such insistent phrases, which more than all else stamp the movement with its own peculiar type of sound, the growth of the music largely depends.

Because in the other three Symphonies each movement falls into well-defined sections the themes could be analysed without much difficulty. With the Fourth, however, it is another matter. In the first movement the music develops from the first note to the last with scarcely a pause for breath anywhere and with a technique so unerring that we can almost imagine it as one long-drawn-out phrase wherein subjects, episodes, counterpoints, harmonies and orchestration all merge into one general fusion of elements : a veritable commonwealth of music's finest attributes. For that reason this movement does not lend itself so readily to analysis. Since each secondary theme or counterpoint at some time or other assumes an almost primary importance, it is difficult to decide what must be left unmentioned.

The opening theme, if viewed along the 1st Violin stave, has a disarming simplicity.

Ex.199

Yet, as Ex. 57 reveals, it carries with it as part accompaniment a pale Wood-wind ghost of itself, which, for eight bars, dogs its footsteps with strange staccato echoes and which reappears in some form or other with every presentation of the theme.[1]

This theme is not everyone's favourite. Indeed, it has been called one of Brahms's weakest inventions. Why, it is hard to say, unless it be that the quaver *arpeggii* on Violas and 'Cellos coupled to the severely plain minims on Basses suggest (within the context) some threadbareness of device. Be that as it may, this theme is the very bulwark of the movement. It contains features that are developed to a remarkable degree of power and beauty ; phrases indicative of most of what is to come, whether from the point of view of expressive digression within the development or of cumulative strength at the coda. Beyond a doubt Brahms's unobtrusive opening is anything but a tentative casting about for means to proceed.

Ex. 199 shows three of these features, marked *a, b* and *c.* None will be forgotten : each will play its part. That marked *a* is the mainspring through which the whole Symphony moves into action ; phrase *b*, with its recurrent nuance ($<>$), serves the claims of richer and more tense expression, while *c* acts as agitated corollary and is destined to become so powerful an influence (13th bar after Q) that it rides roughshod over everything else to carry the movement along to its tumultuous end.

These eighteen bars deserve the closest attention from every angle save that of counterpoint. The theme itself relies on a harmonic background alone, Brahms making no attempt at contrapuntal treatment until it has run its full length. But in these few bars—to quote a general criticism by Henry Hadow in respect to Brahms's music—" even the arpeggio figure, which is usually the easiest and most careless of all harmonic devices, acquires in him a special

[1] See p. 109.

significance and import." [1]   Note, too, that the Oboe enters the Symphony near the conclusion of the theme with a brief phrase soaring high above the other instruments.

At letter A a new element appears.   The music of the opening is now subtly and waywardly varied with delicate contrapuntal traceries of an imitative kind, while the Basses, in a different pitch of notes, toy with the ghost-like echoes already heard on the Wood-wind.   Thus a new significance is added to all that has gone before.   Incidentally, it was this section that at first hearing caused Elizabet von Herzogenberg such concern. [2]

But the forceful, restless nature of the phrases at this point will not permit such delicate treatment for long ; Brahms sees ahead of him many an interesting development once he can indulge his passion for cross-rhythms.   Within a few bars we reach a *crescendo poco a poco* founded on sections *b* and *c* of Ex. 199. [3]   And in the gathering climax we catch a first glimpse of the mountain heights to which the composer assuredly will take us.   The entire section between A and B deserves the closest analysis if we are not to lose sight of the movement as a whole, particular attention being paid to the cross-rhythms abounding in each instrumental part (except the Trumpets) for the fourteen bars preceding letter B.

Ex.200

[1] *Studies in Modern Music,* Vol. 2.
[2] See Ex. 58, p. 110 *et seq.*
[3] The significant fourths already mentioned are now " stretched " into fifths and so enhance the interest still further.

Two points in the above musical quotation stand out in bold relief; (1) the modern cadence in the first bar, and (2) the sense of conflict created by the juxtaposition of certain notes having no apparent tonal agreement. Observe how, with a vehemence unique even for Brahms, A sharp is immediately contradicted by A natural and C natural by C sharp. No wonder that when the *coda* is reached a mighty upheaval is the outcome of such a conflict, for from this moment (Ex. 200) the music assumes a new chromatic character which colours most of what follows. Those diminished and augmented fourths—D to A sharp in the bar before letter B, etc., and C sharp to G (through B and A) in the bars following—sing in the head with strange yet attractive persistence.

Dr. Karl Geiringer, the well-known authority on Brahms, regards the following phrase as the start of the second subject.[1]

But this phrase, important as it is, seems purely episodical and a link to that starker and more determined theme on 'Cellos and Horns that corresponds more nearly to a second subject proper (Ex. 202). Yet this episode (Ex. 201) is important. It contains new features such as the two semi-quavers and the crotchets in triplet formation that are destined for dramatic use and exciting metamorphosis.

Close upon the heels of this brief episode comes the second subject proper—a bold sinewy theme whose limbs

[1] See foreword to the Symphony in Philharmonia Miniature Score.

are entwined with a rhythmical figure carried over from the
previous bars.

Here Brahms concedes nothing to that feminine grace and
elegance so characteristic of most second subjects ; the
theme is as masculine as its predecessors. And to strengthen
the fabric still more he uses the rhythmical figure first heard
two bars before letter C as the bass to his subject, pounding
away at it on Bassoons and Basses and then on the full
Wood-wind instruments while at times we sense fragmentary
(perhaps unconscious) allusions to the opening theme of the
movement—Ex. 199 (a).

As is customary with most second subjects Ex. 202 receives
but scant treatment. After its first appearance on Horns
and 'Cellos it is at once transferred to the Violins in octaves
and thereafter abandoned in favour of the episode which
precedes it. This is not surprising, for the return to this
episode is the logical outcome of all that gathers round the
second subject. Indeed, both subject and episode are held
together by that common bond of the diminished fourth so
characteristic of the melodic line ever since one bar before
letter B (see Exs. 200, 201 and 202). In this way Brahms
approaches and leaves his second subject, dovetailing the
thematic content with great dexterity and fertility of
invention and, by his constant use of this diminished
fourth as an integral part of the melodic progression,
almost persuades us that those cherries mentioned by him
did indeed refuse to ripen in the Styrian orchards at
Mürzzuschlag.

Strong *sforzando* effects off the beat (17th bar after C) now
become a new and important feature of the episode first

heard as Ex. 201, while the recurrent diminished fourths still colour the music with their acerbity, rising from B to E flat (Wood-wind, Horns and Violas), then falling from G to D sharp (1st Violins) and rising yet again from E to A flat (Wood-wind, Horns, etc.), all in the space of seven bars.

Such bold outlines produce the inevitable contrast which now (7th bar before D) takes the form of an unharmonised variant of the opening theme (Ex. 199a), played in stark staccato crotchets and shared between Wood-wind and *pizzicato* Strings. All this is run so cleverly into the context that we are scarcely made aware of the gradual change imposed upon the melodic substance. Then at letter D itself the Flutes, Oboes and Clarinets restate a syncopated phrase first heard at the 13th bar after letter A. This in turn causes an entire change of character in the music which now, for the first time, deserts the minor key for a more lyrical mood.

The contrast is sudden and, with the profusion of major chords that seem to stray into the movement almost too soon, oddly at variance with the previous rugged character of the music. For a brief moment or two the Violins, aided by a Horn, rhapsodize in an ecstatic high-pitched phrase quite new to the Symphony—a phrase that occurs only here and in the corresponding place in the recapitulation. But they are soon cut short by the colder Wood-wind instruments in other phrases which seem sternly to forbid further excursions of the kind, while against them the 'Cellos and Basses sketch in the general rhythmic shape of the opening theme (Ex. 199a).

A close examination of the detail of the score contained in the twenty bars following letter D reveals a certain weakness in the texture. Brahms was evidently in some difficulty over finding the appropriate accompaniment to this ecstatic phrase on the Violins and, what is so surprising for a composer of his resource, could find no better rhythmical background than four bars of triplet crotchets on

Violas and 'Cellos which have no logical bearing on the context.   He is hesitant and inconsistent in style, abandoning the device immediately, conscious, no doubt that this lyrical digression is but a passing fancy which hardly suits the prevailing minor-key mood of the movement and which does not lend itself to satisfactory expression in the secondary parts.[1]

Nevertheless, this sudden change of style serves to consolidate the exposition.   Brahms pegs the music down to the key of B major with but one brief modulation in fifty bars (D to F).   Then, having indulged his lyrical fancy, he once more, and very skilfully, resumes the forward march of the music in the old style.

So far the Timpani have been silent.   With their first note B (3rd bar before letter E) Brahmsian shadows envelop the music with a characteristic *pp*—also the first of the movement.   The weak mood has passed and a climax is in the making.   Wood-wind and Horns are brought to a standstill in tied semibreves while the Trumpets give out the semiquaver rhythm shown in Ex. 201, the strings meanwhile indulging in new quaver figuration that rises and falls with significant effect.   From this mysterious moment the music gradually approaches an important climax : one, it should be noted, that turns the wistful minor key of the opening and those persistent diminished fourths into a succession of joyous major chords—a noteworthy peroration to the exposition.   However, such an ecstatic outpouring of sound cannot prevail for long ; the reflective mood must return.   So (at letter F) we have a short codetta in B major founded on the first subject (Ex. 199a) and then at the start of the development section (9th bar after F) are momentarily led to believe that the recapitulation has been reached. Here, for seven bars, we are back in the key of the movement and seemingly anchored to it.   But at the fourth bar before letter G, Brahms, modulating in masterly style, tells us in no

---

[1] Brahms even revised the 1st and 2nd Violin parts at the 7th and 8th bars after letter D.

uncertain manner how much new ground there is to cover
before he can begin the summing up.[1]

This development section is as extraordinary as anything
Brahms ever wrote.   The several themes and their adjuncts
are subjected to such detailed variation and general metamorphosis that to describe everything becomes an impossibility ; we must follow each line of the score to trace all
that happens.   In general style the development retains the
quieter moods of the exposition ; there are only two ff
outbursts.   But now a new character is given to the music
by some very remarkable variants of the themes heard in
the exposition.

Here are two such variants of the opening theme—the one
legato, the other strongly accented—with which are combined
phrases developed from the second section of the same theme
(Ex. 199*b*).

---

[1] To appreciate this modulatory chord in its full significance, it should be
compared with the harmony of Ex. 199b and the many changing harmonies
between letters K and L (*e.g.*, see Ex. 61, p. 112).

In Ex. 203 the original form of the theme is indicated in small notes underneath. This variant of Ex. 199*a* is in curious contrast to the type of development employed in the finale of the Third Symphony, where a new theme is created by the *omission* of certain notes heard in the original.[1] Here, however, the reverse is the case. The theme is amplified (but not extended in actual length) by the *insertion* of other notes which soon cause as dramatic a development of the music as was the case in the Third Symphony. In fact, no more extraordinary development of thematic material can be found in any Symphony—with the possible exception of the finale to Mozart's " Jupiter " Symphony—than that which begins with Ex. 204 and extends for sixteen bars. It is counterpoint at its finest ; not rigidly academic, but tense with life and variety ; full of devices that amaze and delight the eye as well as the ear. Violins are in canon with Violas and Bassoons ; Horns in close *stretto* with Flutes and Oboes in three-note phrases derived from Ex. 199*b* while 'Cellos and Basses ascend in magnificent strides for an octave and a half till they too find their own version of what the Violins have played a few bars earlier. That is not all ; other similar developments occur. But, except for one point more, enough has been shown here to indicate the extraordinary flights of imagination and contrapuntal skill that inspired Brahms to this great display of virtuosity.

The point still to be considered is that part of the *stretto* which begins eleven bars before letter H. It is here that the 'Cellos and Basses take up what the 1st Violins have played already, which, as we have seen, is derived from Ex. 199*a*. And since Brahms is never happier than when juggling with phrases and intervals inverted from their original form, it is not surprising to find the music taking this course when the Wood-wind contradict by inversion what the 'Cellos and Basses say so emphatically with upward leaps and in canon with Violas and Horns.

[1] See Ex. 188, p. 243.

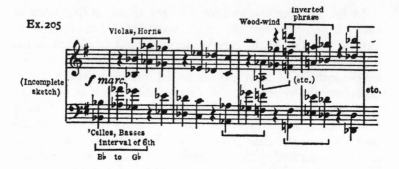

That this remarkable *stretto* owes its whole existence to the ascending interval of the sixth found in the first two bars of the movement persuades us all the more that Brahms's technique did not fail him when he began the Symphony in such unobtrusive fashion.

The section between letters H and I is entirely concerned with music marked *p*, *pp* or *sotto voce*. It is developed from that episode quoted further back as Ex. 201 and, at the fifth bar after H, contains that strange icy-cold passage for Wood-wind quoted on page 111 as Ex. 59. Then the Oboes, accompanied by the Strings in quaver figuration similar to that heard at the fourth bar before E, play haphazardly with scraps of the opening theme.

Yet this is no mere casual reference. The fourth bar of the quotation, with its significant nuance ($< >$),[1] is but a

---

[1] This nuance, used similarly to the above, occurs no less than twenty-nine times during the course of the movement. It is also found in many other places not directly traceable to Ex. 199*b*. Its importance in the expressive scheme of the movement cannot be over-rated.

foretaste of those mysterious, shifting and lovely harmonies that are soon to take us back to the recapitulation almost unawares. But before this happens there is the second *ff* outburst (letter I) in which further variants of Ex. 201, couched in terms almost violent, are developed with points of close imitation and much contrapuntal skill. Finally quiet is once more restored when (8th bar before K) yet another development of Ex. 199*a*—this time robbed of all its energy—gradually prepares us for the recapitulation.

At letter K [1] we learn the full meaning of Ex. 199*b*. The passages alternating between Wood-wind and Strings are like the dews of heaven distilled ; the harmonies so beautiful that analysis must be suspended : no words can describe their magical effect. And through them Brahms approaches his recapitulation *pp*, omitting the nuance ($<>$) at the sixth bar before L (L being the start of the recapitulation).

Everything is indeed strange here, for the opening of the recapitulation is unlike any other ever written ; it suggests in some vague way the last disappearing fragments of a development that has long since receded into the far distance.[2]

Ex. 199*a* is now reduced to minims and semibreves (letter L) and continues thus for some thirteen bars ; *p* and *dolce*, divested of all other expression. And still the development

---

[1] See Ex. 61, p. 112.
[2] Compare the 'Cello part three bars before L with what follows.

seems not to have faded out of earshot. The quaver figuration on Strings—with the ubiquitous diminished fourth —is superimposed on the theme of the recapitulation (Ex. 207) and does not relinquish its hold until the Violins resume much in the old style.[1]

Only some thirty bars are repeated here in the key of the exposition. At the twelfth bar before M a shortened version of the music—*i.e.*, compared to the exposition—brings with it a modulation which guides all that follows, including the second subject (5th bar after M), back into the key of E minor.

Brahms now readjusts his instrumentation to suit the altered pitch of the themes, but for some considerable time keeps the music rigidly to the plan of the exposition. Then the theme which first appeared as Ex. 201 is recharged with energy as never before. Making an unexpected excursion into the key of G sharp minor (8th bar before P) it tears itself away with some violence from following in the footsteps of the exposition. It then plunges from sharps to flats by means of an enharmonic modulation (4th bar before P) ; breaks into a series of dissonant harmonies, and, finally (letter P), arrives at a chord of B major which foretells yet once again the " dominant's persistence till it must be answered to."

But so far this chord is only a pivot ; other modulations must occur before the gage is thrown down and the dominant's challenge finally accepted. So between P and Q Brahms stirs the music up to a fine frenzy. Still developing the same material derived from Ex. 201 he sweeps on through the keys of G and F in a *stretto* irresistible in its cumulative force. Then amid this welter of exciting sounds Timpani, Trumpets and Horns (8th bar before Q) enter *ff* with the note B to consolidate the dominant and drive the music headlong to its climax at Q.

---

[1] Certain differences of harmony at the recapitulation should be noticed. Comparison with the harmonies in the opening bars of the movement will prove instructive.

The coda is nothing short of magnificent throughout its entire length of forty-seven bars.   At Q the opening theme of the movement is hammered out full force on 'Cellos and Basses against canonic imitations on most of the other instruments ; in fact each instrument (except the Timpani), driven with concentrated force to this great peroration, shows an overmastering desire to take control of the theme and make it its very own.   The music well-nigh falls over and into itself in giving rein to its tremendous strength (note the syncopation on 'Cellos, Basses, Bassoons and 1st and 2nd Horns from the 4th bar after Q onwards), while its masterful urge towards some other and, as yet, unattained climax, keeps the whole orchestra in a state of the greatest agitation.

Now (13th bar after Q) Ex. 199c comes once more into action.   But it no longer descends in pitch moodily as it did there and elsewhere.   Marked *sempre più f*, a new courage is given it, which, at this point, takes it higher and higher like the lark nearing heaven's gate, till, in its turn, it is swept aside (letter R) by the theme shown in the second bar of Ex. 200. And still the pressure continues.   The chromatic harmonies associated with Ex. 200 and that restless interval of the augmented fourth need time for their resolution ;   no conclusion can be reached before their force is spent.   And that is not yet.

So in an amazing concatenation of effects, thematic, harmonic and rhythmical, with *sforzando* accents [1] pulled awry in a manner quite brutal,

and where we feel that every theme in the movement but the second subject (Ex. 202) is fighting desperately for the

---

[1] Their origin can be found in the 17th bar after C.

upper hand, the struggle still continues unabated. The familiar quaver figurations of the Violins now traverse the strings as strenuous reiterated semiquavers (Ex. 208) which together with the *sforzandi* from the same musical quotation succeed at last in hustling the movement to its concluding bars. But the mood of the music is true to its general character ; the end is reached with a return to diatonic chords as plain and austere as anything at the beginning, chords delivered with such *fortissimo* emphasis that they seem to deny the right of the major key to any place in the movement whatsoever.[1] Moreover, if we pause to reflect, we can hear the plagal cadence of the two final bars matching to perfection the A minor harmony found in the second bar of the movement.

Ex. 209

"I should choose this movement for my companion through life and death" wrote Elizabet von Herzogenberg to Brahms in a letter praising the beauty of the *Andante moderato*.

It is indeed a remarkable piece of music : eloquent, moving, dramatic ; rich in melody and harmony ; full of those strange patterns in sound that can only spring from the mind of a great inventor ; and, above all, undoubtedly the most beautiful of all the slow movements in the Brahms Symphonies. The plane of thought is much higher ; it forsakes the world. No unworthy phrase or meretricious

[1] Any analysis of this movement must of necessity remain incomplete, the detail being too profuse for a full description thereof. But I cannot let the occasion pass without calling the reader's attention to the remarkable balancing of the sections in respect to *legato, staccato* and *accented* effects.—J. H.

effect mars for a single instant this noble music ; it never descends to any flamboyant trick of orchestration to cloak a poor idea, nor does it rely on superficial romantic feeling for its emotional appeal.

And then there are curious contradictions of tonality unlike anything else ever written by the composer ; peculiar clashes of keys ; a suggestion of the Phrygian mode here and there ; the strong pull of certain notes discordant to the key of the movement yet seemingly part of it, tugging first one way and then another, setting the music on strange paths in a world of its own. On such diverse material Brahms constructs the movement like a true master of his craft.

Though the key is nominally E major it is not properly defined until halfway through the fourth bar, for Brahms begins with a preliminary version of the opening theme [1] set a major third lower and sounding quite Phrygian in the effect.[2]

And, as will be seen from a perusal of the first eight bars, the leading note of the key, D sharp, occurs only once (5th bar, on 'Cellos and Basses) while several notes foreign to the key—C, D, F and G naturals—play a most important part ; not only in Ex. 210, but also in the accompaniment to that lovely and tranquil Clarinet version of the opening theme which twines itself round the 1st Violin *pizzicati*.[3]

[1] See Ex. 62, p. 113.
[2] The Phrygian mode corresponds to the white notes on the Piano from E to the octave above.
[3] The complete *pizzicati* shown in Ex. 62 are not included here.

Ex. 211

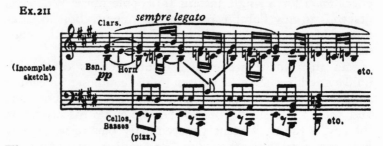

These several notes act as a most definite link with the first movement—we must not forget the F natural in particular—and at the same time become the minor-key framework, both here and again at the end, to a movement set in the *major*.

In such details are heard those curious contradictions of tonality and peculiar clashes of keys referred to elsewhere.

These contradictions bring immediate character to the movement, for all those C, D, F and G naturals adventuring so strangely *below* the actual notes of the E major scale are bound sooner or later to produce a tendency for other notes to proceed *above* that scale. And this is exactly what happens at the ninth bar, at which point the D, E and A sharps and the F double-sharp, running counter to the previous naturals, now cause the music to modulate for the first time.

Ex. 212

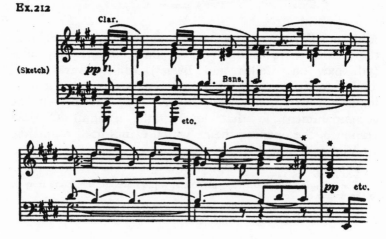

[Note the beautiful cadence marked **.]

But for a while all the modulations are shortlived. Brahms has a good deal to say before he deserts the key of E major. To it he returns momentarily two bars before letter A, where the 1st Horn has a brief echo of Ex. 211. Then at letter A itself he modulates again and in more extended style. Here the Clarinets and Bassoons reiterate at a new pitch the Phrygian phrases of Ex. 210. This sudden change to the more austere version of the theme is highly significant, for it heralds that remarkable contrapuntal development which occurs at the 11th bar after letter D and which (as will be seen later) continues throughout ten bars of intensely vital and stirring music.

At the 7th bar after letter A, Ex. 211 returns, but in slightly different form. Then the Clarinet, four bars later, elaborates the theme of Ex. 212 to a melody of heartfelt lyrical beauty, which, in its dying fall, once more guides the music back to the parent key (letter B).

Now for the first time in the movement the Violins use their bows in a version of Ex. 211 which is so disguised that it might almost pass for a new theme.[1]

This, on its only appearance in the movement, rises to an ecstatic height, and the music, now finally breaking away from all allegiance to the key of E major, modulates towards the second main subject.

But before this subject is reached in its definite form (letter C), something quite unexpected happens ; something, in fact, unique and highly original.

Halfway through the 5th bar after letter B we hear for the first time, on Wood-wind, an arresting rhythmical figure which completely alters the character of the music.[2] In itself this would be interesting enough, for its alternations between Wood-wind, Horns and Strings create an active mood not soon to be forgotten. It is Brahms in full vigour ; though, it must be confessed, the two bars immediately

[1] See Ex. 64, p. 114.
[2] See Ex. 65, p. 114.

before letter C do suggest a premature and unexpected abandonment of this splendid figure. But what makes this passage so remarkable is that it actually contains the nucleus of the second subject itself,

Ex.213

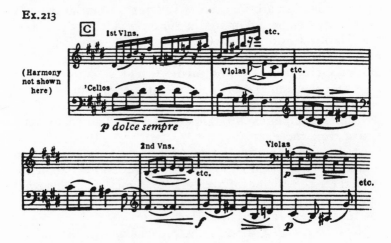

disguised with such effect that we lose nothing of its freshness when, after five bars, we hear it as shown in Ex. 213.

The beauty of this 'Cello melody is beyond all words to describe. It can never be heard too many times ; it is Brahms's most sublime melody.[1] Decorated by the 1st Violins with *dolce* semiquavers which remind me of a similar passage to be found in the slow movement of Schubert's great C major Symphony, this theme lingers through nine bars of sheer loveliness and then, uncompleted, surrenders the thematic interest to other instruments. Note how the

[1] Thus Elizabet von Herzogenberg in her letter to Brahms dated October 10, 1885. "How every 'cellist . . . will revel in this glorious, long-drawn-out song breathing of summer ! And these, I presume, are the cherries which refuse to ripen at Mürzzuschlag." The construction of this melody, both here and on its second appearance, is remarkable in other ways, for the accompaniment itself incorporates sections of the melody. This favourite device of the composer can be heard in the 2nd Violin and 1st Bassoon parts at the 5th bar after letter C, the Viola part at the 7th bar after letter C, and again in the 2nd Violin, 'Cello and Bass parts from the 13th bar after letter E onwards. The last allusion occurs in the Viola part at letter F.

last four notes of the 'Cello melody cause a further development of the music, and, by means such as these,

Ex.214

carry the movement along (by way of a somewhat unconvincing bridge passage) [1] to the recapitulation at letter D.

At the recapitulation Ex. 211 is presented in an entirely different manner. Not only is the orchestration varied— divided Violas taking the place of Clarinets and arpeggiated figuration on Wood-wind and Horns [2] lending a new and darker character to the music—but the harmonies are changed as well. D *sharps* replace the D *naturals* in the harmony of the first two bars and in this way momentarily create a more benign mood, which, however, does not last beyond these two bars. The actual music recapitulated here only amounts to ten bars in all, for, at the 11th bar after letter D, Brahms plunges (letter E) into that remarkable development of the Phrygian phrase already referred to on another page.

Here, against the original theme, he adds demisemiquavers to the score and by this vigorous treatment of the Strings gives the music a strength of movement more compelling than anything heard previously. The theme itself (see Ex. 210) is stated with great emphasis for some ten bars. Tossed about from pillar to post, it is flung between Wood-wind, Horns and Strings, now in the treble and now in the bass, till it culminates in an overwhelming hammering out of that rhythmical figure (Ex. 65) [3] which, metamorphosed, constitutes the second subject proper.

[1] Examine the six bars that precede letter D.
[2] For the origin of this figuration see the String parts in the three bars preceding letter D.
[3] Here Brahms omits one bar. Compare this passage of *four* bars with the *five* immediately preceding letter C.

But now this most moving theme, played this time on the
G string of the 1st Violins (not marked in the score) and in
the tonic key, is divested of that *dolce* semiquaver figuration
which accompanied its earlier presentation on the 'Cellos.
Rich and eloquent harmonies on the other Strings now form
its sole background, for, after the strenuous movement of
the previous fourteen bars, repose is essential to the proper
expression of this lovely melody. Then from this mood of
resignation it quickly changes to one of exaltation as the
theme is repeated *forte* in syncopation against full Wood-
wind harmonies (4th bar before letter F).

At letter F the Strings have one bar which, in new
harmonies, contributes still further to the general beauty
of the music. This leads at once to a *diminuendo* passage for
Clarinets and Bassoons of a loveliness rare even for Brahms.
And then there follows immediately (5th bar after F) that
extraordinary *ppp* allusion to Ex. 212 already described in
the first paragraph of page 115.

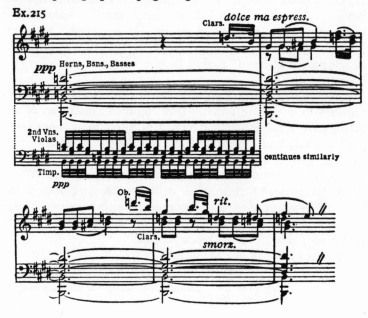

Ex. 215

Such music, unsubstantial and incorporeal, is scarcely of this world. Brahms takes us into some realm of the spiritual where we are lost to every circumstance of earthly existence and where the soul, imprisoned in the darkness of the unreal, waits in patience for the coming of the light.

We have long grown used to the strange ending to this passage in which a D sharp on the Oboe momentarily conflicts with the D naturals of the harmony. But to Elizabet von Herzogenberg it gave so much concern that she could not resist writing to Brahms about it. " On the other hand I have qualms about the passage near the close :

Ex. 216

The D sharp in conjunction with the lower D would not matter in itself, but the whole progression of the three upper parts, as against the marked repose in the bass, jars indescribably. *Must* it be, dear Friend ? " At the end of this passage there is a momentary pause and the Clarinet and Strings resolve the lyrical element in the music into a lovely and contented cadence.

But the movement would not be complete without some return being made to the music of the opening. There is so much in it that is stern that any attempt to end it on the lyrical note would have completely falsified its character. So once more the challenge of the Horns rings out like a dire summons to the judgment seat. Against it Violas, Violins and some Wood-wind instruments strive in vain to keep to the gentler version, pitched, as shown in Ex. 211, a major third higher. The result is a grim struggle between the two tonalities from which there is no respite until the final E major chords are reached two bars from the end. That the

penultimate harmony should be a chord of F (natural) major
and that four bars out of the final six are strewn with
accidentals and chromatic chords in a major key which
had been determined so lyrically but a moment before by
the Clarinet and Strings, go to prove what stress of conflicting
emotions went to the making of this truly remarkable
movement.

Of the four movements the third was the last to be written.
We can only hazard the guess that Brahms was so completely
under the spell of the other movements—the first and finale
particularly, which in general character have much in
common—that he purposely avoided all contact with gay
and rhythmically noisy music until everything else had been
concluded. Then, the load lifted from his mind, he let
himself go, feeling that now was the occasion for a great
exultant outburst in his well-tried key of C major. Moreover, in support of this contention it is worth recording that
the third movement is labelled *Allegro giocoso* and is indeed
the only movement in the four symphonies that opens
fortissimo. Well might Elizabet von Herzogenberg write to
the composer in terms of great enthusiasm ". . . the
irresistible rough humour of the Scherzo " [1] . . .". . . the
old made new by your unfailing skill " . . . and again
(referring to the second subject) . . . " which savours so
clearly of the Volkslied as if some tender youth were piping
it on his flute outside."

Brahms's perfect mastery over the counterpoint that
gathers round the passacaglia theme of the finale must have
filled him with such rare joy that he was only too eager to
set about the third in enthusiastic bravura style. Once
again there is an astounding display of technical virtuosity ;
in fact the detail work is so profuse and the treatment so
galvanic that to describe everything in full becomes an

[1] Nowhere, in my submission, does this movement suggest the spirit of the
Scherzo as we are accustomed to think of it. It is something apart ; tremen-
dously infectious in its virile short-metred rhythms, yet too full of profound
thought to be considered merely a jest.—J. H.

impossiblity. Apart from the two instances given below (see p. 286 and Ex. 223), there is scarcely a trace of academic cerebration, the music slipping into place with all the naturalness of unimpeded inspiration. In its general architecture " it accomplishes a form," writes Professor Sir Donald Tovey in his *Essays in Musical Analysis*[1] " which you may call either a sonata-rondo or a first movement, according to the importance you give to the fact that the first six bars of its theme " (*i.e.*, the opening theme) " return just before the short second subject and the quite fully organized and widely modulating development."

This opening theme, of which the essential phrases are lettered *a*, *b*, *c* and *d* in the following example,

Ex. 217
Allegro giocoso

(staccato rhythm continues)

has its first four bars constructed on invertible counterpoint, the melodic line and the bass exchanging places on two important occasions (see Ex. 219). Further on the bass is also used by itself in slightly varied form as part of that thematic development on the Wood-wind (23rd bar after E) which ushers in the fine *diminuendo* passage for Strings where, to quote Elizabet yet once again—" all the gay apprentices slouch home from work and the peace of evening sets in."

What makes the first subject so absorbingly interesting is

[1] Vol. I., Oxford University Press.

the full use to which each of the phrases is put. Nothing goes to waste ; there is consideration for each detail. Brahms, with true symphonic art, merges one section into another so skilfully that the listener is scarcely aware of any transition whatever.

As the music progresses, great stress is laid on the notes of the fifth bar, F. and A (*b* in Ex. 217). Reference has already been made (p. 115) to the " thunder of the low F " on the Timpani at this point, and also, in an earlier part of this chapter, to the general importance of the note F in its relation to the whole Symphony. It all suggests that here and elsewhere in the movement Brahms is exerting himself to the utmost to throw all care aside, endeavouring, however vainly, once more to recapture the spirit if not the actual letter of his lifelong motto F.A.F. But, deliberate as all these *ffz* and *ff* stresses are—the F and A are joined by a C later on—the motto itself remains unheard. In all probability it never consciously entered the composer's mind.

Nor, indeed, does this F–A chord savour of anything but optimism, for out of it there grows that strongly rhythmical and joyous figure (*c* in Ex. 217) on which so much of the movement's vitality depends. This, in turn, is followed by yet another phrase (*d* in Ex. 217) which has a great bearing on the middle section and climax of the movement. The music plunges without any warning into the key of E flat— a far enough remove to add enormously to the effectiveness of the whole. But no sooner is the phrase given utterance than a swift return is made to the key of the movement. Here the rhythmical *c* of Ex. 217 is accorded a more lyrical treatment,

Ex. 218

foreshadowing similar developments when the impetus has slackened.

All this belongs to the natural ebb and flow of the music. Within a few bars we sense a renewed excitement when disjointed scraps of the opening phrases are spread haphazardly about the orchestra in a strange premonitory way (5th to 7th bars after A *et seq.*), and which, through vigorous semiquaver passages, culminate in one of those brilliant topsy-turvy versions of the opening theme to which reference has already been made.

The excitement quickly subsides, and through further development of existing material we are brought to the brief and gracious second subject, decorated so piquantly with Wood-wind scale passages (9th bar after B).

This (at letter C) is reduced for some twenty bars to a bare outline in crotchets played *staccato ;* a strangely flaccid development that casts something of a shadow over everything. Despite the ingenious device, and, against it, some extremely effective triple-quaver writing for Violas, these bars are the least convincing in the whole Symphony, the effect soon wearing a little thin. The pulse of the music seems to weaken under the strain of so much *giocoso* exuberance ; Brahms is definitely marking time (with the " melancholy of impotence " ?) until he can bound forward

anew with his opening theme. So with evident misgivings
and not a little dry cerebration he abandons the sprightly
staccato and *pizzicato* effects on Strings, turning the meagre
outlines into a somewhat unconvincing display of *legato*
crotchets and minims [1] that hang about like smoke in the
air until zero-hour resounds (at letter D) and Brahms lets
loose his guns with more effect than ever (Ex. 221).

The immensely powerful reiterations of the F–A chord
from the fifth bar after D onwards, together with what
develops therefrom—incidentally we must not forget the
effect of the Timpani and Triangle here [2]—lead to a further
display of Brahms's great contrapuntal skill. All the phrases
of Ex. 217, with the exception of the one marked *d* are
pursued and exploited wtih great fervour. The reader
should examine the full score from four bars before letter E
onwards and discover for himself what pliant strength lies
in the music at this juncture ; how each theme, to which
there is added a descending syncopated scale passage, is
tumbled about from treble to bass and back again in a fine
frenzy of movement.

Out of all this grows that Wood-wind passage (23rd bar
after E) already shown as being a variant of the bass of
Ex. 217. It comes in with something of an inverted sense
of humour : rather a characteristic glimpse of Brahms the

---

[1] See 1st Violin part at the 13th bar and 1st Bassoon at the 9th bar before
letter D.
[2] See Ex. 67, p. 116.

man mirrored in his music. And after the gay apprentices have slouched home (8th bar before letter F)

Ex.222

and twilight descends on the scene in a lovely and eloquent passage (letter F), Brahms lingers fondly on the *d* phrase shown in Ex. 217, giving it out *poco meno presto* in softer outlines and with all the magical feeling that the key of D flat can offer.[1]

But with unlooked-for suddenness and after only eight bars of this music the mood is peremptorily dismissed. A quick transitional passage back into C major, of which the skeleton structure is shown in the following example,

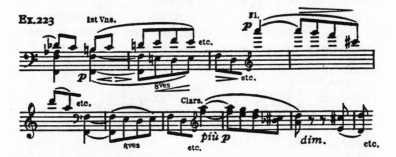

Ex.223

tells us that Brahms must have thought this lyrical digression into D flat to be either irksome to his feelings or (more likely) detrimental, if developed, to the general progress of the movement. The link is none too strong musically ; once more Brahms is marking time, perhaps even deluding himself with the make-believe of all those Gs, which, on the Horns in particular, prophesy in somewhat irritating fashion the return of phrase *d* in Ex. 217. " Believe me "—to quote

[1] See Ex. 68, p. 116.

Elizabet von Herzogenberg yet once again [1]—" it is as if you had played us some glorious thing on the piano, and then, to ward off all emotion and to show your natural coarseness, snort into your beard : ' All rot, all rot, you know ! ' [2] It hurts so, this forcible C major ; it is no modulation, but an operation—at least so I feel it, heaven forgive me ! "

Then, the operation over and a quick recovery made, Brahms busies himself with the recapitulation of the earlier sections of the movement, breaking in, his old vigour renewed, with the now familiar phrase *d* of Ex. 217. Having shortened the recapitulation in this way—and, incidentally, the quick change to the key of E flat gives the music an extraordinary new verve just when we are expecting a return to C—he then proceeds from strength to strength, and, as was said of the Second Symphony, drives everything along to superb climaxes before which those occasional weak phrases seem to disappear as if by magic.

The gracious second subject (Ex. 220), reappearing in the key of the movement at the tenth bar after G, now evokes a triple-quaver rhythm entirely new to the movement.

Ex.224

(22nd bar after G)

This is developed at some length and with growing excitement until, six bars before H, the *staccato* crotchet

---

[1] I cannot refrain from quoting her extensively, for her analysis of the Fourth Symphony is one of the shrewdest pieces of musical criticism ever penned.

[2] " Brahms had a deep-rooted dislike of all display of solemnity, one might even say a sort of shyness of betraying his deepest feelings ; and this occasionally . . . made him burst out with something that sounded unkind, but was in reality only the result of a vain attempt to find a joking expression with which to cover his real feelings." *Recollections of Johannes Brahms*, by Albert Dietrich and J. V. Widmann, translated by Dora E. Hecht (Seeley & Co.).

outline of the subject is heard for the last time in rousing chords.

Ex.225

ff Full Orchestra   etc.

All inertia has now disappeared, the crotchets moving chord by chord with steps firmly founded on a bass descending chromatically.

When the coda is reached at letter H there is a sudden lull from which, on a pedal G in the bass—note the persistent rhythm on the Timpani—there is built up, item by item, a magnificent peroration to the movement. The disjointed scraps of the opening phrases, first heard at the 5th bar after letter A, are now developed far more systematically in a *stretto* that surges along in an unstemmed flood of sound. And the long-held pedal G (the " dominant's persistence " again) seems to promise an almost inevitable return to the key of C.

But Brahms deceives us ; he has two more tricks up his sleeve, and splendid ones at that. Firstly, he modulates most unexpectedly through a B flat (see 9th bar after letter I) and then for the only time in the movement, proceeds to give us phrase *a* of Ex. 217 in the key of F (6th bar before I). This virile handling of the subject-matter, together with further *ff* emphasis (letter I) on the notes F and A—C is added here with enormous effect—produces yet another prodigious development of each phrase shown in Ex. 217 with the exception of the one marked *d*. Moreover, the significance of the note F that causes this further development should not pass unheeded ; as stated elsewhere, it

dominates the music so insistently that at times the very key
of the movement seems jeopardized. Finally, Brahms
furnishes what is perhaps the greatest thrill of all, when, at
letter K, phrase *d* of Ex. 217 is given its one and only
utterance *in the key of the movement*.

Ex.226

Heroic on its first appearance, then passing through a
lyrical moment or two (Ex. 68), this phrase now emerges
triumphant on Trumpets and Horns, and so prepares the
way for the final bars, which, it need scarcely be added, are
founded on the opening phrase. Once again Elizabet hit
the nail on the head when, alluding to the coda, she continued that long letter of hers : " as if you had written it
quite breathlessly or in one long-drawn breath."

The Chaconne and Passacaglia—both originally dances
in triple measure and scarcely distinguishable one from the
other, for each depends on an *ostinato* or ground-bass—have
for centuries proved a lure to the composer. [Anchored to
this device of a ground-bass he could vary the moods of the
music constructed thereon and find full scope for an almost
endless series of variations covering a wide range of expression and often exhibiting great skill and ingenuity.] But
only the greatest masters can be said to have made any
notable success in these dance forms, for the many reiterations of the bass (or the *ostinato* figure when transferred to
another part) demanded much in the way of thematic
interest and harmonic variety. When these were not
forthcoming an irritating monotony of key was often the
result. Purcell was almost pre-eminent in this style of
composition, though he, too, could be dry and uninteresting.

He used the ground-bass time and time again with great effect, as, for instance, in the Grand Dance which ends his opera *King Arthur* or in Dido's poignant lament " When I am laid in earth " from *Dido and Æneas*. In fact, the chaconne, in Lully's time (1639–1687), had become a stock ending to many operas, the convention surviving for at least a century. We find it in Gluck's *Orpheus*, and (with less respect for its form and character), as the concluding Ballet of the same composer's *Iphigenia in Aulis*, written in 1774.

However, it was not in operatic conventions that these two slow dances found their highest expression or in such are nowadays most remembered. In the time of Bach and Handel they became largely identified with purely instrumental writing and even with religious music. No finer chaconne has ever been composed than Bach's famous example for unaccompanied Violin ; no more moving example in church music than the " Crucifixus " from his *B minor Mass*, which, though not strictly conforming to the accepted rhythmic design of the dance, yet makes its presence felt through the composer's adherence to the triple time and his use of the wonderful sorrow-laden ground-bass.

Brahms's lifelong interest in the older forms of music has already been mentioned elsewhere in this volume. His exercises in counterpoint, fugue and canon were to him like the daily eating of his bread ; they brought him new vigour of mind, revitalizing his imagination in such a way that there was scarcely a problem connected with the combination or sequence of musical sounds that could not be solved by him in a manner wholly satisfying. His borrowing of the bass of Bach's *ciaccona* from the 150th Church Cantata [1] as the *ostinato* for the Fourth Symphony's

---

[1] It should be remembered that in numerous examples of ancient church music certain composers did not consider it either irrelevant or irreverent to incorporate features found in secular music or even in street music of the day. The 150th Psalm exhorting the congregation to praise God " with the timbrel and dance " was perhaps their cue and their excuse. Before Palestrina it was quite common for a less reputable composer out to catch the ear of the public (whether in church or not) to found even a Mass on some popular song of the day. That the profane and incongruous forced their way in this manner into

finale, was in keeping with all these exercises, for he was never happier than when experimenting in the variation form, and perhaps happiest of all when anchored to a ground-bass—witness the ending of the *St. Antoni* set.

That no composer before him had envisaged a chaconne [1] or passacaglia as the last movement of a symphony is a strange fact, especially when we remember that the symphony originated from the opera, from that " Sinfonia avanti l'opera " which in olden days served no better purpose than to excite the conversation of theatre-goers whose voices were in danger of being drowned by the unwanted hubbub of a raucous orchestra. So the serious composer of purely instrumental music struck out new paths, tired of wasting what was often his best work on unmannerly and unmusical patrons of the opera. He broke away and made possible the birth of the symphony proper, sowing those seeds which, more than in all other composers of that time, blossomed so gloriously in the works of Josef Haydn " Father of the symphony."

There seems little doubt that Brahms had another and very cogent reason for varying the form of his finale. Unlike the other Symphonies, the first three movements of the Fourth all adhered to that symphonic enlargement of what is termed sonata form ; that is, each movement had its

the sanctuary did not seem to matter, even though it meant the desecration of words whose eternal beauty has stirred mankind since the earliest days of the Christian era. Palestrina, founding a Mass on a song " L'homme armé," was himself tempted and fell. Thenceforward the Church returned to a finer dignity in the style of the music performed, and, as in the " Crucifixus " mentioned above, transformed the best of what the world had to offer into something deeply expressive and more truly religious. For the day of the great contrapuntists had arrived, and with it new tonal values that could not but avoid all flippant expression and wayward extravagance.

[1] Bach's chaconne, following the operatic convention, is the final choral number of the Cantata. Its first verse runs :—

" Meine Tage in den Leiden
Endet Gott dennoch zu Freuden ;
Christen auf den Dornenwegen
Führen Himmels Kraft und Segen ; "

See Ex. 69, p. 117, for the original of the ground bass.

It is interesting to note here that manuscript copies of Bach Cantatas, in Brahms's handwriting, were offered for sale in November, 1884.

exposition, development, recapitulation and final coda. This unadventurous procedure, despite the vital and contrasted themes of each movement, would have engendered a sense of monotony had Brahms constructed his finale similarly to the other movements.

He seems to have had an unerring instinct in regard to such matters, knowing when his bolt was shot, when a drastic change was needed to strengthen still further by some new device the impressions created in earlier movements. He could scarcely have done better then turn to Bach for inspiration, nor to anything more appropriate than this Church Cantata. For is not this Fourth Symphony a Gothic cathedral in sound ?

Brahms did not make use of the word *passacaglia* on the full score of his finale ; he left it to others to note the fact, merely indicating the tempo, *Allegro energico e passionato*. And somehow this indebtedness to Bach's *ciaccona* was for long overlooked ; only in recent years has the fact received general recognition.

In an analysis of this movement we must not, therefore, look for formal symphonic development, for it is not there. At most we can admit a certain likeness to ternary form if we regard the long E major section and the mood created therein as something almost apart from the remainder, something suspended breathlessly between those relentless sections in E minor, where stark nameless tragedy seems to echo down the years and into the vault of eternity.

The passacaglia consists of the theme (see Ex. 70, p. 118), thirty variations and an extended coda, all in the key of E, as would be expected of a movement conforming to a design so strictly classical. The omission of all string tone from the presentation of the theme is in itself a masterstroke ; the passacaglia becomes a bare assertion of fact, uncompromising and stern, unadorned, a challenge to grim action. It is a theme which, in its brief course of eight bars, demonstrates to us the bleak winter of a composer's discontent, a winter holding out no promise of any spring to follow. " The hero is not fighting for his happiness," [1] writes Sir Donald Tovey in his masterly analysis. " He is to die fighting." And the Trombones, entering here for the first time in the Symphony do more than anything else to create this mood.

Let it be admitted at once that no complete analysis of this finale is anything like possible ; the details are so profuse, the touches of genius so many that no words can be found fully to describe all. The interest is twofold : thematic and harmonic, and it is difficult to say which captures the imagination more, so superb is the invention, so superlative the technique.

There must be many like myself who have a passion for analysis ; many who, recognizing beauty in all its intrinsic worth, yet would discover wherein that beauty lies. The bare fact is not enough ; details must be forthcoming. Nevertheless, any bar-by-bar analysis in the present instance will not serve, for by looking too closely at the trees we shall only lose sight of the wood.

The passacaglia divides itself into thirty-one sections of eight bars each (the theme plus thirty variations), four transitional bars which follow, and an extended coda of fifty-nine bars. As befits a movement as truly symphonic in character as anything ever written, the music, despite its self-imposed eight-bar periodicity, never falters, and never, to our surprise, comes to a series of full stops.

Of the danger of this Brahms was aware. But by the variation of his harmonies in the most ingenious yet simple manner he achieves such extraordinary continuity in the music that we are seldom made conscious of these recurrent divisions of eight bars. Given no other choice but E for the key of the movement and that mostly in the minor—he yet avoided the pitfall of exploiting the tonic chord overmuch either at the beginning of each variation or in the final cadence. Even the movement itself begins unconventionally with the first inversion of the subdominant chord—A minor ; it reaches an E minor chord only at the third bar and, in

[1] *Essays in Musical Analysis*, vol. I. (Oxford University Press).

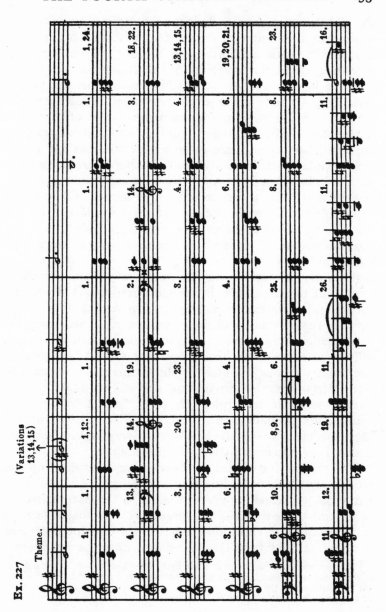

Ex. 227

the eighth, triumphantly flaunts an E *major* ! Not until the ninth bar after letter A do we find a variation (the 4th) that begins with a chord of E minor ; in no less than seventeen of the thirty variations this is avoided.

While further analysis of this kind would become wearisome it is a matter of the greatest interest to indicate in the table given on p. 295 the immense range of Brahms's harmonies. Minor, major, diminished and augmented triads all have their place in both root positions and inversions, while diatonic and chromatic chords are juxtaposed with a balance and precision that we associate more with science than with an art so fallible as music. Of necessity this table must remain incomplete or it would run off the page. But it has been possible to include the main harmonies, many being common to more than one variation.[1]

Scientific as such a display must seem, yet the sheer beauty of the harmonies is beyond question. Only in the theme and variations 1 and 24, and in variations 4 and 5, do they repeat exactly the same sequence. Their strength, their tenderness and pathos, their tragic import, their close affinity to those of the first movement are all born of that inspiration through which Brahms was able to express himself in terms of the highest art and still maintain contact with a scientific principle. He was " urged by a superhuman determination to attain to a Bach-like mastery," says Specht, alluding to the Fourth Symphony. Nowhere is this more apparent than in the passacaglia.

The themes and rhythmic contrasts superimposed on the *ostinato* are on a level with their harmonization. Each new variation, while telling its own story, is the natural sequel to the one preceding it. The music grows in logical fashion from variation to variation ; what in the opening statement is announced in bare dotted minims develops by degrees

---

[1] The numerals shown against each harmony indicate some, but not all, of the variations in which the particular harmony can be found. By dividing the first 248 bars of the movement into 31 sections of 8 bars each, the number of any variation can be identified with ease.

into crotchets, quavers and semiquavers. Nor are the
claims of a modified sonata form altogether ignored, for
themes such as that heard in variation 2—

or that in variation 3 (letter A)

return in other variations ; Ex. 228 in variation 25 (16th bar
after H) and in the coda (9th bar after M) ; Ex. 229 in
variation 26 in a beautiful *legato* version on Horns and
Oboes.

Nothing remains but a brief description of each variation.

I. (9th bar of the movement).   Harmonically, a replica
of the opening eight bars, with Horns and Timpani driving
home the note E in all but one bar, while *pizzicato* Strings,
aided by Trombones, emphasize the theme on the second
beat of the bar.   Note the effect of the *diminuendo* in the last
three bars.

II. In the last bar of variation I an Oboe and Clarinet
begin the theme shown above as Ex. 228.   The lower
Strings, again *pizzicato*, mark the *ostinato*.

III. (letter A).   A version in *staccato* and *marcato* crotchets
for full orchestra (Ex. 229), heavier in style and a forewarning of the general restless, tragic sweep of the music
from variation 16 onwards.,   The 'Cellos and Basses play
arco, the other Strings remaining *pizzicato*.

IV. The 1st Violins, bowing for the first time in the

movement, give out a new theme, one that adds still greater
strength and a new turn to the music by its up and down
leaps across the strings and the introduction of quavers.

Ex.230

Note that the syncopated accompaniment on 2nd Violins
and Violas is carried forward from the Horns of the previous
variation.

V. (letter B). Quaver movement has now become
general in a variation which embellishes the matter of the
previous one. In both these variations the ground forms the
bass of the harmony.

VI. This closely resembles 5 in general characteristics.
For the first time, in bars six and seven, the ground forsakes its strict character, but in doing so it enables the
'Cellos to continue some very effective figuration in triple
quavers.[1]

VII. (letter C). A variation that leaps about in double-
dotted crotchets and dotted quavers with semiquavers
interspersed to give the music a sharp forbidding outline.
Note the remarkable cross-rhythm of the bass in the final
bars.

Ex.231

VIII. The Violins now break into detached semiquavers
while the Wood-wind give out phrases in quavers which are

[1] In Bach's *ciaccona* the *ostinato* modulates from B minor to D ; then through
F sharp minor, A and E back to B minor.

reminiscent of variations 5 and 6.   If ever Brahms " snorted into his beard " it is in the Bass part here and again in variation 9.

Ex.232

The music changes to *legato* and *diminuendo* in the latter half of the variation.

IX. The semiquavers, once more detached, are now elaborated, a mixture of six and four to a beat giving the music its most agitated expression up to this point.   Again the phrases in quavers heard in variations 5, 6 and 8 are a prominent feature, but now, spent in their force, they descend wearily in chromatic style (4th bar before D). The latter half of the variation imitates the *legato* and *diminuendo* effects of 8, reaching a *pianissimo* for the first time in the movement.   The music, no longer active, sinks to a sombre and cheerless close and so prepares the way for a prolonged state of quiet and a growing darkness which enshrouds the next six variations in the deepest mystery.

X. (letter D).   Here the ground returns to its strict form in a variation consisting of the beautiful harmonies shown in Ex. 71 on page 119.   There is no counter-theme here. It ends in an eloquent *pp*.

XI. Even more moving is this variation, which, in its first four bars, decorates in *molto dolce* style the corresponding harmonies of variation 10 and then modulates through a series of hushed chromatic chords till No. 12 is reached. Professor Sir Donald Tovey most aptly describes it as a variation of " April sunshine."   But, it could be added, the sky clouds over at the end.

XII. Now the time changes to 3–2 and with the change comes stealing in a wistful melody on the Flute, one of the most affecting Brahms ever wrote (Ex. 72, p. 119).   For accompaniment it has only detached chords on Violins and Violas, all off the beat, and a pedal E reiterated on Horns. And if the *ostinato* is to be found we must now search for it among the many notes of the melody and, when that fails in the accompaniment. It is almost a case of looking for the proverbial needle in the haystack. The Flute melody explores each register of the instrument and the gradual descent from the high F sharp to the low D is a touch of overwhelming beauty.

XIII. The music, still throughout this variation anchored to the pedal E, now finds solace in the major key. We seem to have left the world behind and to approach some spiritual kingdom where we are at one with the heavenly host. The lovely colloquy between Clarinet, Oboe and Flute brings us near the veil of the temple ; there is the pity of God for man in this strangely affecting music.

The accompaniment, retaining on Violins the detached chords of variation 12, is now rather more ornate. Violas and 'Cellos in imitation remind us that the first three notes of the Flute melody are still of service to the fabric of the music.[1]

[1] Yet another significant example of Brahms's use of the three-note idiom. See Ex. 186, p. 242 *et passim*.

XIV. (letter E). The most solemn moments of the music are now at hand when the Trombones, silent for ten variations, now enter in company with Bassoons and Horns to intone a mystic and awe-inspiring chant.

Ex.235

It is as if we were taking part in the ritual of some sublime service under a sky stretching into infinity. The world exists no more ; we are part of the universe, incorporeal, children of the spirit of God folded in an eternal embrace.

> " Fount of the time-embranching fire,
> O waneless One, that art the core
> Of every heart's unknown desire,
> Take back the hearts that beat no more." [1]

The mysticism of the music is enhanced by the reticent *arpeggii* on Violas and 'Cellos, with the Violins silent until the last bar of the variation. The 1st Horn repeats the lovely strip of Oboe melody shown in Ex. 233.

XV. This variation continues in the same strain and creates even more effect than its predecessor, for the harmonies are more intimate and the orchestration has more grandeur. It fades into the far distance and the celestial vision disappears.

And now for the remaining fifteen variations and the lengthy coda of the movement the music renews the struggle with an intensity even greater than before. Continuity is never broken, each new variation leaping in with

[1] From *Requiem of Archangels for the World*. Poems by Herbert Trench. Vol. I. (Constable & Co. Ltd.)

an insistence that sweeps the music along without definite break anywhere. Examined in bulk these variations show an almost unvaried allegiance to crotchet and quaver movement. No longer could Brahms afford such plaintive interludes as, for instance, variations 10, 11 and 12. Now the drive of the music must be as remorseless as any march of an army over enemy country.

XVI. The *Tempo primo* is resumed in a restatement of the *ostinato*, the key of E minor being restored. Again the Strings are silent. But only for three bars, for at the third and fourth bars they burst in wrathfully, and, but for an odd bar here and there, never leave the music for the remainder of the symphony.

XVII. This variation and the following one (XVIII, letter F) are mainly characterized by Violins and Violas playing *tremolo* against pathetic, despairing phrases on the Woodwind, with, at letter F, Horns and Trombones added.

XIX. and XX deal with a general *staccato* movement in crotchets and quavers, the latter turning into triplet quavers what the previous variation had stated in ordinary quavers.

XXI (letter G). Rough, almost brutal is this *fortissimo* variation notable for scale passages on the Strings and Flute. Its harmonies are far more chromatic than anything heard so far, the *ostinato* itself, as the following quotation shows, turning to intervening semitones for its more urgent expression. Note the almost savage interjections of the Trombones and the sudden and dramatic *pp* two bars before the next variation.

Ex. 236

(Incomplete sketch)

XXII. The tumult subsides for the moment in a *staccato* variation of guileless simplicity in which Strings, Wood-wind and Horns are concerned with an exchange of ideas of a far less chromatic character. From its *diminuendo* close springs the next variation (XXIII, letter H). This is a loud development of what has been heard, far more ornate in style and moving urgently to a crisis.

XXIV. More virile, more shattering than anything heard so far, this variation repeats the harmonies of the opening and variation I. Its *ff marcato* emphasis on the second beat of each bar, with isolated groups of triplet quavers (gathered up from variations 22 and 23) driving the *ostinato* home with sledge-hammer force, makes it an unforgettable experience no matter how many times we hear it.

XXV. Still moving on remorselessly, this variation retains the stern character of the previous one, the *ff marcato* emphasis being transferred to the Brass and a shuddering fearstruck *tremolo* added on Violins and Violas.

XXVI (letter I). Once more the music, now swiftly coming to the end of its tether, subsides to a *piano* which, with little change, continues for the next three variations (XXVII, XXVIII and XXIX). This check to the intensity of the music comes as a much needed relief, for variations 24 and 25 had well-nigh reached breaking-point. These four variations (from 24 onwards) also serve to delay the climax of the movement, fitting into the general scheme in some strange psychological way that can perhaps be likened to that presageful feeling commonly known as " the calm before the storm." Variation 26 is a beautiful *legato* version of variation 3, the Horns and Oboes telling their plaintive story with rare sympathy. Variations 27, 28 (letter K) and 29 seem to come very near the spirit, if not the letter, of the first movement ; there is the same austere restraint imposed on the harmonies.

XXX (letter L). This final variation breaks out *forte* at once. It is a remarkable close *stretto* founded on the previous variation and is in reality a canon at the octave.

Ex.238

One has only to put every fourth note up an octave and there appears a retrospective glimpse of the opening subject of the first movement ! The wheel seems to come full circle.

Ex.239

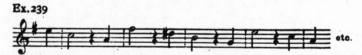

[Compare with the opening of Ex. 199, p. 261.]

Now four transitional bars marked *poco ritardando* link this final variation to the *ff* coda.

Having in thirty variations exhausted the thematic and harmonic possibilities above or around the *ostinato*,[1] what

---

[1] I am not certain I believe my own words here, for it is more than likely that Brahms could have continued inventing new variations on this *ostinato* till kingdom come.—J. H.

remained to this mighty architect Brahms ? Logic demanded
that the coda should consolidate what had been designed
with such meticulous care and such wealth of detail.   So
the composer, just as if he had suddenly remembered an
old umbrella left behind, turns once more to the ground
itself, going over it as with a measure, exploring new
possibilities, examining it now, not for what could be added
to it, but in relation to itself.

His new scrutiny in every way justified itself.   From the
Più allegro to reference letter M the music—all attention now
riveted on the ground—surges passionately through twenty
bars of modulations, its majestic harmonies, swiftly moving
though they are, as simple (when analysed) as any to be
found in Beethoven, Mozart or even Haydn.   After two
dramatic silences (6th and 8th bars after *Più allegro*) the
ostinato gets entangled with itself during the progress of
these harmonies.   A remarkable canon is the result.

Ex.240

(Harmony omitted here)

marc.

marc.

etc.

All finely wrought symphonic music of this kind hastens
to its end with its thematic content closely interwoven.
Such a *stretto* as the above was one after Brahms's own heart ;
given such means to continue, he could not fail to rise to his
superb conclusion.   At letter M (see Ex. 75, p. 121) the
Trombones, in a rousing passage in octaves, foretell the
return, nine bars later, of phrases heard originally in
variation 2.   This phrase is in turn metamorphosed into a
version of the ground that is divided between Wood-wind
and 1st Violins.   Repeated with slightly changed harmonies
and then in cross-rhythm, it drives the music headlong to

its tragic close with the key of E minor unrelenting to the last.

Nothing since Beethoven has approached the immensity of this Symphony ; probably nothing ever will, even to the end of time.

BIBLIOGRAPHY FOR THE ENGLISH READER

ANTCLIFFE, H. *Brahms*. Bell's Miniature Series of Musicians. London, 1905.

BICKLEY, NORA. *Letters from and to Joseph Joachim* (translated). Macmillan, London, 1914.

COLLES, DR. H. C. *Brahms*. Music of the Masters series. John Lane, The Bodley Head. London, 1920.

DIETRICH, A., and WIDMANN, J. V. *Recollections of Johannes Brahms*. Translated by Dora E. Hecht. Seeley & Co. London, 1899.

ERB, J. L. *Brahms*. The Master Musicians series. J. M. Dent & Sons Ltd. London, 1925.

EVANS (senr.), EDWIN. *Historical, Descriptive and Analytical Account of the Entire Works of Johannes Brahms*. Vol. I. The Vocal Works. W. Reeves. London, 1912.

GEIRINGER, DR. KARL. *Brahms, His Life and Work*. George Allen & Unwin Ltd. London, 1936.

HADOW, SIR W. H. *Studies in Modern Music*. Second series. Seeley & Co. London, 1899.

KALBECK, MAX. *Johannes Brahms. The Herzogenberg Correspondence*. Translated by Hannah Bryant. John Murray. London, 1909.

LEE, DR. E. MARKHAM. *Brahms, The Man and His Music*. Sampson Low, Marston & Co. London, 1916.

LITZMANN, DR. BERTHOLD. *Letters of Clara Schumann and Johannes Brahms*, 1853–1896. 2 vols. Edward Arnold & Co. London, 1927.

MASON, DANIEL GREGORY. *From Grieg to Brahms*. The Outlook Co. New York, 1902.

MAY, FLORENCE. *The Life of Johannes Brahms*. 2 vols. Edward Arnold & Co. London, 1905.

MURDOCH, WILLIAM. *Brahms, with an Analytical Study of the Complete Pianoforte Works*. Rich & Cowan. London, 1933.

PULVER, GEOFFREY. *Johannes Brahms*. Kegan Paul Ltd. and J. Curwen and Sons Ltd. London, 1926.

SPECHT, RICHARD. *Johannes Brahms*. Translated by Eric Blom. J. M. Dent & Sons Ltd. London, 1930.

TOVEY, PROFESSOR SIR DONALD. *Essays in Musical Analysis*. Vols. 1, 2, 3 and 5. Oxford University Press.

INDEX

A.

B.